PANCHATANTRA, HITOPADESHA AND STORIES OF TENALI RAMA

PANCHATANTRA, HITOPADESHA AND STORIES OF TENALI RAMA

Editor-in-Chief

Swami Chidatman Jee Maharaj

ANMOL PUBLICATIONS PVT. LTD.
NEW DELHI-110 002 (INDIA)

ANMOL PUBLICATIONS PVT. LTD.
Regd. Office: 4360/4, Ansari Road, Daryaganj,
New Delhi-110002 (India)
Tel.: 23278000, 23261597, 23286875, 23255577, Fax: 91-11-23280289
Email: anmolpub@gmail.com
Visit us at: www.anmolpublications.com

Branch Office: No. 1015, Ist Main Road, BSK IIIrd Stage
IIIrd Phase, IIIrd Block, Bengaluru-560 085 (India)
Tel.: 080-41723429 • Fax: 080-26723604
Email: anmolpublicationsbangalore@gmail.com

Panchatantra, Hitopadesha and Stories of Tenali Rama

First Published 2010

ISBN: 978-81-261-3635-3

PRINTED IN INDIA

Printed at Balaji Offset, Delhi.

Contents

Preface

India colourful and vibrant, a land as diverse as its people. A mosaic of faiths, cultures, customs and languages that blend harmoniously to form a composite whole. One of the world's oldest living civilizations—which gave to the world—the concept of zero, the primordial sound Aum..., Yoga and Buddhism.

She is old. She is young. The two diametrically opposite, different yet unique and dynamic faces of India coexist even at this turn of the millennium. With a history of heritage, learning and civilisation dating back to almost 5000 years or perhaps even more, the modern India presents itself as an ideal country. From snow clad mountains to breezy sparkling blue sea side. From arid deserts with shifting sand dunes to lush green country sides. From ancient relics and architectural ruins dating back into antiquity to modern cities, India has it all.

To the north it is bordered by the world's highest mountain chain, where foothill valleys cover the northernmost of the country's maximum states. Further south, plateaus, tropical rain forests and sandy deserts are bordered by palm fringed beaches. Its southernmost tip is the meeting point of three Oceans.

India is a land of staggering contrast with a mingling of the tradition and modernity that is an unique experience to be in India. One will forever remember the stay in this wonderful Homeland-a land truly of mystery and enchantment. Only India can offer such an astonishing variety of contrasts.

She has given birth to numerous spiritual leaders and founders of some of the popular religions of the present day world. India probably has the most religious diversity in any country. It's the birthplace of Hinduism, Buddhism, Sikhism and Jainism and is among the few places to have a resident

Zoroastrian population. India with her veritable treasure trove of culture, mysticism, philosophy, art, music and architecture to name a few. Much of India's classical music is devotional and the North Indian Hindustani and South Indian Carnatic streams are distinct and both have a complex 'raga' framework. The legacy of dance in India is tremendous. The classical dances of India are numerous such as Kathakali of Kerala, Bharatnatyam of Tamil Nadu, Kuchipudi of Andhra Pradesh, Manipuri and Odissi from Orissa are the prominent dance forms in this country that sways to an altogether novel beat. The Yakshagana, nautanki and puppetry are ancient folk forms that live on till date. The earliest specimens of Indian painting are the ones on the walls of the Ajanta Caves dating back to 2nd century BC. The Mughals had a huge impact on Indian art. The influence of Persian art brought placid garden scenes, illustrations from myths, legends and history into Indian art. Word craft, handicrafts, architecture and sculpture all contribute to this rich and varied domain. Indian literature, both in English and in the vernacular, is ever more popular around the world.

The book aims at presenting perspectives of different aspects of Indian culture. It has topics on Indian classical music and dance, painting, ayurveda and yoga which are traditional and indigenous system of physical and mental wellbeing, language, philosophy and excellence achievements by Indian in the different branches of science and social sciences. It also includes our ancient religious and classic literature.

It is hoped that this book will be welcomed by the general readers as also scholars who are interested in the Indian heritage.

—Editors

1

Panchatantra

The Panchatantra or Kalileh or Demneh or Anvar-e Soheyli or Kalilag and Damnag (in Syriac) or Kalilah wa Dimnah or The Fables of Bidpai (or Pilpai, in various European languages) or The Morall Philosophie of Doni (English, 1570) was originally a canonical collection of Sanskrit (Hindu) as well as Pali (Buddhist) animal fables in verse and prose. The original Sanskrit text, now long lost, and which some scholars believe was composed in the 3rd century BC, is attributed to Vishnu Sarma. However, based as it is on older oral traditions, its antecedents among storytellers probably hark back to the origins of language and the subcontinent's earliest social groupings of hunting and fishing folk gathered around campfires.

Origins and Function

The work is an ancient and vigorous multicultural hybrid that to this day continues an erratic process of cross-border mutation and adaptation as modern writers and publishers struggle to fathom, simplify and re-brand its complex origins. It illustrates, for the benefit of princes who may succeed to a throne, the central Hindu principles of Raja niti (political science) through an interwoven series of colourful animal tales. These operate like a succession of Russian dolls, one narrative opening within another, sometimes three or four deep, and then unexpectedly snapping shut in irregular rhythms to sustain attention (Story within a story). The five principles illustrated are:

- Mitra Bhedha (The Loss of Friends)
- Mitra Laabha (Gaining Friends)

- Suhrudbheda (Causing Dissension Between Friends)
- Vigraha (Separation)
- Sandhi (Union)

Early Cross-Cultural Migrations

The Panchatantra approximated its current literary form within the 4th-6th centuries AD. No Sanskrit texts before 1000 CE have survived. According to Hindu tradition, it was written around 200 BC by Pandit Vishnu Sarma, a sage. One of the most influential Sanskrit contributions to world literature, it was exported (probably both in oral and literary formats) north to Tibet and China and east to South East Asia by Buddhist Monks on pilgrimage.

According to the Shahnameh (The Book of the Kings, Persia's late 10th century national epic by Ferdowsi) the Panchatantra also migrated westwards, during the Sassanid reign of Nushirvan around 570 AD when his famous physician Borzuy translated it from Sanskrit into the middle Persian language of Pahlavi, transliterated for Europeans as Kalile va Demne.

How Two Jackals (in Part One) Branded this (Five Part) Book

Karataka ('Horribly Howling') and Damanaka ('Victor') are the Sanskrit names of two jackals in the first section of the Panchatantra. They are retainers to a lion king and their lively adventures as well as the stories they and other characters tell one another make up roughly 45% of the book's length. By the time the Sanskrit version has migrated several hundred years through Pahlavi into Arabic, the two jackals' names have transmogrified into Kalila and Dimna, and-probably because of a combination of first-mover advantage, Dimna's charming villainy and that dominant 45% bulk-their single part/section/ chapter has become the generic, classical name for the whole book. It is possible, too, that the Sanskrit word 'Panchatantra' as a Hindu concept could find no easy equivalent in Zoroastrian Pahlavi.

Be that as it may, each distinct part of the book contains (as Professor Edgerton noted in 1965) "at least one story, and usually more, which are 'emboxed' in the main story, called the 'frame-story'. Sometimes there is a double emboxment; another story is inserted in an 'emboxed' story. Moreover, the [whole] work begins with a brief introduction, which as in a frame all five... [parts] are regarded as 'emboxed'". Vishnu Sarma's idea was that humans can assimilate more about their own habitually unflattering behaviour if it is disguised in terms of entertainingly configured stories about supposedly less illustrious beasts than themselves.

Another observation that Professor Edgerton makes challenges our persistent assumption that animal fables function mainly as adjuncts to religious dogma, acting as indoctrination devices to condition the moral behaviour of small children and obedient adults. Not the Machiavellian Panchatantra: "Vishnu Sarma undertakes," Edgerton notes, "to instruct three dull and ignorant princes in the principles of polity, by means of stories....[This is] a textbook of artha, 'worldly wisdom', or niti, polity, which the Hindus regard as one of the three objects of human desire, the other being dharma, 'religion or morally proper conduct' and kama 'love'.... The so-called 'morals' of the stories have no bearing on morality; they are unmoral, and often immoral. They glorify shrewdness, practical wisdom, in the affairs of life, and especially of politics, of government."

This realistic practicality explains why the original Sanskrit villain jackal, the decidedly jealous, sneaky and evil vizier-like Damanaka ('Victor') is his frame-story's winner, and not his goody-goody brother Karataka who is presumably left 'Horribly Howling' at the vile injustice of Part One's final murderous events. In fact, in its steady migration westward the persistent theme of evil-triumphant in Kalila and Dimna, Part One frequently outraged Jewish, Christian and Muslim religious leaders-so much so, indeed, that ibn al-Muqaffa carefully inserts (no doubt hoping to pacifiy the powerful religious zealots of his own turbulent times) an entire extra chapter at the end of Part One of his Arabic masterpiece, putting Dimna in jail, on trial and eventually to death. So much for naughty jackals!

Needless to say there is no vestige of such dogmatic moralising in the collations that remain to us of the pre-Islamic original-The Panchatantra. Technically, from the perspective of a more subtle and flexible functionality, Joseph Jacobs in 1888 offers a less coercive interpretation of how the Panchatantra/Kalila and Dimna stories might work more effectively to modify human behaviour: ".... if one thinks of it, the very raison d'etre of the Fable is to imply its moral without mentioning it."

In short the learning opportunity is interactive, voluntary, dynamic, reflective, open, frustrating and risky-compared to the simplified, fixed and often terrifyingly authoritative lessons delivered from priestly heights that briefly excite and amuse, then are soon forgotten, like electric shocks. In such circumstance (which is the norm) the human animal is conditioned to respond to the approved socialising, tagline 'message' of a local time-and-culture-bound 'moral', and prevented from glimpsing anything objective beyond it at an individual pace.

The Shah Nama, How Borzuy brought the Kalila from Hindustan

Initially Borzuy sought his king's permission to make a trip to Hindustan in search of a mountain herb he had read about that is "mingled into a compound and, when sprinkled over a corpse, it is immediately restored to life." The Shah gave his permission, equipped Borzuy fully for the journey and handed over to him a number of gifts, together with a letter for the Ray of India, whom he requested to assist the physician in his search. On his arrival in Hindustan he was received with high honour and granted all facility for his task, including a retinue of local physicians to guide him on his way.

But when Borzuy locates and prepares the miraculous mountain herb and sprinkles it over various corpses provided for his experiments, alas-the magic potion does not work. He is sore distressed at his failure and angry at the false information that has led him so far astray, not to mention the shame which will descend upon him when he returns empty-handed to Persia and faces his king's displeasure. In desperation he asks the Indian physicians accompanying him what to do. Do they know anyone who can help him?

"With one voice they replied: 'There is an ancient sage here who surpasses us in years and wisdom and who in his science is superior to any of the great.'

"They guided Borzuy to this man, whose mind was filled with contemplation and whose lips were ever ready for speech. Borzuy laid all his trials before him, speaking of the book which he had discovered and the words which he had heard from men expert in knowledge. When the ancient sage began to speak he discoursed on every branch of science.

'Kalila is the Herb You Seek'

'I too have found this thing in books,' he said, 'and have moved eagerly, led by the same hopes. When nothing came to light after my travails, I had perforce to listen to a different interpretation. The herb is the scientist; science is the mountain, everlastingly out of reach of the multitude. The corpse is the man without knowledge, for the uninstructed man is everywhere lifeless. Through knowledge man becomes revivified. Happy is he who submits himself steadfastly to labour. In the king's treasury there is a book which the well-qualified call Kalila. When people become weary of their ignorance, the herb for them is Kalila, knowledge being the mountain. If you seek this book in the king's treasury you will find it, and it will be your guide to knowledge.'

"Borzuy rejoiced to hear this and all his past toil appeared in his eyes as empty wind. He blessed the sage and departed for the king's court, and, traversing the road like fire, he arrived in the Ray's presence and lavished compliments upon him.

'May you occupy your throne as long as India exists!' he said. 'Ray, you whose triumphs are widespread, there exists a certain book whose title in Hindu is Kalila. In your majesty's treasury it is sealed as precious and it contains guidance mingled with discernment and wisdom. That herb is a metaphor for this Kalila, nought else. I beg that your majesty, lord of India, may bid your treasurer consign the book to me, if you will not hold that to be irksome.

"The Ray's spirit was rendered unhappy by this request and his body was agitated where he sat.

'Borzuy,' he said, 'no one has ever sought this of me, either recently or in times past. Yet were the emperor Nushirvan to demand my body and soul I would not withhold them from him, nor anything else. I have not any person noble or humble here. But read it in my presence here, lest some malevolent person hostile to me should claim that the book was written by a mortal. Read, understand and investigate it from every point of view.'

The Book's Cultural Migration after Borzuy's Pahlavi Translation

Borzuy's 570 AD Pahlavi translation (Kalile va Demne) was translated nearly two centuries later into Syriac and Arabic-the latter by Ibn al-Muqaffa around 750 AD under the Arabic title, Kalila wa Dimma.

The Brethren of Purity and Part 2 of the Kalila wa Dimna

Scholars aver that the second section of Ibn al-Muqaffa's translation, illustrating the Sanskrit principle of Mitra Laabha (Gaining Friends), became the unifying basis for the Brethren of Purity-the anonymous 9th century CE Arab encyclopedists whose prodigious literary effort, Encyclopedia of the Brethren of Sincerity, codified Indian, Persian and Greek knowledge.

A suggestion made by Goldziher, and later written on by Philip K. Hitti in his History of the Arabs, proposes that:

"The appellation is presumably taken from the story of the ringdove in Kalilah wa-Dimnah in which it is related that a group of animals by acting as faithful friends (ikhwan al-safa) to one another escaped the snares of the hunter. The story concerns a ring-dove and its companions who have become entangled in the net of a hunter seeking birds.

Together, they left themselves and the ensnaring net to a nearby rat, who is gracious enough to gnaw the birds free of the net; impressed by the rat's altruistic deed, a crow becomes the rat's friend. Soon a tortoise and gazelle also join the company of animals. After some time, the gazelle is trapped by another net; with the aid of the others and the good rat, the gazelle is soon freed, but the tortoise fails to leave swiftly enough and is himself captured by the hunter. In the final turn of events, the gazelle repays the tortoise by serving as a decoy and distracting the hunter while the rat and the others free the tortoise. After this, the animals are designated as the Ikwhan al-Safa.

This story is mentioned as an exemplum when the Brethren speak of mutual aid in one rasa'il (treatise), a crucial part of their system of ethics that has been summarized thus:

"And their virtues, equally, are not the virtues of Islam, not so much righteousness and the due quittance of obligations, as mildness and gentleness towards all men, forgiveness, long-suffering, and compassion, the yielding up of self for others' sake. In this Brotherhood, self is forgotten; all act by the help of each, all rely upon each for succour and advice, and if a Brother sees it will be good for another that he should sacrifice his life for him, he willingly gives it. No place is found in the Brotherhood for the vices of the outside world; envy, hatred, pride, avarice, hypocrisy, and deceit, do not fit into their scheme,- they only hinder the worship of truth."

The Crucial Abbasid Classic by Ibn al-Muqaffa'

After the Muslim invasion of Persia (Iran) Ibn al-Muqaffa's 750 AD Arabic version (by now two languages removed from its pre-Islamic Sanskrit original) emerges as the pivotal surviving text that enriches world literature.

From Arabic it was transmitted in 1080 to Greece and in 1252 into Spain (old Castillian, Calyla e Dymna) and thence to the rest of Europe. However it was the circa 1250 Hebrew translation attributed to Rabbi Joel that became the source (via a subsequent Latin version done by one John of Capua around 1270 AD, Directorium Humanae Vitae, or "Directory of Human Life") of most European versions. Furthermore in 1121 a complete 'modern' Persian translation from Ibn al-Muqaffa's version flows from the pen of Abu'l Ma'ali Nasr Allah Munshi.

It seems that any pre-Arabic or post-Arabic format the Kalila and Dimna animal fables take is relative. This loose collection is an oral and literary oddity that flows on, forward and yet also backward into the mists before anything was written down. One simply cannot pin these stories down like butterflies under glass in a tidy Victorian museum display drawer. They exist cross-culturally virtually in perpetual flux, like the 1001 Nights, adapting even now to current conditions to remain fresh and employable, freighting some vestige of an ancient message to new generations. They are alive as conduits of traditional wisdom, of a durable and vital survivalist psychology that requires no formal schooling or even, as remains true to vasts swaths of humanity, literacy.

Modern Adaptions and Difficulties in Establishing a Fixed Attribution

Recently Ibn al-Muqaffa's historical milieu itself, when composing his masterpiece in Baghdad during the bloody Abbasid overthrow of the Umayyad dynasty, has become the subject (and rather confusingly, also the title) of a gritty Shakespearean drama by the multicultural Kuwaiti playwright Sulayman Al-Bassam. Ibn al-Muqqafa's biographical background serves as an illustrative metaphor for today's escalating bloodthirstiness in Iraq-once again a historical vortex for clashing civilizations on a multiplicity of levels, including the obvious tribal, religious and political parallels.

Al-Bassam's imaginative modern work entitled Kalila wa Dimna, while provocative and educational, is technically a misnomer. There is only one brief play-within-a-play tableaux that genuflects towards the actual telling any of the animal fables found in the Arabic original. Understandably this contradictory nuance (where are al-Muqaffa's classic fables?), obvious and even irritatingly puzzling to any literate Middle Easterner, appears to have been intellectualized away by some Eurocentric commentators.

The English literary equivalent would be attending a play called Hard Times expecting to see something of the characters Grandgrind and Bounder by only to find yourself immersed in an imaginary biography of Charles Dickens and the social turmoil of his day, with only a three minute confrontational drawing-room scene alluding to a certain Mr. Grandgrind and his part in the horrors of Victorian factory conditions and child labour.

Yet in the prevailing belief system of the Western post-modernist world, anything goes. Every expression achieves legitimacy. This tolerant climate is ideally suited to the book's sui generis flexibility. Any attempt to re-brand the Panchatantra or Kalila and Dimna or The Fables of Bidpai for the utilitarian Western consciousness, while at the same time avoiding cultural chauvinism, proves elusive and fanciful.

The persistent trend, for more than a hundred years and often encouraged by scholars defending their fields of literary expertise, is to select and promote a single ancient 'source text' as the 'true classic material', whether it be in Sanskrit, Syriac, Arabic or Persian, and ignore, even denigrate, the other three sources. Such behaviour can reach the extreme of one expert within a single language seemingly dismissing the contribution of another, as occurred in the 1990s when two English versions of the Panchatantra translated from separate Sanskrit manuscripts (both, incidentally, dated significantly after al-Muqaffa's 750 AD Arabic version) were published independently as 'classics' of Indian Wisdom by (a) Penquin (1993) and (b) Oxford University Press (1997).

To literate outsiders such prejudicing of texts can appear absurd, even deliberately confusing. "So which translated Sanskrit manuscript," one might ask, "offers the true Panchatantra classic?" And the answer, entering the purest realm of literary quantum reality, must be "Both!". And if we include the many Arabic, Syriac and Persian versions known under the various guises of Kalila and Dimna or Fables of Bidpai and the derivatives thereof, then we can immediately add a couple hundred more versions, all of them also 'classics', yet each with an individual treatment and arrangement in the voice of a different "singer of the song", delivering the goods somewhere in the last 2000 years.

The regional difficulty, as the novelist Doris Lessing says at the start of her introduction to Ramsay Wood's 1980 "retelling" of only the first two (Mitra Bhedha-The Loss of Friends & Mitra Laabha-Gaining Friends) of the five Panchatantra principles, is that ".... it is safe to say that most people in the West these days will not have heard of it, while they will certainly at the very least have heard of the Upanishads and the Vedas. Until comparatively recently, it was the other way around. Anyone with any claim to a literary education knew that the Fables of Bidpai or the Tales of Kalila and Dimna-these being the most commonly used titles with us-was a great Eastern classic. There were at least twenty English translations in the hundred years before 1888. Pondering on these facts leads to reflection on the fate of books, as chancy and unpredictable as that of people or nations."

The Great Panchatantra Tales

For more than two and a half millennia, the Panchatantra tales have regaled children and adults alike with a moral at the end of every story. Some believe that they are as old as the Rig veda. There is also another story about these fables. According to it, these are stories Shiva told his consort Parvati. The present series is based on the Sanskrit original.

A king, worried that his three sons are without the wisdom to live in a world of wile and guile, asks a learned man called Vishnu Sharman to teach them the ways of the world.

Since his wards are dimwits, Vishnu Sharman decides to pass on wisdom to them in the form of stories. In these stories, he makes animals speak like human beings. Panchatantra is a collection of attractively told stories about the five ways that help the human being succeed in life. Pancha means five and tantra means ways or strategies or principles. Addressed to the king's children, the stories are primarily about statecraft and are popular throughout the world. The five strategies are:

- Discord among friends
- Gaining friends
- Of crows and owls
- Loss of gains and
- Imprudence

The stories have been translated into nearly every language in the world that has a script. The story form appeals to children while the wisdom in them attracts adults. The Panchatantra collection represents the earliest folk tale form in the world of literature. There are several versions of Panchatantra tales in circulation in the world but the one that is popular in India is the Sanskrit original of Vishnu Sharman.

The stories will appear in five sections, each representing a strategy for getting over problems in life. They are of interest not just for the ruling class but also for every person. They are all about survival in a complicated world and the several ways to get over problems. The stories based as they are on human nature have an eternal relevance.

The series begins with a parent story that unfolds story after story; each strung to the other by a narrator. Now, it is your turn to enjoy these stories as immortal and fragrant as the soil of India.

First Strategy

The Loss of Friends

Once upon a time, Amarasakti ruled the city-state of Mahilaropyam in the south of India. He had three witless sons who became a matter of endless worry for him. Realizing that his sons had no interest in learning, the king summoned his ministers and said:

"You know I am not happy with my sons. According to men of learning an unborn son and a stillborn son are better than a son who is a dimwit. What good is a barren cow? A son who is stupid will bring dishonour to his father. How can I make them fit to be my successors? I turn to you for advice."

One of the ministers suggested the name of Vishnu Sharman, a great scholar enjoying the respect of hundreds of his disciples. "He is the most competent person to tutor your children. Entrust them to his care and very soon you will see the change."

The king summoned Vishnu Sharman and pleaded with him "Oh, venerable scholar, take pity on me and please train my sons into great scholars and I will make you the lord of hundred villages."

Vishnu Sharman said "Oh, king, listen to my pledge. Hundred villages do not tempt me to vend learning. Count six months from today. If I do not make your children great scholars, you can ask me to change my name."

The king immediately called his sons and handed them to the care of the learned man. Sharman took them to his monastery where he started teaching them the five strategies (Panchatantra). Keeping his word, he finished the task the king entrusted him in six months. Since then, Panchatantra became popular all over the world as children's guide in solving problems of life.

Now begins the Loss of Friends (first of the five strategies) series. These are stories that figure in a dialogue between two jackals named Karataka and Damanaka.

Long, long ago, a merchant named Vardhaman lived in a town in the south of India. As he was resting on his bed one day it struck him that money was the axis of the world and that the more he had of it the more he would be powerful. Even enemies seek the friendship of a rich man, he told himself. The old become young if they have riches and the young become old if they do not have wealth. Business is one of the six ways that help man amass wealth. This was his logic.

Mobilizing all his wares, Vardhaman set out on an auspicious day for Madhura in search of markets for his goods. He began his travel in a gaily-decorated cart drawn by two bullocks. On the way, tired of the long haul, one of the bullocks named Sanjeevaka collapsed in the middle of a jungle near river Jamuna. But the merchant continued his journey asking some of his servants to take care of the animal. But the servants abandoned the bullock soon after their master had left. Joining him later, they told him that the bullock was dead.

In fact, Sanjeevaka was not dead. Feeding on the abundant fresh and tender grass in the forest, he regained strength and began to merrily explore the jungle, dancing and singing in joy. In the same forest lived Pingalaka, the lion. Sanjeevaka, content with his new life in the jungle would waltz and sing uproariously with joy. One day, Pingalaka and other animals were drinking water in the Jamuna when the lion heard the frightening bellow of the bullock. In panic, the lion withdrew into the forest and sat deeply lost in thought and surrounded by other animals.

Sensing the predicament of their king, two jackals, Karataka and Damanaka, sons of two dismissed ministers, were clueless as to what had happened to their king.

"What could have happened to the lord of the forest," asked Damanaka.

"Why should we poke our nose into affairs that are not our concern? Haven't you heard the story of the monkey which pulled out the wedge from the log," asked Damanaka.

"Sounds interesting. Why don't you tell me what happened to the monkey," pleaded Damanaka.

"Now, listen," said Damanaka and began narrating the story of the monkey.

The Monkey and the Wedge

A merchant once started building a temple in the middle of his garden. Many masons and carpenters were working for the merchant. They took time off every day to go to the town for their lunch. One day, when the workers left for lunch a batch of monkeys landed at the temple site and began playing with whatever caught their fancy. One of the monkeys saw a partly sawed log of wood and a wedge fixed in it so that it does not close up.

Curious to know what it is, the monkey began furiously tugging at the wedge. At last the wedge came off, not before trapping the legs of the monkey into the rift of the log. Very soon, not able to get his legs out of the closed wood, the monkey died.

"Therefore," Karataka told Damanaka, "it is not wise to poke our nose into affairs that are not our concern. We have a food store. Why should we bother ourselves about this lion?"

Damanaka retorted, "Food is not the centre of our life. The elders have said that wise men seek the help of the king to help friends and harm foes. There are hundred ways of collecting food. What matters is a life full of learning, courage and wealth. If living somehow is the goal, even the crow lives long eating leftovers."

"True, but we are not ministers any more. The elders have always said that the stupid person who offers uncalled for advice to the king invites not only insult but also deceit," said Karataka.

"No," Damanaka said, "anyone who serves the king with devotion is bound to earn his favour in the long run. The one who does not remains where he is. Those who understand why the king is angry or generous will one-day rise in office. It is necessary to be in the good books of the king.'

"Okay, what do you want to do now?" asked Karataka.

"You know the king is scared now. We will ask him what frightens him and using the six ways of diplomacy get close to him."

"How do you know the king is scared?"

"Changes in posture, signs, pace, actions, conversation, looks and expression indicate the working of the mind. I will approach the fear-struck king today and with my intelligence, I will dispel his fear and once again become his minister," said Damanaka.

"How can you do it when you do not know principles of service?" asked Karataka.

Damanaka told him all he knew and learnt about what makes a good and loyal servant in the service of the king.

"In that case, I wish you all good luck," said Karataka.

Taking leave of Karataka, Damanaka then called on the king. Recognizing that he was the son of his old minister, King Pingalaka told his sentry to bring him into his presence. Damanaka came down on his knees to pay respects to the king.

"We haven't seen you for a long time," the king said.

"I don't know of what use I can be to you, my lord. Yet, according to the learned, there are occasions when every person however high or low will be of use to the king. For generations we have served the king with devotion. Yet I am out of your majesty's favour."

"All right, competent or incompetent you are the son of our old minister. Go ahead and tell me whatever you have in your mind," the king ordered Damanaka.

"May I ask you humbly, my lord, what made you come back from the lake without drinking water," asked Damanaka reluctantly.

"O' Damanaka, haven't you heard the great and frightening sounds in the distance? I want to leave this forest. The strange animal that could make such sounds ought to be as powerful as the sounds he makes."

"Your majesty, if it is only sound that is your problem, I wish to submit that sounds are misleading. I can tell you the story of the jackal, how it overcame the fear of sound."

Let us hear it, said the king.

The Jackal and the Drum

A hungry jackal set out in search of food and ended up at an abandoned battlefield whence he heard loud and strange sounds. Scared, he thought, "I must disappear from here before the man who is making these sounds gets me." After a while he told himself, "I must not run away like that. Let me find out what really the sounds are and who is making them because whether it is fear or happiness one must know its cause. Such a person will never regret his actions. So, let me first look for the source of these noises."

Warily, the jackal marched in the direction of the sounds and found a drum there. It was this drum, which was sending the sounds whenever the branches of the tree above brushed against it. Relieved, the jackal began playing the drum and thought that there could be food inside it. The jackal entered the drum by piercing its side. He was disappointed to find no food in it. Yet he consoled himself saying that he rid himself of the fear of sound.

"Therefore", Damanaka told king Pingalaka, "your majesty should not be afraid of sounds. I seek your permission to go and see what the sounds are." "Okay," said the king. Taking leave of the king, Damanaka proceeded in the direction of the sound.

The king now began worrying himself about Damanaka's intentions. "He may have a grudge against me for dismissing him once. Such persons seek revenge. I should not have taken him into confidence. Let me keep an eye on him. Wise men have always maintained that it is difficult to kill even a weak man who does not easily trust others but easy to kill a strong man who readily trusts others," the king thought.

As the king kept an eye on him, Damanaka moved slowly towards Sanjeevaka, the bullock, and found that he was after all an animal and thought, "This is a good omen. This will help me to get back into the good books of the king. Kings never follow the advice of their ministers unless they are in peril or grief. Just as a healthy man never thinks of a doctor, a strong and secure king also never remembers the need for a minister."

Assured that what he saw was only a bullock, Damanaka returned to the king and told him what he saw.

"Is it true?" the king asked.

"The king is God. The man who lies to a king perishes. He alone has the power to grant favours."

"I believe you. Great men do not harm weaker people. They take on only their equals. That is what is unique about brave people."

"What your majesty says is true. Sanjeevaka is great. If your lordship permits me, I will persuade him to be one of your servants."

"All right, I am taking you back as a minister," said the king, pleased.

Damanaka at once hurried back to Sanjeevaka and told him to stop bellowing and come and meet his king. But the bullock wanted who this Pingalaka was. "What? You do not know our lord? Wait, you will know shortly the cost of this ignorance. There he is, surrounded by his retinue under the banyan tree." Sanjeevaka thought his days were numbered and pleaded with Damanaka, "Sir, you seem to be a man of great wisdom and wit. You alone can save me. I can come only if you can assure me that no harm will come to me." Damanaka told the bullock to wait for the right time to meet the king.

Returning to the king, Damanaka told him "My lord, he is not an ordinary being. He is the vehicle of Lord Shiva. He told me that Lord Shiva had permitted him to feed on the tender grass in the neighbourhood of Jamuna. But I told him that the forest belonged to our lion king who is the vehicle of goddess Chandika. You are our guest. You can see our king and seek a separate space for you to graze. He agreed to this plan provided he has an assurance from your majesty."

"Yes, certainly. But I will need assurance from him in return. Bring him here," the king told Damanaka. Going back to the bullock Damanaka advised him, "You have the assurance of the king. But this new position should not go to your head. We have to work together. That is how we can prosper. Otherwise, he who does not respect everyone, however high or low, will forfeit the favour of kings like Dantila."

"What about Dantila?" asked Sanjeevaka.

The Fall and Rise of a Merchant

In the city of Vardhaman, there lived a wealthy merchant named Dantila. He held a great reception for his wedding attended by the king, the queen, their ministers and all the rich and influential persons in the city. Present at the reception was Gorambha, a lowly sweeper in the royal household. When Dantila saw him occupying a seat reserved for the nobles of the king, he ordered his servants to throw him out of his house.

Thus insulted, Gorambha thought to himself, "I am a poor man and so cannot give a fitting reply to such a wealthy person as Dantila. I must some how see that the king stops his favours to him." Then he hit upon a plan to take revenge on Dantila.

One early morning when the king was still in sleep, Gorambha pretending to sweep the king's bedroom began loudly murmuring, "Oh, how arrogant is Dantila! He has the cheek to lock the queen in his embrace." Hearing this, the king demanded to know whether what Gorambh was murmuring is true. Did Dantila embrace the queen?

"Oh, your majesty, I don't remember nor do I know what I was saying because I was drowsy having spent the entire night in gambling," the sweeper told the king.

Not satisfied with his reply the king thought that it was possible that the sweeper had seen Dantila, who had equal access to the royal household as Gorambha, embracing the queen. He remembered wise men saying that men were likely to talk in their sleep about what they did, saw and desired in the day. Women were chaste because men were not within reach or they were afraid of prying servants. Convinced that Dantila had indeed embraced the queen, the king barred Dantila from entering the royal household.

The merchant began grieving his fate though he had not done any harm to the king or his relatives even in his dreams. One day as Dantila was trying to enter the king's palace he was barred by the king's men. Seeing this Gorambha told them, "You fools, you are barring the great Dantila who has won the king's favours. He is powerful. If you stop him, you will meet with the same fate as I did at the hands of Dantila one day."

The merchant thought that it would do him good to make Gorambha happy and win his confidence. One evening he invited the sweeper for tea and presented him with expensive clothes and told him, "Friend, I had never meant to insult you. You had occupied a seat I had set apart for the learned. Kindly pardon me."

Pleased, the sweeper promised to win the king's favour for Dantila again. The next day, Gorambha repeated the same drama of pretending to talk irrelevantly, raving that the king was eating cucumber in the rest room. "What nonsense are you talking? Did you ever see me doing such things?" the king demanded to know. "No, your majesty. I do not know nor do I remember what I was saying because I was drowsy having spent the entire night in gambling," the sweeper said.

The king then realized that if what the sweeper had said about him was not true what he had said about Dantila also could not be true. A person like Dantila could not have done what Gorambha had told him. The king also found that without Dantila the affairs of the state had suffered and civic administration had come to a standstill. The king immediately summoned the merchant to his palace and restored to him all the authority he had enjoyed before he fell out of king's favour.

Damanaka resumed, "That is why we must know that pride goes before fall." Sanjeevaka agreed. Taking him to the lion king, Damanaka introduced Sanjeevaka to Pingalaka. After exchanging pleasantries, the king asked him to relate his past and the purpose of staying in that jungle. On the bullock relating his story, the king said, "Friend, don't be afraid. I assure you that I will protect you from wild animals here because even stronger animals feel insecure here."

Since then, the king asked Karataka and Damanaka to look after the affairs of the state and began happily spending his time in the company of Sanjeevaka. But the jackals were worried that after Sanjeevaka had become a good friend of the king, the king gave up his royal sports and pastime and became a saint. The jackal twins thought, "the king has stopped taking us into confidence after Sanjeevaka became his best friend. He is also indifferent to his kingly duties. What shall we do now?"

Karataka said, "The king may not heed our advice. But it is our duty to advise him on it if it is good for him. Elders have always held that even if the king is not willing to heed good advice, it is the duty of his ministers to offer him advice. "You are right," said Damanaka. "The mistake is mine. What happened to the sage and the jackal should not happen to us."

Karataka then pleaded with him to tell the story of the sage and the jackal. Damanaka began telling him.

The Crafty Crane and the Craftier Crab

Once upon a time an old crane lived on the rim of a large lake in the middle of a jungle. Because of age, it was not able to prey on fish and other insects. Unable to suffer hunger, the crane stood on the edge of the lake and began crying pitiably. Moved at the sight, a crab passing by asked the crane:

"Friend, what is the matter? Why are you not hunting for food today?"

"Son, you have correctly guessed. I am feeling guilty because I have swallowed too many fish. I have decided to fast unto death and am not harming even the fish that are within my reach," said the crane.

"But why are you so philosophical today," asked the crab.

"What shall I tell you? I have heard that there will be no rains for the coming twelve years. Astrologers have forecast an evil conjunction of the planets. As a result, there won't be rains on this earth for another twelve years. All these years we have all played and lived together. I am now worried about the fate waiting for these poor fish and other creatures in the lake. They will die and I will be alone and without them."

"Is there no way we can save ourselves?"

"At present, fish and other water creatures in other lakes are migrating to bigger lakes with the help of their relatives. Here, nobody seems to worry about the dark future. At this rate, there won't be any kind of fish left."

The crab carried this information to all the fish and other water creatures in the lake. Alarmed, all of them came to the crane and pleaded with him to show them the way to overcome this danger.

"Why not. There is a big lake not far from here that has plenty of water throughout the year and lotuses always in bloom. That lake does not go dry even if there are no rains for twenty-four years. I can ferry all of you one by one to that lake."

The poor fish and other water creatures at once put all the trust in the crane and agreed to be ferried. Every day, the crane would take one of them at a time to a lonely place, smash them against a stone and eat them. He would return to the lake and repeat the trick every day.

One day the crab asked the crane, "Uncle, you are taking everyone to the faraway lake and not me. Why don't you take me there today and save my life?"

Tired with eating fish every day, the crane too was happy to carry the crab to the lake that did not exist. The crab was happy and mounted on the back of the crane. As the crane was flying close to the spot where he ate all the fish, the crab saw a heap of fish bones and asked the crane, "Uncle, we have come a long distance and I see no lake anywhere. Tell me, where is the lake?"

"You are a fool to trust me. There is no lake. Nor is there water. Say your prayers now; I am going to kill you." The crafty crab at once caught the neck of the crane in his claws and tore through it to death. Slowly, carrying the crane's neck, the crab reached the lake where all his friends, worried that the crane did not come back, asked him what made him come back.

The crab said, "you fools, that crane was taking all of us to a lonely place where it would smash the victims against a rock and have them for lunch. I found out his mischief and saved myself by slicing his neck. From today, all of us can live happily without fear."

Then the crows asked the jackal how they could get rid of the cobra that was feasting on their offspring. The jackal told them to go to a big city and snatch any item of jewellery from a palace and drop it in the hollow of the tree that is the cobra's home. In search of the jewellery, the king's men would reach the tree and kill the cobra.

The crow couple flew off to a lake where the women in the king's harem were revealing in water. Before entering water, the women left their jewellery and clothes on the waterside. The female crow skilfully dived and snatched a gold necklace and began slowly flying towards the cobra's hideout. The king's men who saw the crow fly off with the necklace followed the female crow and saw it dropping the necklace into the hollow of the tree. They ran to the tree and pulling it out killed the cobra.

"That's why," Damanaka told Karataka, "elders say that he who is wise is stronger than the strong. That is how a small hare killed the almighty lion."

"How is that?" asked Karataka.

"That is another story," said Damanaka.

The Cunning Hare and the Witless Lion

Bhasuraka was a lion lording over the jungle, killing deer, boars, rabbits, bisons, etc. Yet he was not happy with his kill. The victims too were unhappy and met the lion one day in a delegation. "Oh, lord," they said, "why do you kill so many animals every day when you need only one for your food? Let us come to an understanding. From today, you need not move from your place. We will send an animal every day to you. That will spare you the trouble of hunting and us our lives."

"Our forebears have said that the duty of the king is to rule and not to destroy. Just as a seed sprouts, grows into a tree and yields fruit, a people protected by the king come to his rescue in times of need."

"What you say is true," the lion said and added a condition. "If you fail to send one animal every day, I shall kill all of you."

"Agreed," said the animals and began roaming the forest without fear and sending one of their own folk to the lion for his lunch. One day it was the turn of a hare. He started leisurely on his last journey and saw a big well on the way and saw his own reflection when he peeped into the well from curiosity.

Suddenly an idea struck the hare. "I will somehow tempt the lion to the well and persuade him to jump into it," the hare thought to himself. It was late in the evening when the hare reached the lion's den. The lion was hungry and so angry and decided to kill all the animals when the hare came and knelt before him.

"First, you are too small for my lunch. Second, you have come late. I shall kill you and all the others too," the lion warned the hare.

"My lord, it is not my fault or the fault of other animals."

"Let me know who it is who delayed you and I will kill him at once."

"Our folks have decided that it is my turn today. Since I do not make a full meal, they have sent three more hares with me for your meal. As we were all coming to you, a big lion came out of his den and demanded to know where we were all going."

"We are all going to Bhasuraka as his meal according to our arrangement, we said. The big lion said that this jungle belonged to him and that all animals obeyed its orders. He also told us that you are a cheat and asked us to bring you to him for a trial of strength. Whoever is the victor will become the king. He commanded me to summon you to his fort. That's why I am late. It is now for you to decide," the hare told the lion.

"In that case," Bhasuraka told the hare, "show me that lion. I will kill him and have him for lunch. According to the elders territory, friendship and gold are the rewards of war. Wise men do not go to war unless there are gains."

"Yes, my lord," said the hare, "what you say is true. But the big lion lives in a fort. He knows that the king without a fort is like a cobra without fangs and an elephant without heat."

"Stop that nonsense and bring him here. Don't you know that you have to crush the enemy and disease at the first opportunity? Otherwise, they will grow in strength and crush you."

"But the big lion seems to be very strong. Haven't you heard elders saying that one should not go to war without assessing one's own strength and the strength of the enemy? He who meets the enemy in haste will perish like the locusts in a fire."

Growing impatient, the lion roared, "why all this tall talk. Show him to me." Asking the lion to accompany him, the hare took him to the well. He told the lion that the big lion was there in that fort and showed him the well. The lion then peeped into the well and mistaking his reflection in the water for the big lion jumped into the well to kill him. Thus the foolish lion perished and all the animals in the jungle lived happily ever after.

Damanaka resumed, "This is how with my skills I will create a rift between Pingalaka and Sanjeevaka."

"All right, best of luck to you," said Karataka.

One day when Pingalaka was alone, Damanaka visited him and bowed to him.

"We haven't seen you for a long time," said Pingalaka. "Of what use am I to you? Yet, when your rule is breaking up, I thought I should inform you. Even without asking, offer good advice to him whom you want to protect from indignity, said our elders."

"Whatever you want to say, say it without hesitation."

Gathering courage, Damanaka said, "My lord, Sanjeevaka wants to harm you. Taking me into confidence, he once told me that he would kill you, become the king and make me a minister."

"But Sanjeevaka is a trusted friend of mine. Why should he think of harming me?"

"There is no loyal or disloyal servant. There is no servant who does not covet power. My lord, what made you to take Sanjeevaka into confidence? Don't think he is a strong animal able to kill your enemies. This will not happen because he is a vegetarian and my lord feasts on meat. It is better to get rid of him."

"You remember I gave him the word on your advice. How can I kill him who has won assurance from me."

"My lord, according to wise men, you should not make friends with people you do not know. You know how an innocent flea died for the fault of a bug."

Pingalaka demanded to know the story. Damanaka began to relate.

The Bug and the Poor Flea

Once upon a time a bug named Mandavisarpini made for itself a small home in the folds of the milk-white sheets of linen spread on the king's ornamental bed. One day, the bug saw a flea drifting into the king's bedroom and told the flea that he had come to a wrong place and asked him to leave before somebody noticed him.

The flea, whose name was Agnimukha, said, "Oh venerable sir, it is not proper for you to ask a guest to leave even if he is a wicked person. You must welcome him, ask him about his health, say words that comfort him and request him to take rest. That is how good hosts treat their guests. Besides, I have tasted the blood of a variety of men and animals. Never did I taste royal blood. The king's blood is a compound of rich foods and is bound to taste rich. Please permit me to relish this delicacy."

The flea continued, "Everything we do in this world we do to slake our hunger. I have come to you in search of food. It is not proper for you to siphon off the king's blood all alone. You should share it with me also."

The bug told him, "oh, flea, I suck the blood of the king when he is fast asleep. You are impatient. You have to wait till I finish my job. After me, you can have your fill." The flea agreed.

Meanwhile, the king entered his bedroom to sleep. But the impatient flea began feasting on the king's blood even before he went to sleep. Stung by his bite, the king rose from his bed and asked his servants to look for what was in the bed that caused him discomfort. The king's men pulled the linen off the bed and examined it closely. Before they could him, the flea sneaked into a recess of the bed. The servants found the poor bug and killed him at once.

Damanaka told Pingalaka, "This is why you should kill Sanjeevaka before he could kill you. He who abandons a trusted confidant and trusts an outsider will die like sage Kakudruma."

"How did he die?" Pinagalaka asked him.

The Story of the Blue Jackal

Chandaraka was a jackal living in a forest. One day, driven by hunger, he came to a nearby town in search of food. Seeing him, a group of mongrels began chasing and attacking him whenever possible. The jackal fled in panic and entering the house of a washerman hid in a vat full of blue used for bleaching clothes. When he came out, he became a blue animal. Thinking that he was not the jackal they chased, the mongrels dispersed.

The jackal came back to the forest with his body dyed in blue. When the lions, tigers, panthers, wolves and other animals in the forest saw him, they took fright and ran in all directions. They thought to themselves, "We do not know his power and strength. It is better we keep a distance from him. Haven't the elders warned not to trust him whose conduct, caste and courage are not known."

Seeing them scared, the dyed jackal said, "Why do you run away like that. There is no need to fear. I am a special creation of God. He told me that the animals in the jungle here had no ruler and that he was nominating me as your king. He named me as Kakudruma and told me to rule all of you. Therefore all of you can live safely under the umbrella of my protection."

All the animals in the jungle accepted him as the king. He in turn appointed the lion as his minister, the tiger as his chamberlain and the wolf as the gatekeeper. After distributing office to the animals, the new king Kakudruma banished all the jackals in the forest. The lions, tigers and the wolves killed other animals and brought them as food for the king. Taking his share, Kakudruma would distribute the rest of the kill among his subjects.

One day when the blue jackal was holding court, he heard a gang of jackals howling. Thrilled by the sound of his own ilk, Kakudruma began loudly responding in his natural voice. The lions and other animals immediately recognized that their king was after all a jackal and not a Godsend. They at once pounced on the blue jackal and killed him.

"The moral is," Damanaka said, "he who abandons his own folk will perish."

"But how do I believe that Sanjeevaka has evil intentions," asked Pingalaka.

"He told me today that he would kill you tomorrow. If you notice him carefully tomorrow, you will find him red-eyed and occupying a seat he does not deserve. He would stare at you angrily. If what I say comes true, it is for you what to do with Pingalaka," said Damanaka.

After this meeting with the lion king, Damanaka went to meet Pingalaka. The bullock received him with courtesy and said, "We are meeting after a long time. What can I do for you? They are the blessed who are visited by friends."

"Your are right, sir. But where is rest for servants. They have lost their freedom for the sake of money. They know no sleep, no interest in food nor can they speak without fear. Yet they live. Somebody has rightly compared service to a dog's life," said Damanaka.

"Come to the point, my friend" The bullock was now impatient.

Damanaka said, "Sir, a minister is not supposed to give bad advice. He cannot also disclose state secrets. If he does, he will go to hell after his death. But in the cause of your friendship, I have revealed a secret. It is on my suggestion that you have taken up service in the royal household. Pingalaka has evil designs against you. When we were alone, he told me he would kill you and bring happiness to everyone in the palace.

"I told the king that this was stabbing a friend in the back," Damanaka continued. "The king was angry and said that you were a vegetarian and he lived on a diet of meat and so there was natural discord between you and him. He said that this was enough reason for him to kill you. This is a secret I have kept to myself for a long time. It is now for you to do what is necessary."

Sanjeevaka fainted on hearing these words. Recovering after some time, he said, "It is truly said that a person who serves the king is like a bullock without horns. It is difficult to know the mind of a king who has different ideas. It is not easy to serve a king. Even sages could not read the minds of kings. I think some servants who were jealous of my friendship with the king must have poisoned his mind."

"Don't worry," Damanaka said. "Forget what tales the servants carried to the king. You can still win his favour by your sweet words."

"That is not true. It is impossible to live with wicked people, however small they are. They can always think of a hundred ways to get you in the same manner the jackal and crow trapped the camel."

"Sounds interesting. Let me know what happened to the camel," asked Damanaka.

Sanjeevaka began to tell him the story.

The Camel, the Jackal and the Crow

In a far off forest, there lived a lion named Madotkata served by a leopard, a jackal and a crow. One day they sighted Kradanaka, a camel who lost his way. Thinking the camel they saw was an unusual animal, the lion asked his assistants to find out if he was a wild animal or domestic animal.

The crow said that the camel was a domestic animal fit to be killed and eaten. Refusing to eat Kradanaka, the lion said:

"I shall not kill someone who came seeking hospitality. According to our elders, you cannot kill even an enemy who came trusting you. He who kills so commits the sin of killing hundred Brahmins. Assure him of safety and bring him to me."

The three assistants brought the camel to the presence of the lion. On the lion asking the camel to relate his story, Kradanaka told him how he was part of a trade caravan and how he had lost his way. The lion told the camel, "Kradanaka, why do you go back to your village and become once again a beast of burden? Remain with us without any hesitation and feast on this tender grass." Thereafter, the camel stayed on to live happily with the lion and his three assistants.

One day, the lion was locked in a battle with an elephant. The tusker gored Madotkata and badly injured him. Hebecame too weak to hunt. Without food he was in no position to do anything. Then, the lion asked the assistants to go out and look for some animal for his meal. "Bring the animal here. I will kill him somehow and provide food for you all," said the lion.

The leopard, the jackal, and the camel looked everywhere for an animal but could not find anyone. The jackal told the crow aside:

"Friend, what is the use of wasting time like this? We have Kradanaka, our lord's loyal friend. Let us kill him and survive." "That is fine. Yet we cannot kill him because our lord has assured him protection," said the crow."

"Leave it to me. I shall convince Madotkata to kill the camel. Wait here. I will meet the lord and get his permission," said the jackal and left to meet the lion.

The jackal told his lord, "Oh, lord, we went to every nook and corner of the forest. We could not find a single animal. We are tired, weak and hungry. Since my lord is also in the same condition, I humbly suggest that we make a meal of this camel."

Highly annoyed, the lion said, "You sinner, if you repeat these words, I shall first kill you. I have given him my word. How can I kill him? Haven't our elders said that no gift of land or cow or food is greater than the gift of an assurance?"

"You are right my lord. It is a sin to kill him who has your word. But if the camel voluntarily offers himself as food it is no sin to accept the offer. If he does not volunteer, you can kill anyone of us. You are hungry and close to your end. If we are not of use to you at this time what value have our lives? If anything undesirable happens to our lord, we will immolate ourselves."

"This seems to be more reasonable," said the lion.

The jackal told the other two assistants, "Friends, our lord is in a pitiable condition. There is now no one to protect us from others. Instead of aimlessly searching the forest for food, let us offer our bodies to him. That will deliver us from the burden of debt. The servant who is witness to the helpless death of his master will go to hell."

After the jackal's plea, all of them called on the lion with tears in their eyes. "What's the matter? Did you find an animal?" asked the lion.

"No, my lord. We searched every place, every inch of the forest. We are not lucky. We found nothing. But I request the lord to have me for his meal. That will mean two birds with one shot. The lord will survive and I will go to heaven. He who lays down his life to save his lord will have no rebirth," said the crow.

It was now the turn of the jackal to show his loyalty. He said, "My friend, crow. Your body is too small to slake the hunger of my lord. It amounts to starving him and that is a sin. Get out of my way. I have to submit a plea to my lord."

Addressing the lion, the jackal said, "Lord, I request you to have me for your meal and ensure me a place in heaven. The lord has rights of life and death over his servants. Therefore, it is no sin in exercising his rights."

The leopard intervened and said, "You jackal, you are no great personality. Let me plead with the lord." Addressing Madotkata, the leopard said, "Oh lord, let me give away my life to save your life. Please permit me to earn a permanent berth in heaven. My sacrifice will win fame for me on earth."

All this set Kradanaka thinking, "All these servants of the lord have said what they wanted to say. Still, the lion did not kill anyone of them. Let me also offer to be the lord's food today. I am sure my friends will support me.' He then turned to the leopard and said, "What you have said is right and proper. But you are a carnivorous animal and belong to the same species as the master does. How can he kill you? Let me offer myself."

The camel then came forward and requested the lion to have him for that day's meal. At once, the jackal and the leopard pounced on him tore him to pieces and all of them had a sumptuous feast.

As the story ended Sanjeevaka told Damanaka, "Wicked people surround the king. Good men should not serve such masters. I will need your advice to get out of this problem."

"The best course is to leave the country," said Damanaka.

"It is not wise to leave when the king is still angry. He can reach me anywhere I go. The only alternative I have is to go to war with the king."

Damanaka was afraid that if Sanjeevaka chose to fight Pingalaka the lion might die and that would be a disaster. Let me persuade the bullock to leave the forest, he thought.

"Going to war is all right. But how can there be a war between a servant and a king? If you underestimate the strength of your enemy you will meet the same fate as the Sea met at the hands of the bird pair."

Curious, Sanjeeva asked, "What happened to the birds?"

The Bird Pair and the Sea

Once upon a time, a pair of pheasants lived close to the Sea. They spent their time happily singing and dancing on the branches of the trees by the Sea. One day the female pheasant told her husband that she was expecting their baby and he must look for a safe place to lay the eggs. The husband said, "My dear, this Seaside is enchanting and it is better you lay eggs here only."

The wife said, "When it is full moon, the Sea tide can wash away even wild elephants. Let us go elsewhere."

Amused, the husband said, "What you say is true. But the Sea has no power to harm us. Haven't you heard that there is no fool who could stop the flight of a bird or a fool who would enter fire recklessly. Will anyone be brash enough to challenge Yama (the Lord of Death) to take his life if he can? You can lay your eggs here only."

Listening to this dialogue, the Sea thought, "How vain is this bird which is as small as a worm! Let me drown these eggs and see what he can do."

After laying eggs, the female bird went in search of food. In her absence, the Sea sent a wave that sucked the eggs in to the waters. The female returned to the nest and, not finding the eggs there, told the husband, "You are a fool. I told you that the waves would wash away the eggs. Those who do not heed the good words of a friend will perish like the turtle who fell off the stick."

"What's that turtle and what is that stick?" asked the husband.

Once upon a time a turtle called Kambugriva lived in a pond. He had two swans, Sankat and Vikat, as good friends.

Every day they would meet on the rim of the pond and discuss legends of yore. They would disperse with sunset. That year there were no rains and the water in the pond began slowly disappearing.

Worried, the swans told the turtle, "Friend, What will happen to you? We are concerned."

"I appreciate your interest in me. There is trouble ahead. Please find a way out of this crisis. But it is important that we should not give in to despair. According to Manu, all good men should come to the rescue of friends and relatives in times of need. Look for a stick or a rope. I will hang on to it as both of you hold the two sides of the stick or rope and ferry me to safety."

"We shall do as you say," the swans said. "But you have to shut your mouth. Otherwise, you will crash to the ground."

On Kambugriva agreeing to the plan, the swans brought a stick and asked the turtle to hold it with his teeth. When everything was ready, the swans flew off with the turtle hanging from it. On the way people saw this sight and exclaimed, "see, how clever the birds are." In trying to respond to the people, the turtle opened his mouth and fell to the ground and the people at once killed him.

"The lesson is that those who do not heed the advice of their well-wishers meet their end like the turtle. Any day, the survivors are those who foresee a danger in time and those who deal with it when it comes. Those who leave things to fate and believe in luck will destroy themselves like Yadbhavishya," said the female pheasant.

"What happened to Yadbhavishya?" asked the male bird.

Tale of the Three Fish

Three fish lived in a pond. Their names were Anagatavidhata, Pratyutpannamati and Yadbhavishya. Some fishermen passing by the pond wondered, "Hey, we have never seen this pond. It seems to be full of fish. It is now evening. Let us come at dawn tomorrow and bag as many fish as we can."

Hearing the fisherman, Anagatavidhata (the one who foresees a danger in time) called a meeting of all the fish and told them, "Haven't you heard what the fishermen were saying? We must move out of this pond tonight itself. As the wise men have said weak men should flee when a strong man invades or seek refuge in a fort. There is no alternative."

"The fisherman will come tomorrow. I think we should not be here for even a moment more," said Anagatavidhata.

"That's true. I endorse your suggestion," said Pratyutpannamati. "Let's go elsewhere. Those who are afraid of foreign lands and those who are bound to their soil will die in their own country. He who can prosper anywhere does not die in his own land clinging to sentiment."

Loudly laughing, Yadbhavishya said, "Your plans are not good. Why should we leave this pond, ancient home of our forefathers, because the fishermen have evil intentions. If it is destined, we cannot escape death even if we go elsewhere. Everything is in the hands of God. You cannot dispose what he proposes. Without his blessings people will die even if they have protection. With his blessings nobody can kill them even if they do not have protection.

Unable to convince him, the other two fish left the pond. Coming the next day, the fishermen took a big catch of fish in the pond. Yadbhavishya was one among them.

The female pheasant resumed, "That is why I told you that those who foresee the problem and those who deal with the problem when it arises are always victors and those who trust their luck are the losers."

Her husband asked, "In that case do you think I am as stupid as that Yadbhavishya? Wait and see what I can do. I will siphon off all the water in the Sea and leave him dry."

"Don't try to settle scores with the Sea. It will do no good to you. A weak man's anger will hurt him in the end."

"Don't discourage me. Those who have confidence can confront stronger men. Doesn't the lion who is small in size slash the crown of the mighty elephant? Doesn't a small wick repel darkness? He who has courage is the stronger person. See how I will siphon off all the water in the Sea and make him dry," said the male."

"But hundreds of rivers flow into the sea. Your beak is just as big as a drop of the sea. How can you consume all the water in the Sea? Stop this tall talk," advised the female.

"Not to despair is to win the Goddess of Wealth. I have an iron beak. I will toil day and night to siphon of all the water."

The wife said, "Okay, if you want to engage the Sea, call all of your friends and try to do the job together. When they are united, it is difficult to defeat even a band of weak men. Even blades of slender grass can bind an elephant if they are woven into a rope. Haven't you heard the story of how a sparrow, a woodpecker, a fly and a frog killed an elephant?"

"Let me know how they did it," asked the male pheasant. The wife began telling the story.

The Elephant and the Sparrow

Two sparrows, husband and wife, built a nest on a banyan tree where the female sparrow laid eggs. One afternoon a wild elephant came to the tree seeking shelter from the sun. Unable to bear the heat, the tusker suddenly went berserk and snapped a big branch of the tree, crushing the sparrow's eggs in the nest. The sparrow pair somehow escaped the fury of the elephant but the wife began crying for her eggs.

A woodpecker, a close friend of the sparrow, heard her crying andmoved by her grief asked her, "Why are you crying, my friend? Wise men do not grieve what is lost or what is dead or what is past. That is the difference between a learned person and an unlettered man."

The female sparrow said, "The wicked elephant has destroyed my offspring. If you are a true friend of mine suggest a way to kill him. In my view, he who harms a person in trouble or he who ridicules a person in sorrow deserves to be punished and he who punishes such a person has no rebirth."

"What you say is right," said the woodpecker. "He is a friend who comes to your aid when you are in need. Everyone tries to be friendly when you are prospering. You will see how resourceful I am. I have a friend who is a fly. With his help we can kill the elephant."

Taking the female sparrow with him, the woodpecker called on the fly and told him, "This is my dearest friend. A wild elephant has squashed her eggs. You must somehow find a way to kill that elephant. We need your help."

The fly said, "I have a friend who is a frog. Let us go to him and seek his help also." The female sparrow, the woodpecker and the fly went to the frog and narrated the entire story of the sparrow's grief.

The frog said, "What is an elephant before a united crowd like us? Do as I tell you. O' fly, go to the elephant when the sun is high in the sky and hum a sweet tune into his ears. When he closes his eyes in ecstasy, the woodpecker will scoop his eyes out. He becomes blind and thirsty and will look for water. I will go to a quicksand and begin croaking there. Thinking that there is water, the elephant will come there and sink into the quicksand and die."

All the four played out their roles according to the frog's plan and caused the death of the elephant."

At the end of the story, the female pheasant told her husband, "That is how together the four friends killed the elephant."

Impressed by his wife's wisdom, the husband said, "Okay, we will call our friends and with their help crush the Sea.' As their friends, the cranes, the peacocks, the cuckoos and other birds, gathered, the male pheasant told them the story of how the Sea had killed their offspring and how necessary it was to drain him out. At the end, he said, "We cannot do this job. Let us go to Garuda, Lord Vishnu's vehicle, and tell him all that has happened. He will be angry over what the Sea has done to his species. He will surely take revenge on the Sea."

Wailing and weeping, all the birds went to meet Garuda and told him, "O lord, we need your help. The Sea has destroyed the eggs of the pheasant pair. This is a blow to all the bird community. If you do not intervene, he will destroy our entire tribe. Wise men have always said that one wicked person will be an inspiration to all others with evil intentions."

Moved by their story of grief, Garuda thought to himself, "These birds have a legitimate grievance. I will go and punish the Sea.' Meanwhile, an envoy from Lord Vishnu came and told Garuda that the Lord had sent him as He wanted to travel to Amaravathi on a divine mission. The envoy asked Garuda to accompany him at once.

Garuda told the envoy, "No, I cannot come. I am not a useful servant. Let him take someone else. Please convey my regards to the Lord."

Surprised at Garuda's words, the envoy said, "O Garuda, you have never uttered such words about the Lord. Did the Lord slight you in any manner? Let me know."

"See, this Sea, the Lord's habitat, has swallowed the eggs of the pheasant pair. If the Lord does not punish the Sea for this, I shall not serve Him. This is my decision and you may convey this to the Lord," said Garuda.

Informed of Garuda's pique, Vishnu told himself, "Garuda has reason to be annoyed with me. I shall go myself and receive him with respect. If the king is satisfied he can give only money. But when the master honours his servant, the servant is ready to sacrifice his life for the sake of the master. Therefore, it is wise that I should visit and appease him."

When Vishnu arrived to meet him, Garuda felt guilty that he had said harsh words about the Lord and said, "O Lord, the Sea who enjoys your protection has stolen the eggs of my servants and thus insulted me. Because of respect for you, I delayed taking action against him."

"True, learned men say that a master is responsible for the misdeeds of his servants. Such misdeeds hurt the master more than the servant. Come with me. I shall recover those eggs from the Sea and make the pheasant pair happy again. Later we will go to Amaravathi," said Lord Vishnu.

The Lord then took out his thunderbolt and aiming it at the Sea warned him, "You wicked man, return the eggs to the bird pair. Otherwise, I will turn the sea into a desert."

Frightened, the Sea returned the eggs to the pheasants. The male bird handed them to his wife.

"From this story," Damanaka told Sanjeevaka, "it is evident that he who challenges an enemy without knowing his strength perishes in the end."

"True, but how do I know that Pingalaka has evil designs against me? We have been very friendly. That makes it difficult for me think of killing him," said Sanjeevaka.

Damanaka said, "He stares at you in anger if he has evil thoughts in his mind. Otherwise, you may safely think he is the same old affectionate friend. But if you decide to leave the place do it after sunset. Our elders have said that one must sacrifice an individual for the good of the community, give up caste for the good of the village and surrender a village for the good of the country. It is desirable to save money so that one can spend it in a crisis, spend money to save his wife and give up both his wealth and wife to save himself."

After he gave this advice to Sanjeevaka, Damanaka went to see Karataka. Hailing him, Karataka said, "What happened to your mission?"

"I have just finished sowing the seeds of discord among the two friends. The rest is in the hands of God," said Damanaka.

"Let me know how you did it."

"I have carried tales from one to the other and succeeded in dividing the friends. You will not see them again together."

"Oh, you have not done anything good. You have separated two good friends. You have made them hate each other. A wicked person knows only to harm but not mend."

"You do not know political science. However strong you are, unless you kill the enemy or the disease at the very outset, your enemy or the disease will kill you in the end. Sanjeevaka stole the ministership from us and so he is our enemy. I won the king's assurance for him and brought him to the court of the king. Today, he has ousted us from our office. That is why I have plans to kill him. If he wants to save himself, he should leave this place. Wise men, like Chaturaka, do no hesitate to torment others to achieve their goal. Fools like the lion cannot enjoy even what they have won."

On Karataka's request, Damanaka began telling that story.

The Lion and the Jackal

Vajradanstra was a lion living in a forest. He had two friends, a jackal named Chaturaka and a wolf named Kravyamukha. Because of their friendship with the lion, the jackal and the wolf had a free run of the forest. One day the lion found a female camel separated from its caravan and in labour pains. The lion killed the camel and found a live baby camel inside her womb. The lion and his friends fed on the dead camel but spared the baby. The lion adopted the baby and brought him home.

The lion told the baby camel, "You are now my child. Nobody can harm you. You can freely roam about the forest and have a nice time. You have ears which look like a pair of conches. So I will call you Sankhukarna."

As days passed, Sankhukarna became a young and energetic animal. He was always to be seen in the company of Vajradanstra. One day the lion had to confront a wild elephant and in the fight the elephant badly injured the lion. Now the lion was too weak to go out and hunt. He called his friends, the jackal and the wolf, and the camel and toldthem, "Look for an animal. I will kill it and all of us can have a good meal."

The three scoured the entire forest but could not find an animal. In despair, the jackal thought, "If we can kill this camel we will have a sure meal for several days. But he is a favourite of our king. He will not agree to kill the camel. Yet with my cunning I will see that the lion kills him. The learned have said there is nothing impossible or forbidden for an intelligent being."

The jackal told the camel, "O Sankhukarna, our lord has been without food for a long time and he may die of hunger. His death will mean a disaster for all of us. I have a plan to get over this problem. Listen."

"Go ahead. Let me know what you have in mind. I shall certainly do whatever I can for the lord because if we do good to our master we will reap a reward hundred times more valuable than what we gave to the master," said the camel.

Chaturaka, the jackal said, "O young camel, offer your body to the lord at the double the profit. Your body also will grow in size and the lord also will continue to live."

The camel replied, "I am ready. Let the lord know that he can have my body provided the Lord of Duty is a witness to my sacrifice."

The jackal, the wolf and the camel then called on the lion to inform him of the camel's decision. The jackal told the lion, "We searched the entire forest without sighting even a small animal. It is already sunset now. The camel is prepared to offer his body if you are ready to increase the size of his body and invite the Lord of Duty to be a witness."

On the lion agreeing to the proposal, the jackal and the wolf at once pounced on the camel and tore him to pieces.

Vajradanstra, the lion, told the jackal, "I am going to the river to take a bath and worship the deities. Till I come back, keep an eye on this food.' The minute the lion left the scene, the jackal thought of a plan to have the camel all to himself. He told Kravyamukha, the wolf, "You seem to be very hungry. Go ahead and feast on the camel meat. When the lion comes I shall convince him about your innocence."

As the wolf started to taste the meat, the jackal alerted him and told him that the lord was coming and to allay any suspicion he should stop eating and leave the place. When the lion came, he saw that the heart of the camel was missing. Angrily, the lion roared and said, "Who is the culprit, I will kill him."

The wolf then looked at the jackal suggesting that the jackal should convince the lion of his innocence. But the cunning jackal said, "You did not heed my warning and ate the meat. Why do you now expect me to help you?' Realizing thedanger, the wolf fled the scene to save his life.

Meanwhile, a caravan of camels passing by stopped where the lion and the jackal were planning the next move. The lead camel had a big bell tied to his neck. Frightened by the sound of the bell, the lion asked the jackal to find out what the sound was all about. He had not heard such sounds in his life. Pretending to find out, the jackal went out of the lion's sight and shouted from there, "O lord, run for your life."

"What's the matter," the lion asked him. "Why are you frightening me? Let me know clearly what's happening."

The jackal said, "My lord, the Lord of Death is angry that you have killed the camel before its death was due. He is upset and vowed that he would get from you one thousand times more than the value of the camel we have killed. It is the Lord of Death who hung a bell in the lead camel's neck. He also brought with him all the ancestors of the camel."

The jackal thus tricked the lion into hurriedly fleeing the place, leaving the camel's body all to himself to feast upon.

Damanaka continued, "That is why I told you that a wise man protects his interest even if it is to torment others and never shares his secrets with others as Chaturaka, the jackal did in the above story."

Sanjeevaka began pondering, "Why did I do like this. A vegetarian serving a meat eater! What shall I do and where shall I go? Perhaps, Pingalaka may spare me because he had given me assurance. Trouble may sometimes come to people who walk the path of ethical conduct. Every living being does good and sometimes bad deeds. He will reap the consequences in the next birth. So, we cannot escape what fate has in store for us."

With these thoughts on his mind Sanjeevaka went to see Pingalaka, the lion, and sat down without greeting him. The lion also was surprised at the bullock's arrogance and, believing what Damanaka had told him about Sanjeevaka, pounced on him tearing him with his claws. Sanjeevaka too began goring the lion with his horns.

Seeing that the jackal and the lion were determined to fight to the end, Karataka admonished Damanaka, "You fool! You have created a rift between the two friends. If the lord dies, how can you be a minister? How do you aspire to be a minister when you do not know the principles of diplomacy? War mongers like you can never reach their goals. You should not use force where there is still room for peace. One of the two is bound to die. Save the situation if you can. No, it is my folly to tell you what is good and what is bad. Elders have said that one should not preach to one who is not a disciple. You have the example of the bird Suchimukha."

"I am eager to know what it is," said Damanaka.

Suchimukha and The Monkey

A gang of monkeys made their home in a mountain slope. When winter came, it brought not only severe cold but also heavy rains. Unable to stand the cold, the monkeys collected red berries wildly growing in the mountain slope. They gathered around the berries and began blowing air at them thinking they were embers. Watching their vain effort in amusement, Suchimukha, a bird, told them, "You fools, they are not embers but red berries. Why do you waste your energy on them? This will not save you from cold. Go and look for a shelter in a cave or a place free from wind. The clouds are thick and there will be no immediate relief from rain."

An old member of the monkey gang angrily told the bird, "Why do you poke your nose in our affairs? Go away. Haven't the elders said that he who cherishes his welfare should not talk to a gambler or an inefficient workman. So is the person a fool who talks to an idiot or a pleasure seeker."

Disregarding the old monkey's anger and not giving room to any other monkey to talk, Suchimukha went on repeating his advice to them to seek shelter elsewhere. Tired with the bird's unwanted advice, one of the monkeys sprang at the bird and bashed him against a rock till he was dead.

Karataka said at the end of the story, "If you counsel a fool it will only provoke him and not pacify. If you feed milk to a snake it will increase its store of poison. That's why you should not offer advice to everyone. Look, how two good sparrows lost their home, all due to a foolish monkey."

At Damanaka's request, Karataka began telling the story of the evil monkey.

How a Sparrow Came to Grief

A pair of sparrows made their home on a branch of a big tree and lived happily there. Soon it was winter and it began to rain heavily. Frequent gusts of wind made the cold unbearable. At this time, a monkey completely drenched in the rain and shivering from cold, came scurrying to the tree for cover.

Seeing the condition of the monkey, the female sparrow said, "Gentleman, with your feet and hands you seem to be a human being. Why didn't you build a house for yourself?' Angered by this uncalled for advice, the monkey said, "you stupid, why do not you shut up and mind your business?' The monkey told himself, "My, what impudence! This bit of a creature has the cheek to offer me advice. Makes fun of me. Unnecessary prattle. I must teach her a lesson. Why shouldn't I kill her?"

Turning to the female, the monkey said, "How does it help you to worry about my plight? Haven't you heard this saying of the elders that you should offer advice to those who seek it and cherish it? Advice to him who is indifferent is like a cry in the wilderness. Don't try to do that."

When the female persisted, the monkey climbed up the tree and broke up the nest of the sparrow pair.

"That's why," said Karataka to Damanaka, "you should be careful in offering advice. You are a fool who does not understand the essence of my advice. That is not your mistake. Fools ignore advice and wise men follow it and benefit by it. It is clear that you haven't heard the story of Dharma buddhi and his son Papa buddhi, the story of how the father was killed by smoke due to the son's thoughtlessness."

"Why don't you tell me that story," asked Damanaka.

In a city in the north, lived two friends named Dharma buddhi and Papa buddhi. One day, Papa thought, "I am a man without worldly wisdom and added to that I am also poor. Let me persuade Dharma to take me to far off lands and earn lots of money through his business skills. Later I will deprive him of all his wealth and live happily ever after."

With these plans on his mind, Papa told Dharma, "My friend, you are growing old and cannot manage your business. Unless you go out into the wide world how can you tell your children about the wonders of the world? Elders have said that he is born in vain who does not see the countries in the world, learn several languages and know the dress styles of other people. You cannot earn wealth and knowledge without wide travel."

Dharma liked this advice and taking the blessings of his teachers set out on overseas travel, taking Papa with him. Both of them earned a lot of money abroad due to the business talent of Dharma. It was time for them to return home because it is natural for people who go abroad in search of wealth and learning to think of home when they have achieved both.

As they were entering their native place, Papa told Dharma, "It is not safe to take home all this wealth because relatives and friends in need will seek help if they know about our riches. We shall bury most of our money in some secret place in this forest. Whenever we need money, we can come here and take whatever we need. You know that money tempts even saints."

Dharma agreed to Papa's plan and went home after both of them dug a pit and covered it after burying most of their earnings in it. One midnight Papa went to the secret place in the forest and stole all the money and brought it home. Next morning, he went to Dharma and suggested that they should go to the forest because he was in need of money.

When both of them arrived at the secret spot in the forest and dug there, they found the pit empty. At once Papa began shouting loudly, "Dharma, you stole the money and nobody else. The pit was carefully covered. You must give me half of what we have buried here.' Though Dharma denied it, Papa insisted that they should take the dispute to a court of law.

When the case came before the court, the judge asked them to take oath in the name of God. But Papa quoted experts as saying that relevant documents should be produced first as proof, then witnesses would be summoned to give evidence and oath in the name of God is taken when neither documents nor witnesses are available.

"I can produce the gods of the forest as witnesses. They will determine who is guilty and who is innocent," said Papa. Impressed by this plan, the judges asked both the parties to be present next morning at the forest for a hearing. Happy at the judges' order, Papa went home and told his father, "Father, I have stolen all Dharma's money. There is a case in the court that I can win only with your help. Otherwise, my life will be in danger."

"What have I to do to get that money, son," asked his father.

"There is a big tree there. You have to go now and hide in the hollow of that tree. Tomorrow morning when the judges and others assemble there, I will ask you to tell the truth. Then it is your turn to declare that Dharma is the thief," said the son.

The father left at once for the forest to hide in the hollow of the tree. The morning of the next day, the son took a bath and went to the tree taking Dharma and the judges with him. Papa went near the tree and shouted, "O sun, moon, air, fire, earth, water, the God of Death, day and night, you are all witnesses to the history of humanity. O Goddess of the Forest, declare who among us is guilty."

The father shouted back from inside the hollow of the tree, "Listen all of you, it is Dharma who stole the money." The judges and the king's men heard the verdict and sat down to decide what punishment they should give Dharma. Meanwhile, Dharma filled the hollow with rags and hay, poured oil on them and threw a matchstick into it. The fire forced the half-burnt father to come out of the tree.

"All this is the work of Papa's evil mind," said the father and soon collapsed and died. The king's men at once bound Papa hand and foot and hung him to a tree. They said, "Our elders have always said that wise men should not only be resourceful but also know the consequences of being resourceful. You have the story of how a mongoose killed all the offspring of the crane before his own eyes."

When Dharma asked them to tell the story, the king's men began relating the story.

The Foolish Crane and The Mongoose

A big banyan tree was home to a number of cranes in a forest. In the hollow of that tree lived a cobra, which used to feed on the young cranes which did not yet learn to fly. When the mother crane saw the cobra killing her offspring, she began crying. Seeing the sorrowing crane, a crab asked her what made her cry.

The crane told the crab, "Every day, the cobra living in this tree is killing my children. I am not able to contain my grief. Please show me some way to get rid of this cobra."

The crab then thought, "These cranes are our born enemies. I shall give her advice that is misleading and suicidal. That will see the end of all these cranes. Elders have always said that if you want to wipe out your enemy your words should be soft like butter and your heart like a stone.

Then the crab told the crane, "Uncle, strew pieces of meat from the mongoose's burrow to the hollow of the cobra. The mongoose will follow the trail of meat to the cobra burrow and will kill it."

The crane did as the crab advised her. The mongoose came following the meat trail and killed not only the cobra but also all the cranes on the tree. "That is why," the king's men said, "if you have a strategy, you must also know what the strategy would lead to. Papa buddhi considered only the crooked plan but not what would follow. He reaped the consequences."

Karataka told Damanaka, "That's why like Papa buddhi you haven't foreseen what will happen if you went ahead with your plans. You have an evil mind. I knew it from your plans to endanger the life of our lord. Your place is not with us. If a rat had a 1000-pound scale for its lunch, is it any wonder that a kite carried away a child?"

"What about it," asked Damanaka. Karataka told him the following story.

Jeernadhana was the son of a rich merchant. But he had lost all his wealth. He thought he should go abroad, for, he told himself that he who had once prospered should not live in the same place as a poor man. People who respected him once would now look down upon him and shun him. Deciding to go abroad to seek his fortune, he mortgaged with a local merchant the 1000-pound balance his ancestors had left behind.

He went abroad with the money the merchant gave him and after several years came home and asked the merchant to return him the balance. The merchant said, "O my, where is the balance? The rats have gnawed at it for food."

Jeernadhana replied without emotion, "I cannot blame you for what the rats have done. The world is like that. Nothing really is permanent. Any way, I am going to the river to take the purificatory bath. Please send with me your son Dhanadeva to look after my needs."

Afraid that Jeernadeva would accuse him of theft, the merchant called his son and told him, "Son, your uncle is going to the river for a bath. You accompany him taking with you all the things he needs to take his bath. Men offer help not only out of kindness but also out of fear, greed etc. If one offers help for reasons other than this, you have to be wary of such a person."

The merchant's son followed Jeernadeva to the river. After taking bath, he led the boy into a nearby cave and, pushing the boy inside, closed it with a huge boulder. When Jeernadeva returned from the river, the merchant asked him, "O honoured guest, didn't you bring back my son? Where is he? Please tell me."

Jeernadeva told him, "A kite has carried away your boy. There was nothing I could do."

"You cheat, is this possible? How can a kite carry away a boy? Bring my boy back. Otherwise, I will go to the king and complain."

"Yes, just as a kite cannot carry away a boy, rats also cannot eat away heavy iron balance. If you want your boy, give me back my balance," said Jeernadeva.

Both of them took the dispute to the king's court. The merchant complained to the judges that Jeernadeva had kidnapped his child. The judges ordered him to return the boy to the merchant. Jeernadeva told the judges the entire story. Thereupon, the judges ordered Jeernadeva to return the boy and the merchant to give back the balance to Jeernadeva.

Karataka then told Damanaka, "You have done this foul deed because you were jealous of the king's friendship with Sanjeevaka. It is not without reason that our elders have said:

"Fools hate the learned

The poor blame the rich.

The miser riles the giver

The wicked abhor the virtuous"

"You have tried to help us. But you have hurt us. It is like the well-meaning monkey killing the king," said Karataka.

"What did the monkey do?" asked Damanaka.

The King and The Foolish Monkey

Once upon a time, there was a king who kept a monkey as a pet. The monkey servedthe king in whatever way he could. He had a free run of the royal household because he was the king's pet. One hot day the monkey sat fanning by the side of the king who was sleeping. He noticed a fly on the chest of the king and tried to swish it away. The fly would go away for the moment and come back again to sit on the king's chest.

The monkey could take it no longer and decided to teach the fly a lesson. He looked for a dagger to kill it and when he found it brought it down with all force on the fly. The fly flew away but the king died as result of the dagger blow delivered by the monkey.

Karataka said, "Therefore, the lesson is that a king who cares for his life should not have a fool as his servant.' He went on to relate a second story to show how shrewd people save the lives of others.

Once upon a time a Brahmin lived in a big city and as a result of his misdeeds in his previous birth he became a thief. He saw four other Brahmins from another city selling a variety of goods in his city. He thought he should somehow deprive the four Brahmins of their money and through sweet words become their good friend. He was useful to them in whatever way he could. True, it comes naturally for women of vice to act coy and for charlatans to pretend to be learned.

The four visitors sold all their goods and with the money from the sales bought pearls and precious jewels. The Brahmin thief was keeping an eye on what they were doing even as he pretended to serve them faithfully. One day, in the presence of the Brahmin, the traders cut open their thighs and storing the jewels and pearls inside the thighs sewed them back.

The Brahmin was disappointed that they did not give him even a small part of their wealth. He immediately decided to follow them and kill them in the middle of their journey back home and take all that wealth from them.

He told the traders with tears in his eyes, "Friends, you seem to be ready to leave me behind. My heart is broken because it is difficult for me to snap the bonds of friendship with you. If you will be so kind as to take me with you, I will be very grateful to you."

Moved by his request, the traders started their homeward journey accompanied by the Brahmin thief. They passed through several villages, towns and cities before they reached a village inhabited by thugs. Suddenly, they heard a group of crows loudly shouting, "You thugs, very rich people are coming. Come, kill them and become rich."

The thugs at once attacked the Brahmin traders with sticks and began examining their bags. But they found nothing. They were surprised because this was the first time that the words of the crows turned out to be false. They told the traders, "O traders, the crows always tell the truth. You have the money with you somewhere. Take it out or we will cut every limb of yours and bring it out."

The Brahmin thief pondered, "These thugs will certainly pierce the body of the traders to grab the jewels. My turn also will come. It is better I offer myself to these thugs and save the lives of the Brahmins. There is no point in fearing death because it will come today or after hundred years. One cannot escape it."

With these thoughts on his mind, the Brahmin thief asked the thugs to first kill him and see if there was anything valuable on his body. The thugs accepted the offer and found nothing on him after they pierced his body. They let go the other four Brahmins thinking that they also did not have anything precious on their bodies. As Karataka and Damanaka were discussing the ways of the world, Sanjeevaka engaged Pingalaka in a short battle in which Pingalaka clawed him to death. But the lion was immediately struck by remorse and, recalling the good days he had spent with the bullock, began repenting:

"O I have committed a great sin by killing my friend. There cannot be a greater sin than killing a trusted friend. They who forget a favour or breach a trust or let down a friend will all go to hell as long as the sun and the moon shine in the sky. A king will perish whether what he loses is his kingdom or a faithful servant. A servant and a kingdom are not the same because you can always win back the kingdom but not a trusted servant. In the court, I have always praised Pingalaka. How can I explain his death to the courtiers?"

Damanaka approached the grief-stricken king and told him, "O lord, ruing the death of a grass eater is cowardice. It is not good for a king like you. The learned have always said that it is not a sin to kill a person for treason even if that person is a father, brother, son, wife or a friend. Similarly, one must abandon a tenderhearted king, a Brahmin who eats all kinds of food, an immodest woman, a wicked assistant, a disobedient servant and an ungrateful person."

Damanaka continued, "You are mourning the death of someone who does not deserve sympathy. Though you are talking like a learned man, you forget that learned men do not think of the past or the dead."

These words of Damanaka worked like a tonic providing relief to Pingalaka's troubled mind. Pleased with this advice, the lion king reappointed Damanaka as his minister and continued to rule the forest.

Second Strategy

Gaining Friends

This is the second strategy of Panchatantra known as Gaining Friends beginning with this stanza:

Even without the wherewithal

Learned men and intellectuals

Achieve what they want like

The crow, the rat, the deer and the turtle.

Now the story. There was a city called Mahilaropyam in the south not far off from where was a large banyan tree. Many species of birds came there to eat the tree's fruit. In the hollow of the great tree lived poisonous reptiles like snakes and scorpions. Travellers found the tree a great shelter in their journeys.

A crow called Laghupatanaka made this tree his home. As he was flying one day towards the city for collecting food, he sighted a hunter carrying a net and approaching the tree like a messenger of death. The crow at once sensed danger and, sure that the hunter came to trap the birds on the tree, told all the birds,

"Friends, this wicked hunter has seeds in his bag that he will scatter to lure you don't trust him and avoid the seeds like poison." The hunter came, sowed the seeds and spread the net. He left the spot and sat elsewhere not to arouse the suspicion of the birds. Warned by Laghupatanaka, the birds stayed away from the seeds as though they were poisonous berries.

Meanwhile, Chitragriva, king of doves, saw the seeds from a distance and landed there with his retinue of one thousand doves. They came to eat the seeds ignoring the warnings of Laghupatanaka and soon the hunter spread his net and trapped all of them. That is why elders have said that fools can never foresee peril. People often lose sense when danger lurks in the corner.

Chitragriva and his retinue, however, kept their cool in the face of danger. He appealed to his friends not to panic. Elders have said that they tide over danger, who are not scared by crisis. "Let us fly together and land elsewhere where the hunter cannot reach us. We can then plan a strategy to get out of this net. If we don't fly now, we are all doomed," said Chitragriva. Thereupon, all of them flew together.

The hunter followed the flight of the doves and looking upwards chanted, "They are flying together. But the moment there is a break in their unity they will crash to the ground." Laghupatanaka, the crow, also followed the flying doves to see what they would do. When he lost sight of the birds, the hunter gave up and went home ruing that he had lost his net also.

When he was sure that the hunter had failed to chase them, the king of the doves told his friends, "The hunter has disappeared. Let us all now fly towards Mahilaropyam where I have a friend Hiranyaka, who is a rat. He is our only hope. It is only a friend who will come to the aid of those in trouble." The birds, heeding the advice of the king, flew to the fort of Hiranyaka in Mahilaropyam.

Standing outside the fort, Chitragriva shouted,

"O friend, come quickly. We are in great trouble."

Without coming out, Hiranyaka shouted back, "Who are you sir and what do you want from me? What is the kind of trouble that is bothering you? Let me know."

"I am your friend Chitragriva, king of the doves. Come out soon."

Hiranyaka came out and was happy to see Chitragriva with his retinue and asked what was the matter. The king of the doves said,

"Whatever man does for whatever reasons,

in whatever manner and wherever in his last birth.

He reaps the consequences for the same reasons,

in the same manner and in the same place."

"All of us are trapped in this net because of our weakness for food. Come at once and free us from this trap," urged Chitragriva.

Hiranyaka said, "It is rightly said that a bird can recognise food from fifty miles but cannot see the danger lurking next to him."

After delivering this sermon, the rat set out to free Chitragriva first. But the king of doves pleaded with him to first liberate his friends. The rat was angry and reminded Chitragriva that it was fair that the king became free first and then the servants. "No, it is not like that," countered Chitragriva. "They are all dedicated to my service and have left their families behind to come with me. I have to repay that debt," he said.

Pleased with his friend's love for his servants, Hiranyaka said, "Friend, I know the duties of a king. I was only testing you. I will free everyone now. This will win more doves for your retinue." With the help of his servants, the rat then bit off the entire net and all the doves came out. Hiranyaka saw off Chitragriva and retinue and went back into his fort.

Seeing the whole drama of Hiranyaka liberating Chitragriva and his friends, Laghupatanaka, the crow, thought, "I don't trust anyone. On top of it, I have a fickle mind. I will seek his friendship. Our ancestors have always said that even if a wise man has everything he needs, he should still seek friends. Even if all the rivers flow into the Sea, the Sea still waits for the Moon to come out."

The Crow-Rat Discourse

After he saw how Hiranyaka had helped Chitragriva, Lagupatanaka came down from his tree perch and called out the rat in a voice resembling that of Chitragriva. The rat thought, "What happened? Did I forget to free any bird? The dove king must be calling me for the same purpose."

Not sure who was calling him, the rat shouted from inside his fort, "Who are you?"

"I am Laghupatanaka, the crow."

The rat further retreated into his fort and said, "Go away at once, I don't know who you are."

"I have come on an important business. Why don't you meet me?"

"What do I gain by meeting you?"

"Sir, I have seen you liberating Chitragriva and his retinue. I thought friendship with you would be useful in such a crisis. I am seeking your hand."

"Very odd! You are the diner and I am the dinner. How can there be amity between the two? Where there is enmity, there cannot be friendship. Didn't you hear the elders say:

Friendship or marriage is always
between equals in caste and wealth.
There cannot be any sort of bond
between the weak and the strong.

"He who seeks friendship with someone who is not an equal will earn ridicule. So, please go."

The crow replied, "Hiranyaka, I am waiting here at your doorstep. If you reject my hand, I will starve here to death."

"But friendship with you is not possible. However hot the water, it still kills the fire."

"We haven't even seen each other. How can there be enmity between both of us?"

Hiranyaka then explained, "Enmity is of two kinds. The first is natural and the second is artificial. The second kind disappears when what caused it disappears. But natural enmity ends only with the death of one of the two enemies."

"Can you make it clearer, asked Laghupatanaka.

"Yes, artificial enmity is always based on some reason. Natural enmity is like the one between a snake and a mongoose, water and fire, Devatas and Rakshasas, dogs and cats, the rich and the poor, the learned and the illiterate, between women of virtue and vice."

The crow then pleaded, "Sir, what you say is unreasonable. There is always a reason behind friendship and enmity. That is why a wise man should always seek friendship and not enmity."

"True, it is foolish to think that you will not come to harm because you are a man of character. People who are blinded by ignorance and anger do not consider your character," said the rat.

"Friendship with bad men is like a pot of clay easy to break but difficult to rejoin. With good men it is like pot of gold, difficult to break but easy to mend. I pledge that you will have no reason to fear danger from me," said the crow.

Hiranyaka said, "I have no faith in pledges don't trust an enemy with whom you have made peace. Even if the hole is small, water seeping through it can sink a ship.

don't trust a person untrustworthy

Faith has its own limits

The evil that trust brings

Leaves you totally destroyed

Him who is highly sceptical

The mighty cannot put an end to

Him who trusts others easily

Even the weakest can kill.

After this long sermon, Laghupatanaka didn't know how to reply. Hiranyaka, he thought, was a very knowledgeable being and that was a strong reason for him to seek his friendship. Turning to the rat, he said, "Seven words are enough to bring two good people together.

We have already talked a lot, which makes us good friends. That's why please believe what I say. If it is not possible, I will stay out and you can talk to me from within your stronghold."

Impressed by his sincerity, Hiranyaka said, "Okay, you should not step inside my fort." When Laghupatanaka agreed to that condition, the two became friends and enjoyed their daily meetings and long talks.

They helped each other, the crow bringing pieces of meat and relics of offerings to God at temples for the rat and the rat in turn bringing for Hiranyaka grains of paddy and food items. Thus they became great and inseparable friends.

Meeting a New Friend

Liranyaka, the mouse, and Laghupatanaka, the crow, became great friends. One day, the crow came calling on the mouse with eyes full of tears. Worried, the mouse asked,

"What's the matter? Why are you so sad?"

"I am thoroughly fed up with this country. I want to go elsewhere," replied the crow.

"But what is the reason for this sudden change of mind," asked the mouse.

"There is a famine here. People are dying like locusts. No one is offering cooked rice for the peace of the dead. So, I don't have food. Hunters are busy trapping birds in their nets. I have escaped narrowly. I don't know when my turn will come. I want to leave this country before it comes," said the crow.

"What are your travel plans then," asked the mouse.

"There is a big lake in the middle of a vast forest in the south. I have a friend there, a turtle whose name is Mandharaka. He is a great host who will feed me with fish, pieces of meat etc. I will spend my time happily with him daily discussing small and big things in the world. I don't want to die miserably in a hunter's net."

Laghupatanaka continued, "Elders have always said that they are happy who are fortunate not to witness the destruction of crops and the decline of the people. Nothing is impossible for a competent person. There is no land that does not respond to effort. For a scholar every country is his own country and there is no enemy for a sweet-tongued person. Learning and power are not the same. Remember that the king is respected only in his country but a scholar is honoured everywhere."

Hiranyaka said, "If that is so, I will also follow you. I am also very sad."

"Why are you sad?" asked the crow.

"It is a long story. I shall tell you when I reach your friend's place," said the mouse.

"But how can you come with me," asked the crow. "I am a bird and can fly. You cannot do that," said the crow.

"That is no problem. I will sit on your back and we can fly off," suggested the mouse.

"That's an idea. I will be doubly happy there because I have the company of the turtle and also yours. Come, get on to my back. We will fly together," said the crow.

On a fine day, the crow with the mouse on his back flew to the great lake in the middle of the forest. His friend Mandharaka, the turtle, saw him with the mouse on his back and thought, "This crow is not an ordinary crow. It is better I hide from him." The turtle immediately ducked under water. But the crow saw the turtle going down and understood that his friend did not recognise him. The crow then left the mouse at the bottom of a tree and flying to the top of it loudly addressed the turtle, "O Mandharaka, I am your friend Laghupatanaka. Come out and welcome me who has come to see an old friend after a long time."

Recognising his friend's voice, Mandharaka came out of the water and with tears of joy in his eyes, said, "O Laghupatanaka, I am so happy you have come. Come and hug me. We are meeting after a long time and that's why I could not immediately recognise you. You know the saying that you should not make friends with him whose power and pedigree are not known to you."

The crow then came down from the tree and the two of them embraced each other in joy. They began telling each other about what happened in the long interval of their separation. The mouse, Hiranyaka, too came out of the hole he was hiding in, greeted the turtle and sat by the crow's side. The turtle asked the crow, "O Laghupatanaka, who is this little friend of yours? Why did you bring him here on your back though he is your food."

"He is my friend Hiranyaka. I can't live without him. Just as you can't count the stars in the sky and the sands on the seashore, I can't recount his great qualities. He is fed up with this world. That is why he has followed me on my visit to you," said the crow.

"But there should be some reason for his despair," said the turtle. The crow replied, "I have asked him to tell me the reasons. He said he would tell us after meeting you." Turning to the mouse, the crow asked him, "Now it is your turn to tell us why you are so fed up with the world.

Hiranyaka began telling his story.

The Hermit and The Mouse

"In the southern city of Mahilaropya," said Hiranyaka, "lived a hermit named Tamrachud in a Shiva temple on the outskirts of the city. Every day, he would go out into the city, collect alms and cook his food. After the meal, he would store whatever is left in his begging bowl and hang it to a peg and go to sleep. He would give the leftovers to poor people in return for services rendered to the temple. They would every day wash it, clean it and decorate it with patterns of chalk."

"One day, some of my relatives complained to me, "O lord, the hermit is storing the food in his bowl and hanging it high to a peg. We are not able to nibble at it. You alone can reach any place. Why should we go anywhere else when you are there? Let's go to the hermit's place and with your help feed ourselves."

"Accompanied by my relatives, I went to the hermit's place and springing at the bowl brought the stored food down. All of us then had a good meal. We repeated this act every day till the hermit found what we were doing. He brought a split bamboo and began striking the food bowl with it. That noise used to frighten us and we would spend the whole night waiting for a respite from this noise. But the hermit never stopped striking the bamboo."

"Meanwhile, a visitor named Brihat came calling on the hermit. Tamrachud received him with great respect and did whatever he could to make the honoured guest happy. At night, the guest would relate to the hermit tales about his travels. But Tamrachud, busy scaring the mice with his bamboo, would not pay much attention to what his guest was narrating. In the middle of the story, the guest would ask him questions to which he would give indifferent replies.

"Angry with Tamrachud's absent mindedness, the visitor told him, "Tamrachud, you are not a great friend of mine because you are not attentive to what I am telling you. I will leave your place tonight and seek shelter elsewhere. The elders have always said that you must not accept the hospitality of such a host who does not welcome you gladly, does not offer you a proper seat and does not make inquiries about your wellbeing."

"Status has gone to your head. You do not any more care for my friendship. You do not know that this conduct will take you to hell. I am really sorry for what has happened to you. You have become vain and proud. I am leaving this temple at once," Brihat said.

"Frightened at his visitor's words, Tamrachud pleaded with him, "O worshipful guest, please don't be harsh on me. I don't have any friends other than you. Here is the reason why I was not attentive to your discourse on religion. There is this mouse, which every day steals my food however high I keep it. As a result, I am not able to feed the poor people who do the job of keeping the temple clean. The temple is now in a bad shape. To scare this culprit, I have to keep tapping the food bowl with the bamboo stick I keep with me. This is why I was not able to pay attention to the great and learned tales you have been relating."

"Realising what really was the problem, the visitor asked the hermit, "Do you know where the mouse lives?"

"Sir, I have no idea," said Tamrachud.

"The visitor said, "This mouse must have stored a lot of food somewhere. It is this plenty that gives him the energy to jump so high and eat all your food. When a man earns a lot of wealth, that pile of money increases his strength and confidence."

"Brihat continued, "There is an explanation for everything in this world. There is a reason for Shandili trying to exchange husked sesame seeds in return for degraded sesame seeds."

"Tamrachud asked Brihat to tell him who this Shandili was and the story of sesame seeds."

Shandili and Sesame Seeds

"Brihat began telling the story. "I sought the hospitality of a Brahmin one day for sacred ceremonies connected with the monsoon season. He was kind enough to offer me space in his house and in return I used to render services he found useful in his rituals. As this arrangement continued, one fine morning I heard the Brahmin and his wife Shandili discussing what they should do for the day. The husband told his wife, "Today is the time when the Sun begins his northward journey and a time when the rich and pious people offer gifts to Brahmins. I am going to the next village to receive the offerings. You will do well to invite a Brahmin as guest today and offer him food in the name of the Sun."

"The wife flew into a rage and told him, "How can I offer anything to anyone in your poverty-stricken house? Aren't you ashamed to make such a suggestion? I have wasted my entire life as your wife. I haven't tasted a good meal so far even on a single day. Nor do I have any jewellery."

"Though taken aback, the Brahmin quickly recovered and said, "Such words are not becoming of you. The learned say that if you share even half of your meal with a mendicant, you will get whatever you wish in life. What good the rich reap by liberally giving away, the poor get by parting with even a cent they have. The giver deserves to be served even if he is poor. But a rich miser is shunned. It is like the well and the sea. People drink the water from the well and not the sea. We must always give to him who deserves. Greed can only destroy a person."

"How is it?" asked the wife.

"The husband then told Shandili the story of the hunter and the greedy jackal.

A hunter went to the forest in search of a kill. Spotting a well-fed boar he took his bow and aimed a sharp arrow at the boar. Though severely wounded, the boar made a wild charge at the hunter goring him to death. The boar too died later from the wounds inflicted by the hunter."

"Meanwhile, a hungry jackal, not knowing that he was doomed to die, came on the scene where the bodies of the hunter and the boar lay. He was thrilled by the sight of so much food and thought, "God has favoured me today. That's why he has sent so much food for me. It is not without reason that the learned have said that he who has done a good deed in a previous birth is rewarded in this birth even if he does not make any effort. This great feast is certainly the result of some good I have done in a previous birth. But a man must enjoy his wealth in small doses. Therefore, I will begin my meal with this gut of the bow."

The jackal went close to the body of the hunter and began nibbling at the gut of the bow. The gut suddenly snapped with great force killing the jackal in the end. "That's why," the Brahmin told his wife, "Haven't you heard that a man's longevity, destiny, wealth, learning and death are predetermined by God even as the child is in the womb of the mother."

"If that is the case," Shandili said, "I have some unhusked sesame seeds in the house. I will make a cake from it and serve it to a Brahmin." Happy at his wife's words, the Brahmin left for the next village. The wife soaked the seeds in warm water, removed their husk and left them on a cloth to dry in the sun. As the Brahmin's wife was busy with other chores, a dog came and peed on the seeds left on the cloth to dry."

"When the wife saw what the dog had done, she felt miserable that all her effort had gone in vain. She thought that nobody could undo God's will. She thought, "These seeds cannot now be given away to anyone. I will see if I can exchange them for unhusked seeds. Anybody will agree to this swap."

"Brihat continued his story, "The Brahmin's wife came to the same house which I was visiting to accept offerings. She offered to exchange the husked seeds to anyone ready to accept them. Then the woman in the house came out and was ready to accept the husked seeds from the Brahmin's wife. But her son intervened and told her, "Mother, these seeds are not good. Why should anyone give away good husked seeds for the raw seeds? There must be some reason for it." The housewife at once gave up the idea of taking husked seeds from the Brahmin's wife."

"After Brihat completed the story, he asked Tamrachud, "Do you know the route he (Hiranyaka) takes to come here?"

"I have no idea," said Tamrachud.

"Have you any tool to dig?" asked the visitor.

"Yes, I have a dibble with me."

"In that case, let us follow the mouse trail before it is erased," said the visitor.

Hiranyaka resumed his account and said, "Listening to the conversation between Tamrachud and Brihat, I thought that my end had come. Just as he had found my food store, he is capable of tracking my fort. Learned men can measure the strength of the rival by just looking at him. I decided immediately to take a new route and was on my way with the other mice when a fat cat sighted us. He immediately pounced on us and killed a number of my retinue."

"Excepting me, those of the bloodied mice who escaped being killed by the cat took the same old route to the fort. The visitor saw the trail of blood the fleeing mice left behind and following it reached my fort. There, Brihat and Tamrachud dug and found the food store. The visitor told Tamrachud, "Here is the secret of the mouse's energy. Now, you can sleep in peace." Then they took the store to the temple, the home of Tamrachud."

"I went back to where I had stored food. It was now like a desert. Without food, the spot was a ghastly scene. I did not know where to go and what to do to get back my peace of mind. Somehow, I spent the day in sorrow and when it was dawn went to the temple followed by what remained of my retinue. Alerted by the noise we made, Tamrachud again began striking the food bowl with the bamboo. Brihat, the visitor, asked him why he was doing so. Tamrachud told him about our return."

"The visitor laughed and told Tamrachud, "Friend, don't be afraid now. The mouse has lost his energy. It cannot do any mischief now." When I heard this, I was angry and tried again to jump at the food bowl and crashed to the ground before I could reach the bowl."

"I was dejected by this failure. But my sadness increased when I heard my retinue telling each other that I was no more capable of earning food for them and they should immediately give up serving me. I then realised the importance of riches and decided to somehow steal it back from Tamrachud. When I made another attempt, the visitor saw me and banged the bamboo on my head. I somehow managed to escape."

"Elders have always said that man gets what he is destined to. Even God cannot alter destiny. So, I stopped brooding over what has happened because what is ours can never become others".

"Explain that to us," asked Laghpatanaka and Mandharaka.

Story of The Merchant's Son

"Sagargupta was a merchant living in one of the country's big cities. He had a son, who, one day purchased a book whose only content was a single verse. The verse read:

"Man gets what is in his destiny

Even God cannot prevent it

To me it makes no difference

What's mine can never become others."

"What is the price of this book," the father asked.

"Hundred rupees," said the son.

The father flew into a rage and said, "You are a fool. You have paid hundred rupees for a book that has only one verse. You can never come up in life. Leave my house at once. It has no place for you."

"Thrown out of the house, the boy went to another city and began fresh life there. One day, a neighbour asked him, "What is your native place and what is your name?"

The boy replied, "Man gets what he is destined to." He gave the same answer to whoever asked for his name. From that day onwards, people began calling him Praptavya, meaning the same line he was reciting to indicate his name.

"The summer came and the city was celebrating it with a big fair. One of the visitors to the fair was the city's princess Chandravati and her maids. Chandravati was young and beautiful. As she was making the rounds of the fair, she saw an extremely handsome warrior and immediately fell in love with him. She told one of her maids, "It is your job to see that both of us meet."

The maid ran to the warrior and told him, "I have a message for you from our princess. She says she will die if you do not meet her today."

"But tell me where and how I can see her. How can I enter the harem?" asked the warrior.

The maid told him, "Come to the palace and you will see a rope hanging from the high wall. Climb and jump over the wall with the help of the rope."

"All right, I will try to do it tonight," said the warrior.

When the night came, the warrior lost his nerve and thought, "O this is an improper thing to do. The elders have said, "He who has liaison with the daughter of a teacher, wife of a friend or of a master or of a servant commits the sin of killing a Brahmin. Also, don't do what brings you a bad name or what denies you a place in heaven." In the end, the warrior decided not to meet the princess and stayed back at home.

"Coming out for a walk in the night, Prapta noticed the rope outside the royal palace and curious to know what it is, went up the rope that took him inside the princess" bedroom. The princess mistook him for the warrior and served him dinner and with great ecstasy told Prapta, "I have fallen in love with you at the very first sight. I am yours. You are in my heart and nobody except you can be my husband. Why don't you say something."

"He replied, "Man gets what he is destined to." The princess immediately realised that this man was not the warrior she saw in the day and asked him to leave the palace at once. She made sure that he climbed back the way he came. Prapta left the place and slept that night in a rundown temple.

"The sheriff of the city came to the same temple where he had arranged to meet a woman of vice. He saw Prapta sleeping there and to keep his meeting a secret, he asked Prapta who he was. Prapta recited the verse about destiny. The sheriff then said, "Sir, this is a bad place to sleep. You can go to my house and sleep there tonight in my place." The merchant's son agreed to the proposal.

"At the sheriff's house, his young and beautiful daughter Vinayawati had asked her lover to come and meet her secretly there in the night. When Prapta came there following the sheriff's advice, Vinayawati mistook him in the darkness for her secret lover. She arranged a feast for him and married him according to Gandharva tradition. Noticing that Prapta did not utter a word, the sheriff's daughter asked him to say something. Prapta recited his usual verse. Vinayawati realised her mistake and asked him to leave at once.

"As Prapta once again took to the street, he saw a marriage procession entering the city led by the bridegroom named Varakirti. He joined the procession. The bride was the daughter of a very wealthy merchant of the city. This procession reached the wedding hall sometime before the scheduled time for the wedding.

"The bride's father set up a costly and gaily decorated dais for the wedding. The bridal party came to the scene of wedding a bit in advance. In the meantime, an elephant went berserk and killing the mahout headed for the marriage venue. The bridegroom and his party joined the frightened people who were fleeing the scene of marriage.

"Prapta happened to see the frightened bride alone and abandoned on the dais shivering in fear. He jumped on to the dais and told the merchant's daughter that she need not fear for her life and that he would save her at any cost. With great courage and presence of mind he approached the elephant with a stick and began to threaten him. The elephant luckily left the scene. Prapta took the bride's hand into his as a token of assurance.

"When peace returned, Varakirti and his friends and relatives also returned to the dais and seeing the bride's hand in the hand of a stranger, addressed the merchant, "Sir, you have pledged the hand of your daughter to me. But I see that you have given her away to someone else. This is improper." The merchant replied, "My son, I don't know anything. I also ran away from the dais. Let me ask my daughter."

The daughter told her father, "This brave man saved me from the mad elephant. He is my saviour. I won't marry anyone but him." It was now dawn and hearing the commotion the royal princess also came to the wedding venue to see what happened. The sheriff's daughter also came there learning what had happened. The king also came there and asked Prapta to tell him everything without fear. Prapta as usual recited the verse.

This verse rang a bell in the princess head. She remembered what happened in the night and thought "Even God cannot undo what is destined." The sheriff's daughter also recalled the events of the night and thought "There is nothing to regret nor cause for surprise." Listening to what Prapta said, the merchant's daughter also thought "nobody can take away what destiny gives me."

"The king now knew everything and the mystery of the verse. He then gave away his daughter in marriage to Prapta and also a thousand villages as gift. He also crowned Prapta as the prince. The sheriff also married his daughter to Prapta. The merchant's son lived happily ever after with his wives and parents.

Hiranyaka, the mouse, thus ended his story of troubles and said:

"Even God cannot undo
What is destined
There is nothing to regret
Nor cause for surprise
Nobody can take away
What destiny gives me."

"I am disillusioned. That is why my friend Laghupatanaka brought me to you," said the mouse.

Addressing the mouse, Mandharaka, the turtle said, "O Hiranyaka, the crow is you true friend. Though he was hungry and you were his meal, he did not kill you. On the other hand, he brought you here on his back. You must make a friend of him who is uncorrupted by wealth and who stands by you in time of trouble."

The turtle continued, "Therefore, stay here without fear or hesitation. Forget the loss of wealth and shelter. Remember, the shade of a passing cloud, friendship of the wicked, a cooked meal, youth and wealth do not stay for long. Learned men are never attached to wealth. It does not come with you even for a few feet in your last journey. There is a lot of pain in earning money and protecting it. Money, therefore, brings grief."

"What is not ours will not stay with us. Haven't you heard the story of Somilaka who earned a lot of wealth but could not keep it?"

"How is that?" asked Hiranyaka.

Mandharaka began telling Hiranyaka the story of the unlucky weaver.

The Unlucky Weaver

Somilaka was a weaver living on the edge of the city. He was an expert at making fine garments worthy of kings and princes. He enjoyed the patronage of the nobility. Despite all this, he was poorer than those weavers who were making coarse cloth for the common people. Worried at his condition, he told his wife, "Look dear, how rich these weavers of coarse cloth have become. There is something wrong with this place. I am not a success here. I will go elsewhere."

"No dear. It is not true that you can be successful elsewhere. Our luck is linked to what we have done in a previous birth. If you have done a good deed in your previous birth, you will reap the harvest in this birth without your effort. If you don't have it in your destiny, you will not get it even with effort. Just as sun and shade are inseparable, cause and effect are also linked to each other."

Somilaka did not agree with her. He said, "Without effort, you can achieve nothing. Without cause there is no effect. Even if you get a good meal as a result of a good deed in the past, you have to use your hand to eat it. Wealth comes to a person who toils. There is no point in chanting the name of God. You must do your bit first. If you are not successful despite your effort, you are not to blame. Therefore, I have decided to go abroad."

Ignoring his wife's pleas, Somilaka left his place and reached Vardhamanapuram. Working day and night, he earned three hundred gold sovereigns within three years. He thought he should go home now and started the homeward trek. At dusk he found himself in the middle of a forest. Wild animals began their hunt for prey. The weaver climbed a tall tree and went to sleep on a big branch. He saw a dream:

The God of Action and the God of Destiny were talking to each other. Destiny asked Action, "The weaver is not destined to live in luxury. Why did you give him three hundred sovereigns?" Action replied, "I have to give to those who try and toil. Whether the weaver can keep it or not is in your hands."

The dream jolted the weaver. He looked into his bag and found the sovereigns missing. Heartbroken, Somilaka began crying, "Oh I have lost what I have earned in three years with great effort. I have become a poor man again. I cannot go home in this condition and show my face to my wife." He saw no point in brooding over what has happened and decided to go to Vardhamanapuram and try again.

This time, he could collect five hundred sovereigns in one year. He stored all this money in a small bag and began his homeward journey. When it was sundown, he had already entered a forest. This time, he did not sleep, afraid that he would lose his money. He continued to walk through the forest. This time also he saw those two persons he saw earlier in his dream coming in his direction.

They repeated the same conversation about God rewarding a hard-working person and destiny denying it. He immediately looked into his bag and found there was no gold in it. This time Somilaka lost his courage and thought he should commit suicide. He made a strong rope with the fibres he found in the forest. He tied one end of the rope to a high branch of the tree and made a noose of the other end. Everything was ready for his suicide when he heard a voice in the skies:

"O Somilaka, don't be rash. I am destiny who took away your wealth. I cannot give you more than what is necessary for your bare needs. Not a single cent more. But I am pleased with your adventurous spirit. Ask for a boon. I shall give it."

"Please give me lots of wealth," said the weaver.

"What do you do with so much money," asked the voice.

The weaver replied, "People serve him who is rich even if he is a miser."

"In that case, go back to Vardhamanapuram where two wealthy merchants, Guptadhana and Upabhuktadhana are doing business. After studying them well, decide who you want to become, Guptadhana, the man who earns a lot of money but does not spend a cent of it or Upabhuktadhana, the man who earns but also enjoys the wealth he has amassed."

Somilaka followed their advice and went back to Vardhamanapuram reaching the place in the evening after a tiring journey. With great difficulty he traced Guptadhana's house and entered it despite resistance from the merchant's family. When the time for dinner came, the merchant grudgingly gave food to Somilaka, suggesting that he was an unwanted guest. The weaver found a corner in the house where he could sleep.

Somilaka again had the same dream in which Action and Destiny were debating Guptadhana giving food to him.

Destiny told Action, "You have made Guptadhana give food to Somilaka."

Action said, "You cannot blame me. I had to ensure that Somalika was fed. It is for you to decide who deserved what."

Next day, Destiny saw to it that Guptadhana had an attack of cholera and had to miss his meal. In this manner what was given away was saved.

Later, Somilaka visited Upabhuktadhana's house where the host welcomed him with great love and respect. The weaver had a good meal and slept. He had a dream as usual, the same two figures appearing in the dream.

Destiny told Action, "O Action, the host has spent a lot of money to entertain Somilaka. He even borrowed to make the guest happy. It is not in his destiny to have surplus. How will he repay what he has borrowed?"

Action replied, "My job is to see Somilaka got what he deserved. If Upabhuktadhana crossed the limits in entertaining his guest, that is not my fault. It is for you to decide what should be done."

Next day, a messenger from the royal household came to Upabhuktadhana and gave him a big sum of money on behalf of the king.

Somilaka thought, "It is better to be like Upabhuktadhana. He enjoys life with whatever he has. What's the use of being rich but miserly? I will better be Upabhuktadhana." Pleased, the Gods showered on him the wealth that he needed to enjoy life.

The Rescue of a Deer

Mandharaka ended the story of Somilaka telling Hiranyaka and Laghupatanaka that a rich person who does not spend money is as poor as any poor person can be. Not being able to enjoy is common to both the poor and the miserly rich. Nothing on this earth is greater than charity and there is no greater enemy than miserliness.

The crow then advised Hiranyaka, "Listen to what the turtle is saying. Elders have said that it is easier to get friends who talk sweetly but difficult to find friends who venture to tell you the truth however bitter it is. The latter alone deserve to be called friends.

The crow and the mouse put a brake to their conversation when they saw a frightened deer darting towards the lake. The crow flew to the top of a tree. The mouse scampered into his hole and the turtle sank into the water. From the treetop, the crow could see the deer now clearly and told his other friends, "Friends, he is only a deer who is thirsty. These footfalls are not those of a man."

The turtle replied, "The deer is panting. It seems someone is chasing him. He has not come to quench his thirst. Surely, some hunter might be after him. Please go to the top of the tree and look if you can find any hunter."

Assured that these are friends only, the deer named Chitranga, now said, "Friend, you have guessed correctly. I have escaped the arrow of the hunter and reached here with difficulty. I am in search of a shelter the hunter cannot reach. Please show me a place safe from the hunter."

Mandharaka, the turtle, said, "the scriptures have mentioned two ways of escaping danger. One is to use your muscle power and another is to run as fast as you can. Now, run into the forest before the hunter could come."

"That is not necessary," said Laghupatanaka, the crow.

"I have seen the hunters taking a good catch of food and going the way they came. O Mandharaka, you can now come out of the water."

With Chitranga, the deer, they became now four friends, happily spending time in each other's company. The learned have said that when you have plenty of cordial conversation, to be happy you do not need a woman. The man who has no store of good words is not capable of uttering them.

One day, Chitranga had not come when the other three had gathered at the lakeside for their daily discourse. They thought, "Poor Chitranga has not come so far. Is it possible that a lion or a hunter has killed him? Or, is it possible that he has fallen into a pit?" Well-wishers naturally suspect the worst when their near and dear ones are not seen for a while.

Mandharaka told the crow, "Friend, you know neither Hiranyaka nor I can move fast. You alone can fly and see more things than we can. Please go immediately and find out what is happening to our friend."

The crow did not fly too long before he saw Chitranga trapped in a hunter's net near a small pond. Moved by his plight, the crow said, "Friend, what happened to you?" Trying to check tears in his eyes, the deer said, "Death is chasing me. It is good that you came to see me."

The crow said, "Friend, don't lose courage when we are here. I will rush back and bring Hiranyaka here." Laghupatanaka flew fast to where the mouse and the turtle were anxiously waiting for him to come and tell them what happened to the deer. On hearing his account, Hiranyaka immediately decided that he should go and bite off the strings of the hunter's net.

He got on to the back of the crow and together they flew to the spot where the deer lay helplessly in the hunter's net. When the deer saw his friends rushing to his aid, he realised how necessary it was to collect good friends and how nobody could overcome troubles without the help of good friends.

Hiranyaka asked the deer, "How did you, such a learned being, get into this hole?" The deer replied, "Friend, this is not a time for a debate. The hunter may come any time. First, get me out of this net." The mouse laughed and said, "Why are you scared of the hunter when I am here? But tell me how did you let yourself trapped in this way?"

The deer replied, "Friend, when luck is not with you, you will lose discretion. As the elders say when death is lurking for you and when wickedness overtakes you, your thoughts too take a crooked path. Nobody can save you from what God has in store for you."

As they were discussing their plan to escape, Laghupatanaka and Hiranyaka saw that the turtle also was coming. The crow said, "Look, this slow-footed guy is coming. Neither can we save the deer or ourselves. See this fellow's foolishness. If the hunter comes, I can fly away and you can beat a fast retreat. But how can this turtle escape?"

The hunter came when they were debating this point. The mouse did a fast job of biting off the strings of the net and the deer rushed into the thick forest. The mouse too disappeared into the nearest hole. But the poor turtle was slowly plodding its way to safety. But the hunter saw him and bound him to his bow and slung it across his shoulder and began going home.

Hiranyaka saw this from a distance and began reflecting, "Troubles do not come in singles. I have already lost everything I have. I have lost my relatives and my retinue. Now, this loss of a great friend! We come close to each other only to part. Everything in this world is temporary. Yet, I am grateful to God, for, he has created this sweet relationship we call friendship."

Meanwhile, the deer and the crow came, disturbing the mouse's reverie. Recovering, Hiranyaka said, "Let's not brood over the past. Let us first look for a way to rescue the turtle." The crow said, "Listen, and do as I tell you. Chitranga will go to a small lake on the hunter's way taking him home. He should pretend he is dead and I will sit on his head and pretend pecking his eyes. Seeing the motionless deer, the hunter will then rest the turtle on the ground and reach for the deer. Hiranyaka should at once reach the turtle and bite off the strings binding him to the bow."

"All right, we will do as you say," said the mouse and the deer. Meanwhile, the hunter, seeing the motionless deer, thought it was dead. Leaving the turtle on the ground, he came to the deer. The deer at once ran away and the crow flew away. At the other end, the mouse bit off the strings binding the turtle to the bow. The turtle entered water and the mouse ran to his hole.

Disappointed, the hunter returned to where he had rested the turtle. When he found that the turtle had escaped, he cried bitterly and went home. After making sure that they were far away from the hunter's reach, the four friends gathered and celebrated their reunion.

Concluding his discourse, Hiranyaka said, "It is a lesson to mankind on the value of friendship. One should not try to cheat friends. The elders have said that he who is faithful to his friends shall never taste defeat". Thus we come to the end of the second part of Panchatantra called Gaining Friends.

Third Strategy

Of Crows and Owls

This third part of the Panchatantra begins with a verse:

Trust not even a close friend

Who earlier was your enemy.

This is the story of how the crows burnt the home of a trusting pack of owls.

Once upon a time all the crows in a town called Mahilaropya made a huge banyan tree their home. The tree had hundreds of branches. Their king, known as Meghavarna, set up strong fortifications to ensure security for his brood. Similarly, the owls of the town made a nearby cave their colony. They also had a king, called Arimardana, who ruled with the help of a strong and cunning army.

The owl king kept a close eye on the banyan tree and on account of previous enmity killed every night any crow he sighted outside the tree. Slowly, the owl king managed to kill all crows that could be seen outside the tree. That is why wise men had always said that whoever neglects disease or the enemy perishes in their hands.

Alarmed at the loss of his flock, Meghavarna assembled his ministers and asked them to prepare a plan to fight the owls. He placed before them six strategies and asked them to name the best of the six. The first minister suggested, compromise as a tactic because one had first to survive to gather strength and later destroy the enemy. The elders have said,

"Bend to the enemy when he is strong

Attack him when he is vulnerable.

Don't wage a war if it doesn't bring

Power, or wealth or friendship."

The second minister ruled out compromise and offered trickery as a formula. He cited the example of how Bheema in the Mahabharata had killed Keechaka in the disguise of a woman. He also quoted elders saying,

"Never accept peace with

An enemy who is not just

For, he will break his word

And stab you in the back."

The minister referred to the learned as saying that it is easy to defeat an enemy who is a tyrant, a miser, an idler, a liar, a coward and a fool. Words of peace will only inflame an enemy blinded by anger.

The third minister said, "O lord, our enemy is not only strong but also wicked. Neither compromise nor trickery will work with him. Exile is the best way. We shall wait and strike when the enemy becomes weak."

"Neither peace nor bravado

Can subdue a strong enemy

Where these two do not work

Flight is the best alternative."

The fourth minister opposed all these tactics and suggested the king of crows should stay in his own fort, mobilize support from friends and then attack the enemy. He quoted the learned as saying,

"A king who flees is like

A cobra without fangs.

A crocodile in water

Can haul an elephant."

Therefore, the minister said, "An ally is what wind is to fire. The king must stay where he is and gather allies for support." The fifth minister offered a strategy similar to that of the fourth and said, "Stay in your fort and seek the help of an ally stronger than the enemy. It also pays to form an axis of less strong allies."

After listening to all the ministers, Meghavarna turned to the wisest and senior most among his counsels, Sthirajeevi, and asked him for his advice. The wise man told Meghavarna,

"Oh, king of crows, this is the time to use duplicity to finish the enemy. You can thus keep your throne."

"But learned sir, we have no idea of where Arimardana lives and of what his failings are."

"That is not difficult. Send your spies and gather information on the key men advising the king of owls. The next step is to divide them by setting one against the other."

"Tell me why did the crows and owls fall out in the first place," asked Meghavarna.

Sthirajeevi said, "That is another story. Long, long ago all the birds in the jungle-swans, parrots, cranes, nightingales, owls, peacocks, pigeons, pheasants, sparrows, crows etc.- assembled and expressed anguish that their king Garuda had become indifferent to their welfare and failed to save them from poachers. Believing that people without a protector were like passengers in a ship without a captain, they decided to elect a new king. They chose an owl as their king.

As the owl was being crowned, a crow flew into the assembly and asked them why and what they were celebrating. When the birds told him the details, the crow told them, the owl is a wicked and ugly bird and it is unwise to choose another leader when Garuda is still alive. To crush enemies it is enough if you mentioned Garuda's name or for that matter the name of anyone who is great. That was how the hares managed to live happily by taking the name of the moon."

The birds asked the visiting crow, "Tell us how this has happened."

"I will tell you," said the crow and began telling them the story of the hares and the elephants.

Elephants and Hares

Once upon a time a great elephant called Chaturdanta ruled over a vast stretch of forest as the king of his subjects.

They were not happy because for several years there had been no rains and all the lakes, tanks, ponds and water holes in the forest became arid. The subjects went in a delegation to the king and appealed to him, "O mighty king, there is no water to drink in the forest. Many of the younger ones are on the verge of extinction. Please look for a lake full of water and save us."

The king told them, "I know of a hidden lake that is always full of water. Let us go there and save ourselves."

The elephants then set off for the hidden lake and after plodding through the jungle for five nights reached the great lake. They colonised the land around the lake and once again started their revelry in water. But as the elephants daily marched their way to the lake, they trampled upon hundreds of hares that made the land around the lake their home. Hundreds of them died and thousands more were maimed.

One day the hares assembled to chalk out a plan to save themselves from the menace of the wayward elephants. An older one among them said, "these elephants will come every day and every day many of us will die. We must find a solution to this problem."

A wiser one among them said, "The great Manu had said that it was better to abandon a person to save the whole community, abandon the community to save the village and abandon the village to save the country. Even if the land were fertile, a wise king would abandon it if it were in the interests of his subjects."

But the other hares protested and said, "How can we do that? We have been living here for several generations. Let us find an alternative. Let us see if we can scare the elephants by some means."

Some of them said, "We know of a trick that works with the elephants. However, we need a very intelligent person."

Pressed to reveal the plan, they said, "Our ruler Vijayadatta lives in the lunar sphere. Let us send a messenger to the elephant king. The plan is to tell the elephant king that the

Moon does not like the elephants visiting the lake for water because they are killing and maiming hundreds of hares. The Moon has declared the lake out of bounds for the elephants."

Some others agreed and said, "Yes, there is a hare whose name is Lambakarna. He is an expert negotiator. He can do the job with success."

After a lot of discussions, the hares decided to send Lambakarna to the elephant king. Addressing the king, Lambakarna said, "O heartless king, I live in the lunar sphere. The Moon has sent me as envoy to you. This lake belongs to the Moon. He has forbidden all of you from drinking water from the lake. So, go back."

"But where is you lord, the Moon," asked the elephant king.

Lambakarna said, "He is very much in this lake. He has come to console the survivors of your rampage."

"Then, let me see him," the elephant king challenged the envoy.

"Come alone with me, I will show you."

"Let us go then," said the elephant.

Lambakarna took the elephant king one night to the lake and showed the reflection of the Moon in the lake and said,

"Here he is, our King, the Moon. He is lost in meditation. Move quietly and salute him. Otherwise, you will disturb his meditation and bring upon you his wrath."

Taking him for the real Moon, the elephant king saluted him and left quietly. The hares breathed a sigh of relief and lived happily ever after.

The crow told the birds gathered to elect a leader, "that is why it is important to choose a wise and experienced person as your leader. If you do not, listen to this story of how a hare and a partridge destroyed themselves because they chose a wicked mediator."

"Very interesting," said the birds and asked the visiting crow to tell them the account of the mediator.

The visiting crow began narrating the story.

The Cunning Mediator

A sparrow was living in the hollow of a big tree that I had made my home. His name was Kapinjala. We became good friends and used to spend our time discussing characters in our literature and the unusual things we saw in our travels. One day, my friend left the tree with other sparrows in search of food and did not return even after nightfall. I began to worry. "What happened to him? Did any hunter take him away? He never leaves my company even for a while."

Days passed without any trace of my friend Kapinjala. One fine morning, a hare named Sighragha, came and silently occupied the hollow that my friend made his home. It did not worry me because there was no word about Kapinjala and I had lost all hopes of his return. But one day, he returned looking healthier than he was when he had left and found that the hare had taken his place.

Kapinjala told the hare, "O hare, what you have done is improper. You have displaced me. Leave the place immediately."

Sighragha hit back saying, "What are you talking? This is my place. Haven't you heard the elders saying that nobody has rights over a public well, a temple, a pond and a tree? Whoever enjoys land for more than ten years also becomes its owner. That needs no evidence or documents of proof. This place is not yours any more."

The sparrow told him, "Oh, you are quoting legal scriptures! Let us go to an expert in law and ethics. We will abide by his ruling."

The hare agreed to this proposal and both of them went in search of an expert. Curious to see what would happen, I also followed them. Meanwhile, word about their quarrel had reached a wicked and wild cat. Knowing the route that the hare and the sparrow would take, the cat set up a camp on the way. He spread a mat of grass on the ground and went into a posture of meditation. Facing the sun and raising his hands in worship, the cat began reciting scriptures,

"This world has no essence. Life is passing. All liaisons with lovers are like a dream. Your ties with the family are illusory. There is no alternative to following the right path. The learned have said,"

"This wretched body will soon perish
Material wealth is not permanent
Death is knocking at your door
Free thyself from earthly chains
He who abandons the right path
Is the same as the living dead."

"I will end this long discourse and tell you in a nutshell what the right path is. Doing good to others is virtue. Tormenting others is vice. This is the essence of our philosophy. I am in the service of God and have given up all desires. I will not do you any harm. After hearing your account, I will decide who among you is the rightful owner of the place in the tree. But I am now very old and cannot hear you properly. So, please come close to me and narrate your story."

When the poor and innocent sparrow and hare came within the reach of the cat, he pounced on them and grabbed the sparrow in his teeth and slashed the body of the hare with his jaws and killed them.

The visiting crow then told the birds, "That is why I tell you if you rest your faith in this wicked and blind owl, you will meet the same end as the hare and the sparrow." The birds then dispersed, deciding to discuss the matter again carefully before electing the owl as the king.

Meanwhile, the owl was sitting restlessly on the throne waiting for his coronation.

He asked his wife Krikalika, "What is all this delay in crowning me."

The wife told him, "My lord, it is this crow which has sabotaged the coronation. All the birds have dispersed. Only this crow is lingering here. Come, let us go. I will take you home."

Furious, the owl shouted at the crow, "You wicked crow, what harm have I done to you? You have wrecked the coronation.

This is enough reason that from today there shall be enmity between owls and crows. One can heal wounds inflicted on the body but not the heart."

Dejected, the owl went home with his wife.

The crow began reflecting, "Oh, what a foolish thing have I done? Unnecessarily, I have made enemies. I should not have advised the birds not to elect the owl as the king. Elders have aptly said,

"Words out of tune with times

Words that bring grief in the end

Words that bring pain to others

Are, any day, as good as poison."

Regretting what he had said and done, the visiting crow also went home. This is how enmity began between the owls and the crows.

After listening to the story, Meghavarna asked Sthirajeevi, "What should we do in such a situation? Sthirajeevi, the wise crow, told him, "There is a strategy better than the six I had already told you. With its help, I will myself go and conquer the owl king. The learned have said that men with great common sense and a little bit of cunning can subdue stronger enemies like the tricksters who cheated the gullible Brahmin of his lamb."

On Meghavarna's request, Sthirajeevi began telling him the Brahmin's story.

The Brahmin and The Crooks

Mitra Sarma was a Brahmin living in a small village. He used to daily worship Fire. It was the month of Magha (February). The sky was full of clouds and it had already started raining. Sarma left for a neighbouring village at that time to seek the gift of a sacrificial lamb from some rich man. He called on a well-to-do man in the village and requested him to make him a gift of a healthy lamb for sacrifice to Gods. The wealthy man gave him one of the well-fed lambs he had.

Carrying the lamb on his shoulders, the Brahmin began his homeward journey. Three crooks, very hungry and emaciated, crossed his path and seeing the healthy lamb on the Brahmin's shoulders thought, "Ah, God has sent us good food. Let us trick the Brahmin into parting with it and free us from hunger and cold." At once, they began to act.

One of them changed into a disguise, and overtaking the Brahmin by another route, stopped him and said, "O what a fool you are? Such a great worshipper of Fire, why are you carrying this dog on your shoulders? This will bring you ridicule. Don't you know that it is a sin to touch a dog, or a rooster, or a donkey?"

The Brahmin lost his temper and said, "You stupid fellow, are you blind? Why do you call a lamb a dog?"

The first crook replied, "Don't be angry, if you think he is not a dog, please carry on. I have no objection."

The Brahmin hardly walked a little distance when the second crook greeted him and said,

"O respected sir, it is highly regrettable that you are carrying a dead calf on your shoulders, however dear it is to you. The man who touches dead animals or birds has to undergo purification rites."

The Brahmin challenged him, "Are you too blind? This is a live sacrificial lamb and you say he is a dead calf."

The second crook said, "All right, sir. Please excuse me. I am an ignorant fool. Do as it pleases you."

Now it was the turn of the third crook to cross the Brahmin's path.

Turning to the Brahmin, the crook said, "Sir, it is highly improper. You are carrying a donkey on your shoulders. This is not done. The elders have said he who touches a donkey, knowingly or otherwise, has to take a bath fully dressed. So, please leave him before anybody notices it."

Thinking that he was really carrying a donkey, the poor Brahmin threw the lamb to the ground and went home. Sthirajeevi, continuing his advice to Meghavarna, said,

"There is hardly any person
Who is not misled by
The servility of a new servant or
The sweet words of a guest or
The mock tears of a wily woman."

"Also, remember not to quarrel with weak men when they are united because they cannot be defeated. See, for example, how a deadly snake becomes prey of a united army of ants. That is why I want to tell you a few words of caution. Follow them."

"We shall do as you command us," said Meghavarna.

Sthirajeevi then began revealing his plan, "Apart from the four strategies I had told you, there is a fifth one. In the presence of everyone, abuse me and punish me branding me as the friend of your enemy. That will convince the spies of our enemy that you don't trust me any more. Bring some blood and spray it on my body. Then exile to the Rishyamooka hills."

"I shall remain here bruised and when the enemy comes, I will try to earn his mercy and trust by blaming you. You stay in the hills till I find their fort and give you a signal when all the owls are sleeping in the day. Then you can come and with the help of your army kill all the owls. This plan is the result of great thought. We have no alternative."

On Meghavarna approving the plan, Sthirajeevi started a mock fight with the king of crows. The king's men and others, mistaking it for a real duel, were ready to kill Sthirajeevi when Meghavarna told them, "Don't interfere. Go away. I will have the pleasure of punishing this unfaithful fellow." Meghavarna then pretended to attack Sthirajeevi with his beak and doused him in blood he brought with him and left for the hills.

Then Krikalika, wife of the pretender who was spying on the crow camp, carried this news of the assault on minister Sthirajeevi and the king's departure for the hills, to the owl king Arimardana. Soon after sunset, the owl king, accompanied by his ministers and followers, set out to kill all the crows. They reached the tree, home of the crows, and surrounded it.

Not finding a single crow there and happy for that reason, Arimardana told his men to look for the crows so that they could chase them and kill them. Meanwhile, Sthirajeevi, who suffered mock injuries, began weakly moaning to attract the attention of the owls. When the owls saw this and rushed to kill him, he pleaded, "Sir, my name is Sthirajeevi and I am minister of Meghavarna, the king of crows. Before you kill me, I have something to convey to your king."

Arimardana came to see the minister at once and asked him the reason for his plight. Sthirajeevi told him, "Our king wanted to avenge the massacre of his subjects by your men. When I knew he was bent upon waging a war with you, I advised him not to be rash and not go to war with you. I asked him to sign peace with you. My king thought that I was on your side and in great anger inflicted these injuries on me. As soon as I recover, I will show you where he and his men are hiding. You can destroy them."

The king of owls called a meeting of his elders and his five ministers for consultations. He asked his first minister, Raktaksha, "Friend, our enemy's minister is in our custody. What shall we do with him?"

The minister said, "What is there to discuss? Kill him instantly without hesitation. It is always better to destroy the enemy before he acquires strength. Such opportunities come once in a while. If you lose it now, you will never get it back. Don't be carried away by Meghavarna's minister's show of affection. Because once lost, love never returns."

To drive home the point, Raktaksha related to the king of owls the story of a cobra and a Brahmin.

The Brahmin and The Cobra

Laridatta was a Brahmin living in a hamlet. He was a farmer but the piece of land he cultivated gave him very little to survive. One day, unable to stand the heat of the summer sun, he went to a big tree in his land to rest for a while. Before he could spread himself on the ground he saw in the nearby anthill a huge cobra swaying with his hood open.

He thought, "This cobra must really be the Goddess of this land. I have never worshipped her, which is why I am not able to get anything from the land. From today, I will worship her."

At once he went back to his village and returned with a glass full of milk.

He poured it in a bowl and turning to the anthill said, "O ruler of the land, I did not know you were living in this anthill. That is why I have not paid my tribute to you. Please excuse me and accept this humble offering."

He then placed the bowl of milk at the anthill and left the place.

Next day when the Brahmin came to his land before the Sun was up, he saw a gold coin in the bowl he had left at the anthill. Henceforth, he came alone every dawn, collected the coin, offered the milk in the bowl and left. One day the Brahmin, leaving for another village on business, asked his son to go to the anthill and offer milk. When the son went the next day, he found a gold coin in the bowl.

He collected the coin and thought, "This anthill must be full of gold. If I kill the cobra, I can collect all the gold in one go instead of coming here every day."

He then struck the cobra with a big stick. But the cobra deftly dodged the blow but stung the son to death with his poisonous fangs. Returning to his village the next day, Haridatta heard the story of his son's death and at once realised that greed was behind it.

The Brahmin went to the anthill the day after his son's cremation and offered milk to the cobra. Without coming out of his hole, the cobra told Haridatta,

"You have come here for gold forgetting that you had lost a son and that you were in mourning. The reason is greed, pure greed. From today, there is no meaning in our relationship. Blinded by his youth, your son has struck me and I bit him back. How can I forget that blow? How can you suffer the grief of your son's death? Finally, I am giving you this diamond, don't come back again."

Ending the story of the Brahmin and the cobra, Raktaksha told Arimardana, "The lesson is that love once betrayed cannot be regained. If you kill this minister (Sthirajeevi) you will have no problems left."

After listening to Raktaksha patiently, the king of owls turned to his second minister Kruraksha and asked him for his opinion.

The second minister said, "O my lord, I don't agree with the advice Raktaksha gave you. It is very unkind. We should never kill a person seeking asylum. There is a fine story about how, knowing that a hunter who sought shelter had in fact come to kill him, a dove offered himself as food to the hunter."

On the king asking him to relate that story, Kruraksha told him the following tale.

Once upon a time there lived a merciless hunter in the heart of a forest, terrorizing birds and animals. Because of his cruel nature he had no friends or relatives. The elders have said,

"It is unwise to be close to

Men who are wicked and cruel.

Avoid such heinous persons as

You avoid poisonous snakes."

The hunter went out into the forest every morning with a stick and net. One day, he threw his net and trapped a female dove in it. Soon, thick and black clouds appeared in the sky and it began raining cats and dogs. Scared and shivering, the hunter looked for shelter and found it under a huge banyan tree. The rain and wind stopped suddenly. The skies became clear with stars shining. The hunter said loudly,

"If there is anyone on the tree, I seek shelter and food from him. I am hungry and may faint any moment. Please save me."

At the same time, a dove that had his nest on the same tree was worried that his wife who had gone out had not come back. He prayed to Gods that his wife should not come to any harm in this wind and rain. He began telling himself,

"Blessed and happy is the man
With a caring and loving wife.
A home is not a home without a wife;
A wifeless home is like a jungle."

The wife trapped in the hunter's net heard her husband's sorrowful words and, happy that her husband loved her so much, thought,

"Don't call her a woman
Whose husband is unhappy;
Where happy husbands live
Heavens shower blessings."

Later, addressing her husband, the female dove said, "Listen to me, my dear. Even at the cost of your life, you must come to the rescue of someone seeking shelter. This hunter is suffering from cold and hunger and has sought shelter under our tree. You must serve him with devotion. Don't hate him because he has trapped your beloved wife. In reality, the strings of destiny have bound me. Give up all thoughts of revenge and serve the hunter with care."

In accordance with his wife's desire, the dove suppressed grief and told the hunter, "Sir, you are welcome to our modest home. Please let me know what I can do for you. Treat this as own home and feel free to command me."

The hunter told the dove that he was suffering from cold and needed relief. The dove flew out, brought fire from somewhere and a lit a small fire with dry twigs and asked the hunter to warm himself.

The dove told the hunter, "Because of my past deeds, I am born poor and unfortunate and do not have enough to feed myself. What is the point in a host living if he cannot entertain a guest? It is better he renounce this world."

Yet he thought that it was better to die than say no to a host. Determined to die, the dove told the hunter to wait for a while and that soon he will have food. Then circling over the fire, the dove jumped into the fire he lit for the benefit of the hunter.

Moved by this sacrifice, the hunter told himself, "I am responsible for this tragedy. I will no doubt go to hell. This dove is a great soul, he has shown me the right path. Hereafter, I will give up all wants and desires and slowly destroy this body. Nothing, neither cold nor sun nor wind, matters to me. I will fast and see my slow end."

The hunter then threw his net and stick and released the female dove from the net.

The wife then saw how her husband had jumped into the fire to provide food for the hunter. She thought that life without her husband was worse than death and at once jumped into the same fire that consumed her husband. After her death, she saw her husband in the heaven wearing royal regalia.

On seeing her, the husband said, "O my darling, you have done well to follow me into the fire. Women like you live happily with their husbands for 35 million years."

The dove couple lived happily ever after. The hunter, shunning worldly pleasures, went to a forest for realising God. As penance had cleansed him of all desires, the hunter burnt himself in a forest fire and attained nirvana.

After Kruraksha ended telling the king the hunter's story, Arimardana asked a third minister, Deeptaksha for his advice on dealing with Sthirajeevi.

The minister told the king, "My lord, Sthirajeevi does not deserve to be killed. He will be of use to us in revealing the secrets of the enemy. There is this story of how even a thief could help an old man."

On the king commanding him, Deeptaksha began telling him the story of the old man, his young wife and the thief.

The Old Man, His Young Wife and The Thief

There lived an old widowed merchant in a city in the south. Though old, he did not give-up his desire for another wife. Therefore, he gave lots of money to a poor merchant and married his young daughter. She never loved her old husband. One day, when the husband and wife were sleeping on different sides of the bed, a thief entered their house. Shocked by the sight of the thief, the wife embraced her husband in fear.

The husband was both thrilled and surprised by the embrace and began thinking about what made her do so. He searched every nook and corner of the house and at last found the thief lurking in a corner. He then realised that his wife had embraced him because the thief had frightened her. The husband told the thief, "My dear young man, today I had the fortune of being hugged by my wife. Thanks to you. Take away whatever you want."

The thief replied, "My dear sir, I do not find anything in your house that I could take with me. But I will come back soon and see if there is anything to carry away. Or, you could call whenever you need love from your wife."

"That is why," Deeptaksha said, "when even a thief could do some good for someone, why not this Sthirajeevi who has sought asylum? He will give us useful information about the handicaps of the enemy. Therefore, in my view he should not be killed."

Then Arimardana turned to another minister, Vakranasa, and asked him, "Tell me what should we do with this crow?" Vakranasa told him that "the refugee's life should be spared because it may benefit us when two rivals fight each other like the quarrel between a thief and a monster had saved the life of a Brahmin and his two calves."

"How was that?" asked the owl king.

Vakranasa narrated him the following story.

Drona was a poor Brahmin who was living in a small town. He was so poor that he never wore good clothes, or used cosmetics, or indulged in the luxury of eating apaan (betel leaves). He had matted hair, an unshaven beard and uncut nails. He was extremely weak and emaciated because he had no cover from cold, sun or wind or rain. Taking pity on him, a rich man donated two calves to him.

With all care and love, he fed them well with butter oil and grass. The calves grew into two fine and healthy animals. A thief set his eyes on them and decided that he should somehow steal them. As he set out for the Brahmin's house, he saw on the way an awesome figure with loose teeth as long and sharp as fangs, an arched nose and blood-red eyes. He had a lean body with varicose veins and his hair and beard looked like two torches.

Though he was frightened, the thief asked him, "Who are you, sir?"

"I am Satyavachana, a monster. Let me know who you are."

"I am a thief. My name is Kroorakarma. I am going to steal the calves of the Brahmin."

The monster trusted the words of the thief and told him that he took only one meal a day in the evening and that he would kill the Brahmin for his dinner.

Both of them went to the Brahmin's house that night and waited for the Brahmin to go to sleep. When they were sure that the Brahmin had slept, the monster stepped in to kill the poor Brahmin. The thief held him back saying it was unjust to kill the Brahmin before he (the thief) could take away the two calves.

The monster said, "If the sound of the resisting calves disturbs the sleep of the Brahmin, all our effort will be in vain."

The thief replied, "Suppose there is some obstacle in your killing him, I cannot take the calves. Therefore, wait till I finish my job first."

The thief and the monster began quarrelling about who should be the first to finish his job.

The Brahmin woke up due to the commotion they were making and asked them who they were and what was the matter.

The thief told him, "This monster wants to kill you."

The monster denied and said, "O Brahmin, this thief wants to steal your calves."

The Brahmin then invoked his deity through prayer and the power of the prayer forced the monster to flee. The Brahmin then took a stick and drove off the thief.

"That is why," Vakranasa said, "I had told you that if two rivals quarrel among themselves, we would be the beneficiaries." Then the king asked his fourth minister, Prakarakarna for his opinion.

The minister said, "My lord, I think we should spare the life of the crow. It is possible that he will cooperate with us and that will be a gain for us. Where there is no cooperation, people will perish like the two snakes."

The king said, "In that case, let us hear that story."

The Tale of Two Snakes

Once upon a time there was a king named Devasakti. He had a son who was very weakand growing weaker by the day. It was found that he had a snake in his stomach. Experts, physicians and surgeons tried to nurse him back to health without success. Dejected, the son left his palace one night and took shelter in a lonely and dilapidated temple in another town ruled by a monarch called Bali. Every day, the son would go out to beg and return to the temple in the night.

King Bali had two daughters who came of age. Following a tradition, the two daughters would get up every dawn and touch the feet of their father in reverence.

One day, after paying respects to the king one of his daughters said, "Victory to the king. We are happy in every way."

The second daughter said, "O king, reap the harvest of your actions."

The king, very angry at the words of the second daughter, called his ministers and told them, "Take this foul-mouthed woman away and marry her off to some stranger. Let her reap the consequences of her actions."

In compliance with the orders of the king, the ministers took her away and married her without pomp or ceremony to

Devasakti's son living in the old temple. The daughter considered the king's son as God's gift and after persuading him, left for another country.

The princess and the son of Devasakti reached a city where they camped close to a lake. She asked her husband to take care of the camp and went into the city with her maids to buy daily needs like rice, salt, butter oil and vegetables. After shopping, she returned to the lake where she saw a surprising spectacle.

The prince was sleeping, resting his head on an anthill. The serpent in his stomach came out to breath fresh air. Then another serpent emerged from the anthill for the same reason. Both of them glared at each other.

The anthill inmate said, "You wicked creature, why do you torment such a handsome prince."

The other serpent retorted, "Why are you polluting the two golden urns in your hole."

Thus in their row, they revealed the secrets of each other.

The serpent in the anthill told the other serpent, "Don't be arrogant. Who does not know the secret of your death? If the prince drinks a concoction made of gruel and mustard you will die unsung."

"Oh, is that so? You will also perish if someone pours hot oil or hot water in your anthill. Don't be too proud," said the serpent in the prince's stomach.

The princess, who heard all that passed between the two serpents, poured hot oil into the anthill and took the two golden urns and gave the mustard concoction to her husband and killed the serpent inside his stomach. Both Divyasakti's son and his daughter-in-law returned to his kingdom and lived happily ever after.

After listening to this story, owl king Arimardana accepted his advice that Sthirajeevi's life should be spared.

Raktaksha, the first minister, was sad and told the ministers, "You have misled the king by giving wrong advice and paved the way for his destruction. The learned have said that where wicked men are honoured and wise men are insulted, there will be fear, famine and death."

Disregarding the warning of Raktaksha, the king's men set out to take Sthirajeevi to their fortress.

On the way, Sthirajeevi said, "My lord, in my condition, I cannot be of any help to you. Why do you unnecessarily carry me to the fortress? I will jump into a fire and perish. Please permit me to do that."

Sensing his internal thoughts, Raktaksha asked him why he would want to end up in fire.

Sthirajeevi said, "It is for your cause I met this fate in the hands of Meghavarna."

Raktaksha said, "You are a cheat, good at spinning words. You were really born as a crow and even if you are born as an owl in your next birth, you will still be a crow in nature. Haven't you heard the story of the mouse, which even when she was born as a girl in another birth, chose to marry not a human being but another male mouse?"

The ministers and other king's men pressed Raktaksha to tell them that story.

T here was a hermitage belonging to the sage Salankayana. He went one morning to river Ganga to bathe. As he was reciting stanzas in praise of the Sun, he saw a kite carrying a mouse in its claws. At once, the sage aimed a stone at the kite. Hit by the stone, the kite released its prey and the mouse at once ran to the sage asking him for protection.

The kite addressed Salankayana and said, "O sage, you have hit me with a stone, which is not proper. Are you not afraid of God? Surrender that mouse to me or you will go to hell."

The sage said, "You wretched bird, my duty is to save God's creations, to punish the wicked, to respect the good, to honour the teacher and worship the Gods. Why do you preach all those irrelevant rules of conduct to me?"

The kite delivered a big lecture to the sage on the right path. "You have no idea of what is good and what is bad. God created all of us and at the time of creation also prescribed what should be our food. God has marked mice, other rodents and insects to be food for us. Why do you blame me for seeking what God has meant for me? There is nothing wrong for anyone to eat the food marked for him. The danger comes when one eats what is not food for him. What is meat for someone is poison for someone else."

"It is not proper for sages to be violent. They are not presumed to notice what is happening around them. They are detached from this world. Nothing that happens in the material world should interest them. They should not discriminate between vice and virtue. They are above everything. But by your deed today you have lost all the gains of your penance. Learn from this story of three brothers how to attain that state of detachment."

Salankayana asked the kite to relate that story to him. The kite told him the following story.

The Wedding of The Mouse

Once upon a time, three sages, who were also brothers, chose a riverbank to do penance. Their names were Ekata, Dwita and Trita. The clothes they washed every day used to dry in the sky without a clothesline lest they should drop and become soiled. One day a kite was carrying a female frog like I (the kite) carried a female mouse.

Ekata saw this and shouted at the kite, "Leave it, Leave it."

At once his clothes drying in the sky dropped down to the ground.

When Dwita saw this, he shouted at the kite, "Don't leave it, Don't leave it" and soon his clothes also came down hurtling.

When Trita saw that the clothes of his elder brothers fell down, he thought it would be better not to say anything and remained silent. That is why it is better not to notice the happenings around and concentrate on self.

The sage Salankayana replied, "O foolish kite, your story has happened in the Age of Truth when even if you spoke to a wicked person you became a sinner. The clothes came down because the first two sages addressed the wicked kite. We are now living in the Age of Kali, an age in which everyone is a born sinner. In this age only those who commit a sin become sinners and not those who speak to sinners. Now, don't waste my time. Disperse or face my curse."

The kite flew away disappointed.

The female mouse then prayed Salankayana, "O sage, please give me shelter in your hermitage. Otherwise, some wicked bird will kill me. I will spend the rest of my life with whatever leftovers you choose to feed me with."

The female mouse's prayer moved the sage but he thought that if he took her home, people would laugh at him. So, he turned the mouse into a beautiful girl and took her home.

"What is this you have brought," asked the sage's wife. Where did you bring this girl from?"

"She is a female mouse. She needed protection from wicked birds. That's why I turned her into a girl and brought her home. You will need to shower all care on her. I will make her a mouse again," said the sage.

"Please don't do that," pleaded his wife, "You have saved her life and therefore you have become her father. I don't have a child. Since you are her father, she becomes my daughter." The sage accepted her plea.

The girl grew into a beautiful woman and became an eligible bride. Salankayana told his wife, "The girl has come of age. It is not proper for her to remain in our house. The learned have said,

He who keeps an eligible bride in his house

Forfeits a place in heaven. So do his ancestors.

"It's all right. Look for a boy," said his wife.

Salankayana immediately summoned the Sun and told him, "This is my daughter. If she is willing to marry you, get ready to marry her."

He then showed the Sun to his daughter and asked her if she would marry him. She said that the Sun was very hot and she would prefer someone else. The sage then summoned the God of Clouds, the God of Wind and the God of Mountains. The girl rejected every one of them on one ground or the other.

Then the God of Mountains told the sage, "The most suitable candidate for your daughter is a mouse. He is more powerful than I am."

The sage then turned her into a mouse and gave her away to a king of mice in marriage.

"That's why," Raktaksha resumed, "I want you know that a crow is a crow and cannot become an owl."

Yet, disregarding Raktaksha's warnings, the king's men took away Sthirajeevi to their fortress not knowing that they were bringing ruin upon themselves and the king. Sthirajeevi thought on the way to his destination, "This man (Raktaksha) alone advised the king to kill me. Of all of the king's men he alone knows statecraft. If they had heeded his word and killed me the king would have escaped disaster."

When Sthirajeevi's procession arrived at the entrance of the fortress, king Arimardana ordered his men to accommodate him in a comfortable place of his choice. But Sthirajeevi had other ideas. If he had to hatch a plan to kill the king, it was not possible within the fort because he and his movements would be constantly under watch. That would alert his hosts. So, he thought, it was better to be outside the fort.

He told the king, "My lord, I am grateful for your generosity. But I am a politician and belong to the enemy camp. Yet I am your devotee and faithful servant. It does not become of me to live inside the palace. I will stay at the entrance of the fort and every day sanctify my body with the dust of your feet."

The king of owls accepted his request and let him stay where he wanted to. The king's men took extraordinary care of his needs and very soon Sthirajeevi became as strong as a wrestler. Seeing Sthirajeevi's new personality, Raktaksha told the king and other ministers, "I regard all of you as very unwise. Haven't you heard the learned often repeating the words of the bird Sindhuka? The bird used to say, ""First, I am a fool. Then the hunter and then the king and his ministers."

"How was that?" asked the ministers and Raktaksha began telling them the story of Sindhuka.

Tale of The Golden Droppings

On a big tree in the lap of a mountain lived a bird named Sindhuka. His droppings used to turn into gold as soon as they hit the ground. One day, a hunter came to the tree in search of prey and saw Sindhuka's droppings hit the ground and turn into gold.

The hunter, struck by wonder, thought, "I have been hunting birds and small animals since I was a boy. I am now eighty years old. I have never seen in my life this kind of miracle."

He decided to get the bird some how and set a noose for him. Not aware of the trap, the bird stayed on the branch merrily singing. Soon, the noose tightened and the hunter caught the bird and pushed him into his cage.

The hunter took it home and considered, "If the king comes to know of this wonder, he will certainly take away the bird from me. Instead, I will go to the king and present the unique bird to him."

The hunter took the bird the following day to the king and presented it to him with great reverence. The king was extremely happy and told his men to keep the bird in safe custody and feed him with the best bird food. But his minister was reluctant to accept the bird.

He said, "O Rajah, There is no use in trusting the word of this hunter and accepting the bird. Has anyone seen a bird dropping gold? Therefore, I request you to release the bird from the cage."

The king ordered the bird to be set free. As soon as the door of the cage opened, the bird perched himself on a nearby doorway and defecated. The dropping immediately turned into gold. Sindhuka then recited that line about fools, "First, I was a fool. Then the hunter and then the king and his ministers."

Raktaksha continued, "That's why I tell you that we are all fools in sparing the life of this minister of the crows,

Sthirajeevi." Despite Raktaksha's warnings, the owls continued to look after Sthirajeevi with great devotion. The crow minister became strong and powerful. Giving up all hopes of reforming his king and ministers, Raktaksha called his close colleagues and told them,

"Friends, our king and his men are beyond reform. We have given whatever advice a minister has to give. We shall now leave this dangerous place and pitch our tents elsewhere. The elders have said, "He prospers who anticipates danger and escapes it. He who does not destroys himself." I have been living in this jungle for so long, I have become old. Yet, in all my life I have never heard a cave speaking like a human being."

"What, a cave speaking like a human being! Surprising. We have never heard of it. Please tell us all about it," asked his followers.

Raktaksha then told them the following story.

Deep in the rain forest lived a lion named Kharanakara. One day, he was very hungry and looked for a prey in every nook and corner of the forest. There was no animal, big or small, as far as he could see. As he was wandering in search of food he found a big cave and thought, "There must be some animal living here. If so, it is bound to return to the cave in the evening. I will hide myself in the cave and when the animal returns, pounce on him and have a good meal."

Then as sun began to set, Dadhiputcha, a jackal, came to the cave that was his home and saw the footprints of the lion entering the cave. There were, however, no traces of footprints to show that the lion had left. Scared, the jackal wanted to make sure that it was a lion or some big animal that went into the cave. But how should he know? He hit upon a brilliant idea.

The jackal went near the cave and began shouting, "Hello cave, I am your friend here." There was no reply from the cave. He did not know what to do. He again shouted, "Hello cave, don't you remember the arrangement we made? I have to shout when I arrive at the cave and you will ask me to come in. Without your green signal I do not enter the cave. Since you are silent, I will go to some other cave."

The lion heard the jackal speaking and thought, "Ah, there seems to be an arrangement between the cave and this animal. Let me get him into my trap. I will shout back a welcome to him and he will walk in happily." The lion then roared, "Hi jackal, come in. You are welcome."

The jackal at once knew it was a lion inside the cave and hurriedly fled the place, remembering the lines of the learned,

"He survives who anticipates a danger and acts to avert it,

He who does not comes to grief."

Raktaksha said, "That is how we must also anticipate danger and act. Let us leave now before it is too late."

Listening to his advice, his ministers and others followed him to a far off place.

Seeing that the main obstacle in his way has disappeared and that the remaining king's men were all stupid, Sthirajeevi began piling up twigs on the pretext of building a nest. He heaped them at the entrance of the cave in which the king and other owls lived. When the pile was big enough, he waited for daybreak when the owls would become blind. Then he flew off to Meghavarna and told him that before word could reach the enemy camp of this plan, he and his followers should accompany him (Sthirajeevi) each carrying a piece of burning wood.

Accordingly, Meghavarna and his men followed Sthirajeevi, each carrying a burning twig in his beak. When they reached the entrance of the cave, which was now blocked by the pile of twigs Sthirajeevi built, they threw the burning twigs on the pile, which began to burn fiercely killing all the owls trapped inside.

When Megahvarna and his men returned to their kingdom, he asked Sthirajeevi to tell him how he could plan to kill the enemy.

Sthirajeevi said, "It was not an easy job living in the enemy camp. Luckily, except Raktaksha, every one of Arimardana's ministers was a fool. Yet it was like walking on the edge of a sword. But if you want to achieve your goal you will have to put up with all inconvenience and discomfort like the snake which carried the frogs on its back."

Frogs That Rode a Snake

A black snake named Mandavishya lived in a forest on the Varuna hills. He was becoming old and worried that he would not be able to snare frogs any more and that would make him weak and bring his end closer. With a plan in his head, he went to a lake and resting on its edge pretended that he had lost all interest in worldly matters.

A frog in the lake came out and asked him, "Uncle, why are you not preying for food as used you to do in the past?"

The snake said, "Listen, my son, I am very unfortunate. How can I have any fervour for food? Last night when I was on my rounds looking for food I sighted a frog. When I tried to get at him, he jumped into the middle of a group of Brahmins reciting the Vedas. I could not track him. But soon I saw something like a frog near the Brahmins and at once jumped at him and bit him. It turned out to be the thumb of a Brahmin boy. The boy died immediately."

"When his father found that I had killed his son, he cursed me, "You wicked snake, you have killed my innocent son. From now onwards you will serve as a vehicle for all frogs. Your life will be at their mercy." I have now decided to serve my sentence. That is why I am here," said the snake.

The frog ran into the lake and told every one about the snake and his offer to serve as a vehicle. Happy at the prospect, all the frogs went and met their king Jalapada and told him about the snake. "What a wonderful news," thought the king and trooped out of the lake with his ministers and subjects. The king was the first to get on to the hood of the snake, followed by his ministers. In the order of seniority and prominence, the kings' subjects also climbed the back of the snake. Those unfortunate frogs that could not find space on the vehicle followed the snake in a procession. To entertain them, Mandavishya showed several feats he could do.

Thrilled by the experience of riding a deadly snake, Jalapada, the king of the frogs, thought that the ride had no parallel. No ride, whether on an elephant or a horse or a chariot or a palanquin, can match this experience, he thought.

On the second day, Mandavishya slowed down the pace of his haul. Noticing the change of pace, Jalapada asked the snake why he was not moving as briskly as he used to. The snake told the king of frogs that he had no food that day and being weak he was not able to carry so much load.

Jalapada, taking pity on the snake, said, "You can have the younger frogs for your food."

Thrilled at this offer, the snake said, "O king of frogs, my plight is due to the curse the Brahmin gave me. Your magnanimous concession has released me today from the curse. I am so happy."

The snake thus began eating a few frogs every day and soon became strong and healthy. He was also worried that if he began eating the frogs at that rate there would not be any frogs left for him in the future.

Meanwhile, a big cobra chanced to come that way and seeing the snake carrying the frogs and struck by wonder asked the snake, "This is very unique though unnatural. How is it you have become a vehicle for frogs which are our natural food?"

"That's a long story resembling the story of the Brahmin who pretended to have become blind after eating the good food his wife had made," said Mandavishya.

The cobra asked the snake to relate that story.

Once upon a time, a Brahmin named Yagnadatta lived in a city. He had a wife who was not trustworthy. She had a lover to whom she would secretly send every day delicious food she made. One day, her husband found out what she was doing.

He asked her, "My dear, you are making every day some special dish or the other and taking it out of the house. Tell me, what is the truth."

With great presence of mind, she told Yagnadatta, "Every day I am fasting and taking this food to offer to the Goddess." To allay suspicion, she collected food and telling her husband that she was leaving for the temple, left home. The husband began following her secretly and when she went to the tank to bathe, he went to the temple of the Goddess and hid behind the idol.

After taking bath in the tank, the Brahmin's wife came to the temple from the tank and began praying the Goddess, "O mother, tell me how can I render my husband blind?"

The Brahmin, hiding behind the idol, changed his voice and said, "O great devotee, you feed your husband daily with good and delicious food. Very soon he will become blind."

From then onwards, the wife began feeding her husband with delicacies. Soon, the Brahmin complained to the wife that he was not able to see clearly. The wife thought that the Goddess had at last fulfilled her desire.

Encouraged by the Brahmin's blindness, his wife's lover began visiting her without any fear. One day, Yagnadatta saw him and his wife together. The lover ignored him thinking the Brahmin was blind. Yagnadatta then thrashed the lover so hard that he died. The Brahmin then cut the nose of his wife.

"That's why," Mandavishya told the cobra, "I am pretending to be friendly with the frogs." Jalapada, the king of frogs overheard this conversation and asked Mandavishya if what he had heard was true. The snake at once realised his mistake and told the king of frogs that it was all fun. The king of frogs foolishly believed the words of the snake and the snake slowly swallowed all the frogs.

Sthirajeevi told Meghavarna that he followed the tactics of Mandavishya in misleading his enemies. Pleased, the king of crows said, "What you have said is correct. Great men do not give up what they have begun even in the face of obstacles. Cowards, afraid of failure, do not venture at all. There are some that begin a task and give it up when there is a problem. But courageous people do not give up whatever dangers they face."

"You (Sthirajeevi) have crushed the enemies and brought security to my kingdom. The learned have said,

"It is dangerous to leave

A fire unextinguished

A debt unredeemed

An enemy uncrushed and

A disease untreated."

Sthirajeevi said, "My lord, virtue belongs to him who is charitable, learned, courageous and friendly. Virtue brings wealth. Wealth brings power. It is a king with these qualities who can rule and expand his kingdom. I have done my duty. I need rest. But I humbly seek to offer one word of advice. All this power should not go to your head. Follow the path of duty and rule your subjects for a hundred years. May God bless you."

This is the end of the third strategy Vishnu Sarma disclosed to his royal wards.

Fourth Strategy

The Croc and The Monkey

Vishnu Sarma begins his fourth Tantra with the following stanza:

"He overcomes all problems

Who does not lose his cool

Even in the face of adversity

Like the monkey in the water."

Raktamukha was a monkey living on a blackberry tree near the coast. That tree was always full of fruits. One day a crocodile named Karalamukha came out of the waters and loitering on the sands came to the tree.

Seeing the croc, the monkey said, "O croc, you are my guest. I will feed you with these delicious blackberries. Enjoy the fare. The learned have said,

"That man is blessed who hosts

A lover or an enemy or a fool.

Angels will desert the home

That fails to host a guest."

The monkey then gave the crock a lot of berries. After he had his fill, Karalamukha went home. Thereafter, it became a habit with the croc to daily visit Raktamukha, enjoy the fruit he offered, spend time with him discussing the world and then go home.

One day, the croc's wife asked her husband, "Where do you get this fruit, they are so sweet. I have never tasted such mouthwatering fruit."

"I have a close friend, a monkey, who gives me the fruit every day," said the husband.

"If the fruit are so sweet, the heart of your friend who eats them everyday must be as delicious as the fruit. Please get his heart for me, if you have love left for me. I will always be young and immortal if I eat that fruit," said the wife.

"My dear, it is improper for you to speak like that. I have accepted him as my brother. It is not possible for me to kill such a host. Please be reasonable. The elders have said,

"From mother we get our first relative,

A good word brings the second relative

Who is more precious than a brother."

Angry, the wife said, "You have never defied my word. It must be a female monkey who is your friend. That's why you are spending so much time with him every day. I have now understood you thoroughly. Your heart is full of that monkey. You are a cheat."

Karalamukha, wanting to pacify his wife, said, ""My dear, why are you angry? I am your most obedient servant and ready to carry out your order at any time."

"No, she is dear to you. If you really love me, why don't you kill her and get me her heart. If you don't get it, I will fast and die," threatened the wife.

Worried, the croc went to the monkey. Seeing that the croc was late for his daily meeting, Raktamukha said, "You are late and do not seem to be cheerful. What's the matter?"

"O my friend, how can I tell you what happened at home. My wife is very angry. She told me that I am an ungrateful friend and that every day I eat the fruit you offer but never had the courtesy of inviting you home. You have no redemption; she told me and warned me that if I did not bring you home, I would see her only in the other world. These arguments with her have delayed me. Please come with me. My wife has decorated the house fit to receive you. She has hung welcome buntings at the entrance. She is eagerly waiting for me to bring you home."

The monkey said, "Your wife has said the proper thing. You should leave a man who loves you for your wealth like the spider attracts his prey. She might as well have quoted the elders saying,

"Where there is no give and take

Where there is no exchange of secrets

And of hospitality either

There is no true friendship."

"There is a problem, however. We are all land animals. You live in water. It may not be possible for me to accept your kind invitation. I advise you to bring her here," said the monkey.

"It's really no problem," said the croc. "Our house is on a sandbank. It's a beautiful place. Sit on my back. I will carry you."

The monkey happily sat on the back of the croc and the journey began. As the croc was entering deep waters, the monkey got scared and told the croc to go slowly.

Thinking that the monkey was his prisoner now, Karalamukha told Raktamukha, "It is now safe to tell you our plan. My wife wanted me to create trust in you first and persuade you to accept our invitation and then kill you so that we may have the good fortune of feasting on your heart."

With great presence of mind, the monkey said, "My friend, if this is what you and your wife wanted, why didn't you tell me in the beginning itself? My heart is safely stored in the burrow of the tree. What is the use of your taking me home without my heart? Let us go back. There is nothing happier for me than giving my heart to your wife." Happy, the croc turned back and brought the monkey to the shore.

The monkey at once leapt to the top of the blackberry tree and thought, "We should not trust an untrustworthy person, even if we did, it should not be total. Such trust will destroy us completely. This is a rebirth for me."

The croc was in a hurry and asked the monkey, "What is the delay? Get you heart. My wife will be very happy."

The monkey angrily told him, "You idiot, have you seen anyone who has two hearts? You are ungrateful. Get out of my sight and never come this way again. People who are hungry stoop to any level like Priyadarsana." The croc asked him to tell the story of Priyadarsana.

Raktamukha told him the following story.

The Greedy Cobra and The King of Frogs

A big well was the home of Gangadatta, king of frogs. Unable to bear harassment by his relatives, the king abandoned his kingdom and came out of the well and thought,

"He who certainly retaliates

Him who harmed him in peril

And ridiculed him in misery

Is a man without rebirth."

Deeply lost in such thoughts, the frog king saw a big cobra entering the burrow of a tree and thought, "We must set an enemy to fight an enemy, set a strong person to crush another strong person. Their end will bring us happiness."

With this aim in view, he went to the burrow and called the cobra, "Priyadarsana, please come out."

The cobra, however, was careful. He thought, "Who is this fellow? He does not seem to be one of us. I don't have any friends outside my circle. I will stay inside and find out who the caller is. He could be a magician or someone seeking my help in killing his enemy."

Then, the cobra shouted from inside, "Who are you, sir?"

"I am Gangadatta, king of frogs. I have come to seek your help," said the caller.

"I cannot believe you. Can there be friendship between a blade of dry grass and fire? Haven't the learned said that he, who is natural prey to the predator never, even in a dream, gets closer to him? I cannot trust your words," said the cobra.

"O Priyadarsana, what I tell you is true. You are my born enemy. But I have come to you seeking help to avenge my humiliation. The learned have said,

"When your life is under threat

When danger stares you in the face

It is better to bend before an enemy

And save life and property."

"Who humiliated you," asked the cobra.

"It is my relatives."

"Where do you live? Is it a well or a pond or a tank?"

"It is a well with stone walls."

"But I have no legs. How can I reach the well and kill your enemies?"

"Sir, please don't say no. I will show you how to enter the well. There is a crevice in the wall that opens into the well. It's a nice hiding place for you. Come, I will show you," said Gangadatta, king of frogs.

The cobra then thought, "I have become old. Rarely can I get a frog to eat. This fellow has come to give me a new lease of life. I will go with him and have a daily feast of frogs."

Addressing the king of frogs, the cobra said, "Let's go."

"But there is a condition," said Gangadatta, "Priyadarsana, I will take you there and show you the place. But you should spare frogs that are close to me. You should eat only those I select as food for you."

The cobra replied, "You are now my friend. I give you my word. I will eat only those marked by you as my food."

The cobra then emerged from its burrow and accompanied the king of frogs to the well. The frog king showed him the crevice in the well and his relatives who deserved to be killed.

The cobra happily settled in the crevice and finished in course of time all those frogs their king had marked for extermination.

Now, without frogs to eat, the cobra told the king, "I have destroyed all your enemies. Now show me prey for food. It is you who brought me here."

Gangadatta told him, "You have done your job to help me. Now, it is time for you to leave this place."

"How can I leave?" protested the cobra. "Someone else will occupy my place. So, I will not go, I will stay here only. You offer me one frog every day from your circle of relatives."

Repenting for making friends with a natural enemy, Gangadatta thought it was better to offer the cobra one friend a day, remembering the saying that "he who befriends a stronger enemy invites certain death. A wise man does not lose all his wealth to save a paltry sum."

Accordingly, the king of frogs began offering the cobra a frog a day. But the wicked cobra swallowed all the frogs. One day, it was the turn of Yamunadatta, son of the king of frogs. The king cried bitterly over the loss of his son. His wife then told him that there was no point in crying over the past and that he should immediately leave the place and look for ways to end the menace of the cobra.

As days passed, the cobra finished off the entire tribe of frogs with the exception of king Gangadatta. So, he asked Gangadatta, "Look, my friend, there is now no frog left for me to eat. I am very hungry. Show me where and how can sate my hunger."

The king replied, "Priyadarsana, don't worry about food as long as I am your friend. You get me out of this well. I will go and look for wells full of frogs. I will tempt them to come here and you can have your fill."

The cobra said, "You are like a brother to me, Gangadatta. I can't kill you. But if you bring me food, you will be as good as my father. I will get you out of this well." Thus, the king came out and disappeared. The cobra was eagerly waiting for the king to bring him food. When Gangadatta failed to turn up even after a long time, the cobra sought the help of a chameleon.

"My friend, you know Gangadatta very well. Please go to him and tell him that it does not matter if he cannot bring me a frog. Let him come. I cannot live without such a trusted friend."

The chameleon carried the message of the cobra to the king of frogs and told him, "Your friend Priyadarsana is eagerly looking for you to return."

Gangadatta told him, "Excuse me sir, who can trust a hungry man. You may please go."

Concluding the story, Raktamukha, the monkey, told the crocodile, "You wicked creature, I will never visit your home."

Karalamukha, the croc, pleaded with him, "My friend, this is not proper. Please come and sanctify my home. Otherwise, I will be guilty of ingratitude. If you don't come, I will fast and die."

The monkey said, "You are an idiot to think that I would, like Lambakarna, invite death knowingly."

"O my friend, let me hear that story of Lambakarana," asked the croc.

Then the monkey told the croc the story of Lambakarna.

The Lion and The Foolish Donkey

A lion named Karalakesara was living in a forest, loyally served by Dhoosaraka, a jackalthat used to accompany the lion wherever he went. One day, an elephant badly injured the lion in a fight. The injuries were so serious that the lion could not go out hunting. As a result, the jackal also had to go without food. Both the master and the servant became very weak. Unable to bear hunger, the jackal pleaded with the lion to get him some food.

"You know my plight. I cannot move out of this place. However, if you manage to lure some animal to come here, I will kill him and both of us can have a good meal," said the lion.

So, the jackal set out in search of some animal and saw a donkey feeding himself on weeds. The jackal approached him and said, "O my friend, please accept my regards. I have not seen you for a long time. You have become very weak. What is the reason?"

The donkey said in sad tones, "How shall I tell you my suffering? The washerman is tormenting me by placing too much weight on my back. He does not feed me at all. I exist on weeds. That is why my body is weak."

The jackal said, "If that is the case, why don't you come with me? I shall show you a place where you can have your heart's fill of green and fresh grass. We can happily spend our time there."

"You have given me good news. But there is a problem. We are domestic animals and you are all wild animals. One of them will certainly kill me," said the donkey whose name was Lambakarna.

Allaying his fears, the jackal said, "O uncle, don't say like that. This place is in my control. Nobody can enter this area. Just like you are suffering at the hands of the washerman, there are three female donkeys in this area, which are waiting for a suitable husband. They are all young and told me, "If you are really our uncle, go and get a suitable husband for us." It is on that mission I have come here and seen you."

The donkey replied, "If that is the case, let's go now."

That is why the elders have said,

"If the very thought of a woman
Brings ecstasy to a young man
How thrilled would he be?
If he actually is in her presence."

In the end, the jackal and the donkey reached the forest and came to the lion. When Lambakarna saw the ailing Karalakesara, the lion, he began running away from him. The lion made a great effort to reach him and strike him with his paw but failed to get the donkey.

Angry at the lion's failure, Dhoosaraka, the jackal protested, "O my lord, you are useless. If you cannot tackle a foolish donkey, how can you fight an elephant? I have now realised how powerful you are."

Ashamed, the lion told the jackal quietly, "O my friend, I was not ready for attack. Otherwise, even an elephant cannot escape my strike."

Satisfied, the jackal said, "All right, let us forget the past. I will bring the donkey here again. You must be ready and strike him this time."

"But how can Lambakarna forget his experience and come back here again," asked the lion.

"You leave it to me," said the jackal and set off to look for the donkey. Lambakarna was there on the bank of a lake feeding on grass.

He came to the jackal and said, "Friend, you have taken me to a nice place. I escaped death by inches. Who is that animal who had nearly killed me?"

"You are mistaken," said Dhoosaraka, "It is, after all, the female donkey I promised to take you to. She was getting up to come and embrace you. You ran away in scare. She cannot live without you and so was trying to reach out to you. She told me that if you do not marry her, she would commit suicide. So please come and spare me the sin of causing the death of a woman. The God of Love will punish you if you do not heed my word."

Beguiled, the donkey followed the jackal. The lion was prepared for the attack this time and when the donkey came; he fell on him and killed him instantly. The lion asked the jackal to keep an eye on the donkey's body and left to take a bath in the river. Unable to resist the temptation of fresh flesh, the jackal snipped off the ears of the donkey and scooped his heart out and made a good meal of them. When the lion returned, he noticed that the ears and heart of the donkey were missing.

The lion angrily asked the jackal to tell him what had happened to the ears and heart of the donkey. Dhoosaraka told him that the donkey had no ears and heart. If he had, he would not have come again. The foolish lion believed every word of the jackal and shared the donkey with him.

"So, like the donkey in the story, you too are a fool," said Raktamukha, the monkey to Karalamukha, the croc.

"You have deceived me but like Yudhishtira in the story I am going to tell you, you too spoke the truth when you ought not to and lost everything."

"Please tell me everything about this Yudhishtira," pleaded the croc.

The Story of The Potter

Once upon a time, there lived in a village a potter named Yudhishtira. One day, he drank a lot of liquor and got intoxicated and began running. He lost his balance and fell on broken pieces of a pitcher. The sharp edges of the pot pieces cut a big and bloody gash in his forehead. Somehow, he got up and went home. The wound took a long time to heal because he neglected to follow the instructions of the doctor.

Suddenly, a famine struck the whole country. The potter left the country with some others of the royal household. In the new country, he found a job with the king of that country. The king saw the mark of the big wound on his face and thought that Yudhishtira must have been a great warrior who suffered wounds in a battle. The king began showering special attention and affection on the potter, which the king's sons envied. They could not harm him because he was the king's favourite.

When everything was going smoothly for the potter, a war came and the king was summoning all known warriors to honour them and prepare them for the war. The king's men were readying the elephants and horses for the combat while the soldiers were busy staging rehearsals. It was now time for the king to know everything about Yudhishtira.

He sent for the potter and asked him when no one was around, "What is your name, o warrior? In what battle were you injured?"

The potter told the king, "My lord, this is not a wound inflicted on me in a battle. I am a potter and my name is Yudhishtira. One day, when I was drunk, I ran and fell on sharp pieces of a broken pot. This scar on my face is the result of that fall."

Ashamed that he deceived himself by the speech and garments of the potter, the king asked his servants to throw out the potter.

But Yudhishtira appealed to the king, "My lord, please don't throw me out. See how well I will fight."

The king said, "I admit you are a warrior. But you are born in a potter community and hence cannot kill an elephant."

"How is that," asked the potter.

The king then told him the following story.

A lion couple lived in a forest. In course of time, the lioness delivered two lion cubs. Every day, the lion went out and brought food for the lioness. One day, the lion wandered all over the forest in search of food but could not find any prey at all. At sunset, the lion gave up his search and was returning home when he found a jackal cub. The lion took a fancy for him and took him home and gave him to his wife.

The lioness asked her husband, "Did you get us any food today?"

"I found this cub. That's all," said the lion.

"I haven't killed him because he is a child. But if you are very hungry, you can have this child for your meal."

The lioness was angry and asked her husband, "How can I kill him when you spared him his life?"

The elders have said:

"Don't do an unworthy deed

Even in the face of death;

Don't give up a worthy deed

Even if it means suicide."

"I will treat him like my third son," said the lioness.

Thereafter, the new jackal cub became one of the family and the three ate, drank, played and slept together. One day when they were playing, an elephant passed by. At once, the two lion cubs got ready to attack the elephant. The jackal cub told them that the elephant was an enemy of the lions and that it was better for them to leave. The lion cubs were disappointed at the words of their jackal brother.

They went home and told their father the details of how the jackal brother fled from the scene. The father was not happy with his children and admonished them. The lion took the jackal cub aside and told him not to discourage the lion cubs who, she said, were his younger brothers.

The jackal was hurt and asked his lion mother, "How am I different from them in beauty or education or bravery? Why should the two ridicule me? I will kill both of them."

Amused by the words of the jackal cub and wishing him long life, the lioness said, "You are still a child. I brought you up taking pity on you. Your brothers are also young. Before they grow old and know that you are different from them, leave this place and join your own folk."

Realising the danger ahead, the jackal cub left the lion family in search of his own folk.

"That's why, before other warriors find out that you do not belong to the warrior caste, leave this place," the king advised Yudhishtira. The potter immediately left the palace.

Raktamukha, the monkey, told Karalamukha, the croc, "You have tried to kill me heeding your wife's plea. But one should never trust women. I deserted my family for the sake of a woman and gave her half of my life. But in the end she left me to join a lame lover. That's why never trust a woman."

"Interesting," said the croc and asked the monkey to tell him that story.

A Three-in-One Story

Once upon a time, there was a popular king called Nanda. His people respected him for his learning and valour. He had a prime minister called Vararuchi who was well versed in diplomacy and statecraft. Vararuchi's wife was one day annoyed with her husband and kept away from him. Extremely fond of his wife, the prime minister tried to please her. It was no use. He did not know what to do to regain her affection.

He pleaded with her, "Tell me what can I do to make you happy."

The wife at last opened her mouth and said, "Shave your head cleanly and prostrate before me if you want to regain my love."

The prime minister complied with her wish and succeeded in winning back her favour.

The king's wife also played the same drama of shunning his company. Nanda tried every trick he knew to win her affection without success.

When everything failed, the king fell on her feet and prayed her, "My darling, I cannot live without you even for a while. Tell me what should I do to win back your love?"

The queen said, "I will be happy if you pretend to be a horse, agree to be bridled and to let me ride you. While racing you must neigh like a horse. Is this acceptable to you?"

"Yes," said the king and did, as his wife demanded.

Next day, the king saw his prime minister with a shaven head and asked him, "Vararuchi, why did you have your head shaved on a day when tonsure is forbidden."

Vararuchi replied, "O king, is there anything that a woman does not demand and a man does not readily concede? He would do anything, shave his head or neigh like a horse."

Raktamukha, the monkey, then told Karalamukha, the croc, "You wicked croc, you are a slave of your wife like Nanda and Vararuchi. You tried to kill me but your chatter gave away your plans."

That's why the learned have said,

"Parrots sing and betray
Their presence to the hunter.
The crane eludes the hunter
By keeping his beak tightly shut."

"See how a donkey despite his disguise in a tiger skin betrayed his origin by braying and got killed. Here is the story if you want to know," said Raktamukha and began telling the story of the donkey.

In a small village lived a washerman named Suddhapata. He had a donkey that was very weak because he did not feed the animal regularly. One day, the washerman found the dead body of a tiger while he was collecting wood from the forest. Suddhapata was very happy and thought, "I am lucky. I can skin the animal and cover my donkey with that skin and drive it into wheat farms where he will have plenty to graze. Thinking that he is a tiger, people will keep away from him. This way, my donkey will have plenty of food."

He acted on his plan and the donkey would go to the wheat farm every evening, have his day's fill and return to his master's house in the morning. This went on for sometime. The donkey became so strong and sturdy that it became difficult for the washerman to pull him to the peg and tie him to it.

One day, when he was happily grazing at the wheat farm, the donkey heard the voice of a female donkey and began to respond to it in ecstasy. Then the watchman and others at the farm at once recognised him as a donkey in a tiger skin and killed him.

Raktamukha then addressed the croc and told him, "You have seen how the donkey met his end because he opened his mouth where he should not. Now, will you leave me or do you want to meet with the same fate as Syamalaka?"

"No, please. I want to know the story of Syamalaka," said Karalamukha, the croc. Raktamukha told him the following story.

A very wealthy merchant named Eswara lived in a city called Vikantakapuram. One day, his four sons-in-law arrived from Ujjain with their families to enjoy the hospitality of their father-in-law. Eswara did everything to make them happy and contented. Six months passed but the sons-in-law did not show any sign of leaving for Ujjain. Eswara was angry but could not directly tell his sons-in-law that they had overstayed.

One day, the father-in-law told his wife, "These guys are enjoying their stay here and are reluctant to leave. I am sure they will not leave unless we offend them in some way. Tomorrow, when they come for dinner, don't offer them water to wash their feet. They will regard this as an insult and will certainly leave."

Eswara's wife did, as her husband wanted her to do.

The first son-in-law was offended because water was not ready for him to wash his feet and left in a huff.

The second son-in-law was not happy with the place assigned to him at the table and left ranting.

The third complained about the quality of food and packed his bags.

Syamalaka, the fourth son-in-law, however, did not mind these insults and stayed on. The father-in-law had, therefore, to throw him out of his house by force.

"I have seen how wicked you are and I am not a fool to still trust you like the carpenter," said Raktamukha. At once Karalamukha insisted on hearing that story.

The Carpenter's Wife

Once upon a time, a carpenter lived in a village with his wife. He had heard bad stories about her and wanted to know the truth about those rumours.

Next day, pretending he was going to the village nearby, he told his wife, "I have to leave the place early morning tomorrow for a village not far away from here. I may have to stay there for a few days. Please get things ready for my travel."

The wife's joy knew no bounds. She cooked his favourite dishes and packed some of it for his travel.

Next morning the carpenter left. His wife put on her best clothes, daubed perfume on her body and thrust flowers in her hair and spent the rest of the day with great difficulty.

When it was dusk, she went to her lover's house and told him, "My wicked husband has left for some place and will not come back for a few days. So, come to my place after every one has gone to sleep and we will have a happy time."

After this invitation, she returned home.

Meanwhile, the carpenter spent the day in a nearby forest and came back before his wife had returned from her lover's place. He hid himself under a cot. Soon, his wife's lover came and joined her. As the wife was talking to her lover on the bed, her dangling legs hit something hard. She at once thought it could be her husband hiding under the bed to test her.

"I will show my husband how clever I am," she thought.

When her lover moved close to her, she told him through signs that her husband was under the bed and said, "Sir, you should not touch me. I am a very faithful wife. If you touch me I will turn you into ash."

"In that case, why did you invite me," he asked her angrily.

"Please listen, this morning, I went to the temple of the goddess where I heard a divine voice saying, "O woman, I know you are my devotee. But you will become a widow in six months."

Then I prayed her to tell me a way by which I could save my husband and make him live for hundred years.

"There is a way which is in your hands," the goddess told me.

"If that is so, I would give my life to save my husband", I told the goddess.

She told me, "If you go to bed with a stranger, the danger to your husband's life will shift to the stranger who will die soon."

The foolish carpenter believed every word of his wife and happy that he had such a faithful wife, he came out of his hiding and told her, "O sacred woman, I paid heed to rumours about you and doubted your character. I wanted to test you and put you on the wrong track making you believe I had left the village. Now I have seen what you are. Come, let us enjoy," he said and embraced her. In that happiness he carried his wife and the carpenter on his shoulders and paraded the streets of the village.

At this stage Raktamukha, the monkey, told Karalamukha, the croc, "O wicked croc, I now know your evil thoughts. How can I come to your place? It is your nature to be wicked. Friendship with good men will not change your nature. You are too attached to your woman. You are her slave. Such people never hesitate to lose their wealth and friends for her sake."

As the monkey was telling this story of the carpenter to the croc, someone from the sea came and told the croc that his wife who was fasting had died. The croc felt that living in a house without a wife was like living in a jungle.

He told the monkey, "Friend, pardon me. I have done you harm. So, I have lost my wife. I deserve to die."

The monkey said, "I know you are a henpecked husband. But this is no time for grief because you are rid of a greedy wife. You must celebrate." The elders have said:

"Consider that evil woman

Who has no character and

Who always quarrels with you

As a curse in the form of a wife.

That man who wants to be happy

Should not even take her name.

He who loves a woman of vice

Perishes like a moth kissing fire."

The croc said in grief, "My friend, I have lost your friendship and also my wife. All this is the result of betraying a friend like you. I think I am wise. But it is like the wisdom of the foolish woman who lost her lover and her husband also."

"How is it?" asked the monkey.

The croc began telling him the story.

There was an old farmer who had a young wife, who always had other men on her mind. She never attended to household jobs. She was always looking for younger men to spend time. One day, a trickster saw her and seeing that she was alone went to her and prayed, "O beauty, I am a widower. The minute

I saw you I lost my heart to you. Please give me the pleasure of your company."

Delighted, the woman told him, "O handsome, my husband has a lot of wealth. He is old and of no use to me. I will bring all the money and jewellery at home to you. Let us run away to a far off place and live there happily ever after."

The trickster was very happy and asked her to bring all that money and gold to a place where he would be waiting for her. "We will then leave the place quietly," he told her.

The farmer's wife waited till it was dark and when her husband fell asleep stole all the money and gold, packed it in a bag and left the house at dawn to meet the trickster at a place he had indicated. The trickster took the bag full of money and gold from her on the pretext that he would carry it and began their journey. After two miles, they stopped because there was a river to cross.

The trickster thought, "What do I do with a woman? If someone else were to set eyes on her, I have to protect her. It is better I give her up but take the money with me."

With these thoughts in mind he told the woman, "Look, my dear, it is very difficult to cross the river. I will first ferry the money bag to the other side of the river and keeping it there I will come back and carry you on my back."

She said, "Okay" and gave the bag to the trickster. He asked her to give her clothes also because he said clothes would hinder swimming. She gave away her clothes also. The trickster left with the bag and her clothes.

Covering her naked body with her hands, the woman began waiting restlessly for the trickster to return. Just then a jackal with a piece of meat in his mouth happened to pass by. The jackal saw a fish that had come out of water and in trying to get at it he dropped the meat piece and ran towards it. But the fish, seeing the rushing jackal, jumped back into water. Disappointed, the jackal went back to pick up the piece of meat. But a kite dived down fast and took it away before the jackal could reach it.

The woman laughed at the jackal that had lost the fish and also the piece of meat. Hurt by the woman's behaviour, the jackal said, "You may be twice as intelligent as I am. But what is the use? You have lost your husband, your lover and your wealth also."

In the middle of the story, some one from the sea came and disturbed Karalamukha and told him that another big croc had occupied his house. The croc did not know what to do. He had lost a friend (Raktamukha), his wife and the house. He began to wonder how he could throw out the big croc from his house. He went to the monkey who had already climbed back to the top of the tree and asked him for his advice.

Raktamukha told the croc, "You fool, why do you still bother me? You have tried to kill me to make your wife happy. Now, you have come for advice. I cannot give it to such fools like you who ask for advice but do not follow it. He who does not heed the advice of wise men will perish like the camel at the hands of the lion."

Without any shame, the croc asked the monkey to tell him that story. The monkey told him the following story.

The Price of Indiscretion

In the city of Nagara, there was a carpenter whose name was Ujjwalaka and who was extremely poor. One day he was pained to realize that every one else in his profession was rich and happy and that he alone was very poor. He thought Nagara was not the proper place for him to prosper and that he must go out and seek his fortune elsewhere. Then he left that city and began his journey to a new country. When the sun was fading, he reached a cave in a forest.

There he saw a female camel that separated from her caravan and just then delivered a child. The carpenter gave up his plans to go to another country and went home taking the camel and her calf with him. Every day he would go into the forest and bring back with him bundles of tender leaves for the camel and her child to eat. The she camel regained and her strength and the calf now became an adult. The carpenter began selling camel milk and making good money.

Ujjwalaka loved the camel so much that he bought a bell and hung it to her neck. One day he thought to himself, "If one camel can bring so much money for me, how much more would I earn if I buy more camels and sell their milk?" He told his wife that he would borrow some money to go to Gujarat and buy a she camel and that she should take care of the she camel and her calf till he returned from Gujarat.

He went to Gujarat and returned home with a she camel. Slowly, the number of camels he had increased several times. He appointed a keeper to take care of the camel herd he had on the condition that he would give one camel to the keeper every year as remuneration. The keeper was also free to drink camel milk twice a day. Now, everything was fine for the carpenter and he and his wife thus lived happily ever after.

The camels used to go every day to a nearby forest to feed on the fresh green leaves available in plenty in the forest. After spending a lot of time in the forest, eating and playing, the camels trekked back home. But the senior she camel stayed on in the forest and joined the herd later. The other camels thought that the she camel was a fool to go her separate ways and what would she do if a wild animal attacked her.

One day a lion saw all the camels leaving the forest in a herd and the she camel staying back and loafing about. By the time she finished her leisurely grazing, the others left and reached home. The she camel lost her way and was in panic when the lion, which was following her, pounced on her and soon tore her to pieces.

"That's why I tell you that he who does not follow the advice of wise men perishes like the camel," said the monkey.

The croc replied, "You are right, if you follow advice given for your good you will face no danger either here or in the heaven above. Yet, what is great about doing good to a person who is good? He who helps a person who has done him harm is considered great by learned people. That's why take pity on me and give me advice."

The monkey said, "In that case, you go and fight that big croc who has occupied your home. If you die in that battle, you will go to heaven. If you win the battle, you will get back your house. Know this from me:

"Conquer a good man with humility,

Vanquish a hero with strategy,

Overcome the poor through small gifts

And crush equals with power."

"How is that possible?" Karalamukha asked Raktamukha. Another story begins.

The Jackal's Strategy

Mahachataraka was a jackal living in a forest. One day, he found the body of an elephant and was happy that it would have food for many days. However, he was not able to bite into the thick hide of the elephant and was circling around the body when a lion came that way. The jackal humbly prostrated before the lion and said, "My lord, I am your obedient servant. At your command, I am keeping a vigil on the body of the elephant. Please help yourself."

The lion said, "You know my friend, I do not eat something others have killed. You may take it as my gift to you."

"I am touched by your magnanimity, my lord," said the jackal.

After the lion had left, a tiger came on the scene. The jackal thought, "I got rid of one menace through humility. How do I escape this fellow? He will not yield to any strategy I know. The only way of keeping him at bay is cunning. Let me try it."

The jackal then went half way to greet the tiger and said, "O uncle, why are you entering this area of death? The lion has killed this elephant and asked me to keep watch on it. He has gone to take bath. Before going, he told me to inform him if any tiger happened to come here. He vowed to kill all the tigers because long time ago a tiger had nibbled at an elephant he had killed. He told me that from that day he had sworn to kill all tigers."

These words frightened the tiger.

He told the jackal, "Son, save my life. When the lion comes, don't tell him I had come this way. Please."

On receiving an assurance from the jackal, the tiger hurriedly left the scene. Then came a leopard.

The Jackal thought, "This fellow has strong and sharp teeth. I will persuade him to pierce the hide of the elephant."

Addressing the leopard, the jackal said, "My son, you have come this way after a long time. You seem to be hungry. Why don't you be my guest? See this body of the elephant killed by the lion. He has asked me to keep an eye on the body. So, have a feast before he returns."

The leopard said, "Uncle, how can I accept your invitation. If I want to live long I should not touch this elephant. I will leave now."

The jackal assured him, "Don't worry, you go ahead. I will alert you when the lion comes."

The leopard then began attacking the elephant and when he tore the hide, the jackal cried, "Run. The lion is coming."

In this way, the jackal managed to get rid of the leopard also.

When the jackal began feasting on the elephant flesh, another jackal came that way. He was very angry and looked very strong. The first jackal remembered the last line of the stanza "crush equals with power" and attacked the trespasser with great ferocity and killed him.

Raktamukha told Karalamukha, "In the manner of the jackal in the story, you also kill that encroaching croc. Otherwise, it will be your end. But you must be wary like Chitranga, the dog, of your own kith and kin."

"Who is this Chitranga? Can I learn anything from his story," asked the croc.

"Why not?" said the monkey and began telling him the story of Chitranga.

Chitranga was a dog living in a city in the south visited by famine for many years. Dogs began dying by the hundreds because there was no food. There was a danger that they would disappear as species. So, Chitranga left that city and came to a far-off city in search of food. There he found the house of a wealthy man whose wife was a lazy and careless woman who would not close the doors of the house.

Every day, Chitranga would sneak into the open house and have his fill. But he really could not enjoy his food because as soon as he came out of the house, street mongrels attacked him and severely wounded him. Chitranga thought, "Oh, I made a mistake in coming here. Home was better even if there was no food. There was no struggle like this for food. Let me go home." In the end, Chitranga left that city and returned home.

Seeing him return from abroad, Chitranga's friends asked him, "Tell us everything about the country you have visited. How are the people there? What is their culture?"

The dog said, "The less said the better about that country. Everything is freely available because the women are careless. Yet your own kith and kin deprive you of this joy."

The croc was then impressed by the monkey's good advice and decided to fight the encroaching croc. He fought his enemy with great valour and killed him and regained the house occupied by him. The elders have said:

"There is no true happiness in

What you get without effort.

Even an old bullock survives

On food that comes his way."

Thus ended the dialogue between Raktamukha and Karalamukha. With that ends the fourth Tantra of Vishnu Sarma.

Fifth Strategy

Imprudence

The fifth strategy begins with the following verse:

"Whoever without judgement

Does what the foolish barber

In this chapter did

Comes to eternal grief."

This is the story that shows how true is the above verse. Manibhadra was a merchant living in the southern city of Pataliputra. He was a man of principles who had lost all his wealth. His poverty madehim very sad and one night he reflected on his condition and thought:

"Neither character nor patience

Neither humility nor pedigree

Dispels a poor man's gloom."

Even if a man has merit, the pressures of earning a livelihood overshadow such merit. The need to look after the family wears out one's brilliance. A poor man's house is like a sky without stars, a lake without water.

"A poor man is shunned even if

He has character and pedigree.

A wealthy man shines in society

Without merit and caste roots.

What he does is never shameful

But to be poor is always a crime."

After thinking a lot about his condition, Manibhadra decided that death alone could solve his problems. With these thoughts he fell asleep and saw a dream. In his dream, a Jain monk appeared and said, "O merchant, don't give in to self-pity. I am Padmanidhi, the treasure collected by your ancestors. Tomorrow morning when I will visit you in this guise, you will hit my head with a stick and I will turn into gold. You can live happily ever after."

When the merchant woke up next morning he wondered whether what he saw in the dream was real or unreal. "This may not be true. It could just be an illusion because I have been thinking about money all the time," he thought and remembered the following poem:

"Their dreams never come true

Who are sick, grief stricken,

Lovelorn and infatuated."

Meanwhile, a barber came to the merchant's house because his wife had called him for pedicure. Very soon came the Jain monk who appeared in the merchant's dream. Manibhadra was happy to see him and at once reached for the stick and struck him on his head. The monk turned into a statue of gold. The merchant then gave clothes and money to the barber and told him not to pass this information to anyone.

The barber went home and thought, "if a monk turns into gold if I strike him, I will invite all the monks and kill them and I can have lots of money." He passed the night with great difficulty. Next morning he went to the Jain monastery, went round its precincts three times and prostrated before the idol of Jinendra and sang the praise of the Jains thus:

"Victory to the Jain monks

Who keep lust and love at bay

Who turn the mind into a desert

Where desire does not grow.

Blessed are the hands that worship

The enlightened Jinendra

And blessed is the tongue

That praises the great Saint."

After this prayer, the barber met the chief monk and knelt before him seeking his blessings. The monk blessed him and asked the barber the reason that brought him to the monastery. The barber pleaded humbly that the chief monk and others should accept his hospitality.

The chief monk said, "O my son, we are not Brahmins who are invited home to be honoured. We are mendicants who visit Jain homes and accept what is necessary to keep us alive. Please go away and don't embarrass me."

Disappointed, the barber said, "O great seer, I have made all preparations to receive you. Yet I cannot press you. You will do what you think is best."

The barber went home and kept a stick ready after checking the exits of the house. He went to the monastery again and stood there pleading with the monks to accept his offerings. Taking pity on the barber, the monks agreed to visit his home. The elders have rightly said:

"Man becomes old and infirm,

Loses his hair and teeth and

Cannot even hear and see properly.

Everything in his body

Degenerates but not desire."

When the poor monks trooped into his house, the barber closed all the exits and began assaulting them. Some of them died while some were crying with pain. The sheriff, passing by, heard this commotion and asked his men to immediately find out what was happening. The men saw what the barber had done and presented him before a magistrate. The barber admitted that he had killed some of the monks. The magistrate ordered that the barber be impaled.

The judges then said that no one should do like the barber without understanding the situation for the learned have said that he who does things without discretion or prudence regrets his action like the Brahmin's wife.

The Brahmani and The Mongoose

In a city in the north lived a Brahmin whose name was Deva Sarma. His wife delivered a son at the same time as a she-mongoose gave birth to a male child. The Brahmani (Brahmin's wife) adopted the mongoose's son and began bringing him as she would her own son. Yet the Brahmani never left her son alone because she did not trust the mongoose, fearing that she would some day harm her son. The elders have said that one's own son, however immoral, ugly, foolish and wicked, are his parent's darling. It is said that

"The bonds of a son are stronger than

The bonds of a friend, father, or well wisher."

One day, leaving for the lake to bring water, the Brahmin's wife told her husband to keep a watch on their son. Soon, a cobra entered the house. Fearing danger to the son of the Brahmin, the mongoose attacked the cobra and killed him. Hearing the footfalls of his mother Brahmani, the mongoose, with a mouth smeared by blood, went to greet her. When the mother saw the mongoose with his mouth oozing blood, thought that what she had feared had happened. Without a second thought, the Brahmin's wife threw the pot of water on the mongoose and the mongoose died as a result.

Mourning the death of the mongoose, the woman entered the house and found that her child was soundly sleeping in the cradle and also the cobra bitten to pieces by the mongoose. The woman was struck by grief that she had killed the mongoose that was like a son to her. Meanwhile, her husband returned and she began cursing him, "You miser, you didn't heed my word and went out for alms. Self-interest is good. Too much of it will earn a man the fate of Chakradhara," the Brahmani said.

"Who is Chakradhara and what is his story?" asked the husband. Following is his story as told by the Brahmin's wife.

Four young Brahmins were living in a city, suffering utter poverty.

Unable to bear it, they thought, "It is better to live in a forest where only wild animals live and no human beings than to suffer poverty. Sleeping on a bed of grass is better than leading forever a life of want and suffering."

So, they packed their bags and set out in search of prosperity and happiness. The learned have always said that the grief-stricken man always gives up truth, relatives, mother and even motherland. It was no wonder that the four Brahmins left their place and after several sojourns reached the great city of Ujjain. They bathed in Sipra river and went to the Maha Kaleswar temple. When they emerged from the temple after the worship of Kaleswar, Bhairavananda Swami, a sadhu, greeted them. All of them prostrated before him in reverence and accompanied him to his monastery.

The Swamiji asked the young men, "From where are you coming and where are you going? What brought you here?"

"We are in search of prosperity. For us, it is either death or wealth. You know that adventurous people achieve their goals even if they have to sacrifice their lives. Destiny is all-powerful. Still, nothing can be achieved without human effort. Wells, tanks and ponds become full when it rains. But man too brings water out of the earth by digging deep wells. So, please show us a way to achieve our goal," the Brahmin boys pleaded with the Swamiji.

Moved by their plight and determination, the Swamiji gave them four sanctified tablets and told them, "Each one of you takes a tablet and travel towards the Himalayas. Stop where the tablet slips out of your hand and look at that spot for treasures. Dig the treasures out and bring them back home and be happy."

They began their journey and after some days of travel, the tablet dropped from the hand of one of the four Brahmins. They stopped there and after digging the earth, they found plenty of copper. The first Brahmin told the others that all of them could mine as much copper as they could and take it home. The others said, "What is there in copper. Let's go ahead." The first Brahmin said they could go if they wanted but he would go home taking all the copper he could carry.

The other three continued their journey till a tablet dropped to the ground from the hand of one of the three. They dug there and found plenty of silver. The second Brahmin suggested that they should be happy with the silver they found and go home. The other two said he could take all the silver if he wanted. They would, however, continue their search for gold. The second Brahmin, happy with what he had found, took silver and went home.

Now, the remaining two Brahmins trekked some more distance until a third tablet dropped. The two dug there and found gold. The third man said that gold was better than copper and silver and they must now go back because there was nothing more precious than gold. The fourth Brahmin did not agree and replied that he would continue his search. The third man took the gold and went home.

It was now the turn of the fourth man. He was now tired and thirsty, and on top of it he had lost his way and began wandering aimlessly. Then he saw a man completely soaked in blood and a wheel whirring over his head like a halo. The Brahmin went near him and asked, "Sir, who are you and what is this wheel over your head? Can you show me a place where water is available?" As he finished his questions, the wheel shifted from the stranger's head and came over the Brahmin's head.

Then followed a dialogue:

"What is this wheel which has come over my head," asked the Brahmin.

"I have no idea. It tormented me as it is doing to you now," the stranger said.

"At least tell me how I can get rid of it. It is so painful."

"If any person like you with a tablet comes here and talks to you, the wheel will shift on to his head."

"How long have you been bearing this hurt," asked the Brahmin.

"I have no idea. But I think it was in the reign of Lord Rama," said the stranger.

"Who gave you food and water?"

"This place is where Kubera has stored all his wealth. Those who trespass on this area will have no thirst or hunger but a lot of pain inflicted by this wheel. Only such persons who have a magic tablet like you had can come here," said the stranger and took leave of the Brahmin.

When the last Brahmin, whose name was Chakradhara, did not return, his friend Suvarnasiddhi went back following the trail left by his friend and found him bleeding and in great pain with a wheel over his head. He asked him how he got into that plight. Chakradhara told him what had happened so far.

Suvarnasiddhi then said, " I told you in many ways not to be greedy. You did not heed my word. You are learned but not wise. Wisdom is always superior to learning. Foolish people perish like the Brahmin boys who brought the lion to life."

"How is that?" asked Chakradhara.

The Lion That Sprang to Life

Four friends lived in a city. Three of them were very learned in all sciences but had no common sense. The fourth boy named Subuddhi was not well-versed in scriptures or sciences but had a fund of common sense. One day all of them thought that there was no use of their learning unless it brought them money to live happily. Therefore, they decided to go out and seek the patronage of kings. They set out to meet patrons of learning.

On the way, the eldest of them pointing out to the fourth man told the others, "Friends, this fellow is an unlettered fool. He has common sense and nothing else. I am not going to share my earnings with this fellow. Let him go home."

The second man also supported the eldest boy's suggestion.

But the third boy said, "Friends, it is not proper to send him back. We played together and he is one of us. Let us share our gains with him because elders have said:

"He who has a narrow mind

Thinks this is mine, this is his.

To a large-hearted person

The whole world is his family."

In the end, the other two agreed with the third boy's suggestion and let the common sense man accompany them. As they continued to travel they reached a forest where they saw a heap of bones. One of them told the rest, "Look, here is an opportunity to test our learning. Some animal is dead. Let us bring it to life using the knowledge we have acquired."

The first man said, "Okay, I will use my learning to assemble the bones into a skeleton." With the power of learning he ordered all the bones to come together and become a skeleton.

When the skeleton was ready, the second man commanded flesh and blood to fill the skeleton and skin to cover it.

When the third man was about to bring life to the body, Subuddhi, who had only common sense, warned him, "Look, this looks like the body of a lion. If it comes to life, he will kill all of us."

The man who was to put life into the body of the animal told Subuddhi, "You are a fool. Do you think I will lose this opportunity to test my learning."

Subuddhi then told him to wait so that he could climb up a tree for safety and went up a tree. When the first man gave him life, the lion came alive and killed all the three learned men.

Suvarnabuddhi continued, That's why I have always said:

"Even if one is very learned

If he is without common sense

Becomes the butt of ridicule

Like the learned in this story."

"What is that story? Please tell me," asked Chakradhara. Suvarnasiddhi began to tell the story.

There lived four young Brahmin boys in a city. They were good friends eager to go out and acquire knowledge. They went to a place called Kanyakubj. They joined a monastery and began studying sciences and scriptures. After twelve years of learning they thought it was time to go home and asked their guru for permission to leave the monastery. After taking his permission,. they started their homeward journey.

After a few days of travel, they reached a point where the road forked. They were not sure which road would take them home. Then they saw a funeral procession. One of the boys opened his book of learning and read out "Follow the path taken by great men."

The boy told his other friends, "Let us join and follow these great men leading the funeral procession."

They thus followed the procession to the cremation ground where they met a donkey.

The second Brahmin boy opened his book of shastras and found this verse in it:

"He who comes to your aid

In times of danger, famine,

Cremation and invasion

Is truly a friend in deed."

Then he told his friends that the donkey was, therefore, their best friend. At once one of them held on to the neck of the donkey. Another washed his feet. After this ceremony, they looked around and found a camel. The four of them began figuring out what the animal is. The third man opened his book of knowledge and read out, "What moves fast is righteousness" and decided that the camel must be the embodiment of righteousness.

The fourth man referred to his book and found that righteousness and friendship should always be together. They then tied the donkey and the camel together. Informed of this, the donkey's owner rushed to beat the four Brahmins. But they escaped before he came. They continued to travel till they reached a river and found a big leaf floating over the water.

One of them saw it and, remembering a line from a verse describing how a leaf helped a man cross the river, jumped on it and was being carried down by the current. A second Brahmin saw his friend in distress and remembered a verse:

"When total loss stares in the face

A wise man sacrifices half and

Manages with what remains."

So, with a view to save half of his friend, the second Brahmin cut off the head of the drowning man.

The remaining three resumed their travel only to stop when three villagers invited them for a feast. When the host served a dish resembling noodles to the first Brahmin, he thought "what is long should be discarded" and left the place without food.

The second man was served pancakes. He thought, "What spreads is not good for health" and refused to eat.

Doughnuts were served to the third Brahmin. He remembered that "There is peril where there is a hole" and left. The three Brahmins later went home.

Suvarnasiddhi ended the story and turned to Chakradhara and told him:

"Even if one is very learned

If he is without common sense

Becomes the butt of ridicule

Like the learned in this story."

Chakradhara protested, "That is not true," and quoted this verse:

"What God chooses to save

Survives sans human effort and

No human effort can save

What God ordains to perish."

As the frog said, "the one with thousand tricks sat on the head of the fisherman, the one with hundred tricks is hanging by the fisherman's arm and I with only one trick am happily swimming in the water."

"How is that?" asked Suvarnasiddhi. Chakradhara begins the story.

The Tale of Two Fish and a Frog

Two fish named Sahasrabuddhi and Satabuddhi made a lake their home. They had a frog as a friend whose name was Ekabuddhi. Every day, they used to meet on the bank of the lake and discuss everything under the sun and disperse at sunset. One day, they saw some fishermen equipped with nets and each carrying a basket full of fish came that way and saw the lake and noticed that it was full of good fish. They told themselves that they should come early the next morning and bait the fish.

The fish heard their conversation and were very worried. Then the frog asked Satabuddhi for advice.

"O Satabuddhi, you have heard what the fishermen were planning. Now tell us what we should do. Should we remain in the lake or go somewhere else."

Sahsrabuddhi answered the question, "Don't worry. You should not be scared by just words. The learned have said "The world is still safe because the dreams of snakes and wicked men never come true." The fishermen may not even come tomorrow. If they come, I am here to save you."

Satabuddhi said, "You are a genius. What you say is correct. There is nothing that accomplished men cannot conquer. Remember how Chanakya had killed all the armed Nandas.

"Where one cannot pierce sun and wind

The wits of a resourceful man enter.

One should not leave motherland, for,

Nothing is happier than one's own land."

Then, Ekabuddhi, the frog, said, "Friends, flight is the only thing I know. So, I and my wife will leave this place tonight itself."

Accordingly, the frog left the lake immediately. Next day, the fishermen came and netted lot of fish, frogs, crabs, turtles etc. and also Satabuddhi and Sahasrabuddhi and killed all of them. One of them carried Satabuddhi on his head because he was heavier and slung Sahsrabuddhi to his arm because he was long.

Ekabuddhi showed this scene to his wife and said, "Didn't I tell you what the fishermen will do? Now, see the plight of Satabuddhi and Sahasrabuddhi."

At the end, Chakradhara said, "O Suvarnasiddhi, you said that wisdom is superior to knowledge. But I say that wisdom alone without education does not serve any purpose."

"True," said Suvarnasiddhi. "But it is not wise to rule out the advice of a friend. Greed made you ignore my advice. Haven't you heard how the donkey ignored the advice of the jackal and got a millstone around his neck?"

There was a donkey named Uddhata living in a village, carrying clothes and other burdens for his master.

At night when there was no work, he used to trespass into farms outside the village and would come home at dawn for fear of assault by farm owners. One day Uddhata happened to meet a jackal in a farm outside the village and both soon became friends.

Every night they would go together to the cucumber farms and sumptuously feed on cucumber. At dawn, they would go home after they had their fill. One day, in a happy mood, the donkey told the jackal, "My son, look, how pleasantly serene the night is. It inspires me to sing. Tell me what raaga would you like me to begin with?"

The jackal said, "Uncle, why do you unnecessarily invite a peril? We have come here to stealthily rampage cucumber crop. Pimps and thieves must always observe silence. Haven't the learned said:

"He who cannot control cough

Or cannot keep sleep at bay

Or cannot resist good food

Should not burgle a house."

"Your music has no melody. One can hear it like a trumpet from a mile. The watchmen here are asleep. If your music wakes them, they will either impound us or kill us. So, give up that bright idea and let us eat these sweet cucumbers."

"You stupid child, you live in the wilderness. That's why you don't know to enjoy music. It is only the very lucky people who are destined to listen to music sung in moonlight," said Uddhata.

The jackal replied, "True. But you do not know what is music. You know only to bray loudly. So, please give up your foolish idea."

The donkey was angry and retorted, "You are an idiot to say that I don't know music. Sage Bharata was the author of music, which is regarded as the fifth Veda with hundred and eighty-five notational patterns. To Gods, nothing is dearer than music. It is through music that Ravana won favours from Lord Shiva. "

The jackal said, "All right uncle, let me first get out of this farm and keep a watch outside to alert you if anyone comes this way. You can then leisurely sing to your heart's content." The jackal then left the scene quietly.

The moment the donkey began singing, one of the watchmen woke up and struck it with a stick till he dropped to the ground. The watchman then brought an old millstone and hung it to the donkey's neck. The donkey soon recovered from the blows the watchman showered on him and managed to run with the millstone around his neck.

The jackal saw his plight and said, "You haven't paid heed to my advice. See how you have got a millstone around your neck."

After he finished this story, Suvarnasiddhi said, "Friend, you haven't cared to listen to me."

Chakradhara agreed with him and said, "What you say is true. The learned have said:

"He who has no wits of his own

Or does not heed advice of friends

Perishes like the weaver, Mandhara."

On Suvarnasiddhi showing interest, Chakradhara began Mandharaka's story.

The Story of The Weaver

There was a weaver called Mandharaka in a southern city. One day, when he was weaving clothes, the wooden frames necessary for weaving were totally damaged. He went to the forest to bring wood to make new frames. From the forest he drifted towards the seashore where he saw a gigantic tree and thought that if he could cut wood from the tree it would stand him in good stead throughout his life.

As he started to cut the tree, a Yaksha living on that tree said, "O weaver, this tree is my home. So I have to protect it.

I am very comfortable here enjoying the cool breeze coming from the sea."

Mandharaka said, "Sir, If I do not cut the tree and take home its wood, my family will starve and die. So, please go somewhere else. I have to cut this tree."

"All right, if you do not cut the tree, I will give you a boon of your choice," said the Yaksha.

The weaver said, "Sir, in that case, I will go home and consult my wife and friends. You can give me the boon later."

On the Yaksha agreeing to it, Mandharaka went home and on his way he met his friend who was a barber and asked him, "Friend, a Yaksha has given me a boon of my choice and gave me time to consult friends and my wife. What boon do you want me to ask him?"

"Ask him to give you a kingdom. You will be the king and I will be your minister. Both of us can enjoy life here and hereafter," said the barber.

"True. But let me ask my wife also," said Mandharaka. The barber warned the weaver against consulting his wife and said quoting learned people:

"A wise man can give to his woman

Fine clothes, pearls and diamonds;

But never consult her on his affairs

Because women have low wits."

And as Shankaracharya said that home that is run by women or children or tricksters will meet ruin in the end."

The weaver gently ignored the advice of the barber saying that he would nevertheless consult his wife and went home. He told his wife the whole story of the Yaksha and the boon he had offered.

Mandharaka also told his wife that his friend, the barber, had advised him to ask for a kingdom. His wife said, "O my lord, how intelligent is a barber? Never listen to his word. No wise man would consult children or barbers or servants or beggars. Also,

"Kingship has too many problems;
Conspiracies take away your peace.
With the crown come not only thorns
But also sinister plots and treason.
It was for the sake of kingdom
Lord Rama lived in the woods,
Pandava brothers fled into exile,
The Yadava dynasty disappeared,
King Nala embraced anonymity."

"Therefore, no wise man will invite kingship that leads to killing brothers, friends and relatives," said the weaver's wife.

The weaver replied, "My dear, what you say is true. But you haven't told me what boon I should choose."

The wife said, "Every day you are able to weave a single piece of cloth. That's barely enough to meet our daily needs. Therefore ask the Yaksha to give you another head and two more hands. That helps you to weave two pieces of cloth every day instead of one. The first piece will help us meet our daily needs. The second one will help us meet special needs. We can sail through life comfortably and happily."

The weaver was happy with the advice his wife gave and went to the Yaksha and prayed to him, "Sir, you have kindly given me a choice. I request you to give me two more hands and an extra head."

At once, he had four hands and two heads. Happily, he began his homeward journey. On the way people saw him and mistaking him for some monster hammered him with sticks and stones. The poor weaver died on the spot,

Chakradhara continued, "That's why, as I have said earlier:

"He who has no wits of his own
Or does not heed advice of friends
Perishes like the weaver, Mandhara."

"When the devil of greed dances on their head, people will become objects of ridicule like me." The elders have said:

"He who covets the impossible
Or builds castles in the air
Comes to certain grief like
Poor Soma Sarma's father."

Suvarnasiddhi asked him how. Chakradhara tells him the following story about Soma Sarma's father.

The Miserly Father

Swabhavakripan was a Brahmin living in a city in the south. He was known for his miserliness. Every day, he would go out begging and save some corn flour people gave him as alms. He stored such flour in an earthen pot and when it was full he hung the pot to a peg above his bed so that he could keep an eye on it.

He returned home one day very tired and went to sleep and began dreaming: "This pot is full of flour and if there is a famine it would fetch me a very high price. With that money, I will buy two she goats that in course of time will become a big herd. I will sell them for a huge profit and buy cows with that money. Then I will buy buffaloes and later horses. And, when the stables are full of horses I will sell them and buy lots of gold."

"With this gold, I will build a huge house with four floors. Seeing my riches one Brahmin will offer the hand of his beautiful daughter to me. She will soon deliver a son and I will name him Soma Sarma. When he is a year old, I will go and hide in the stable and call out to him to find me out. But the son drifts dangerously towards the horses. I shout at my wife to come and take him away. Busy with domestic chores she ignores my call. Then I shall kick her."

The dream shattered when he kicked the pot of flour hanging from the peg and spilled all its contents over his body. He now looked like a white ghost.

Chakradhara resumed, "That is why, I said:

"He who covets the impossible
Or builds castles in the air

Comes to certain grief like

Poor Soma Sarma's father."

"I don't see anything in this to blame you," said Suvarnasiddhi. "Every one becomes a slave to greed. As the learned have said,

"He who is overwhelmed by greed

And doesn't weigh its consequences,

Will become a victim of deceit

Like King Chandra in this story."

Suvarnasiddhi then told the story of King Chandra to Chakradhara.

Once upon a time there was a king named Chandra ruling a small state. His children were fond of playing with monkeys. So the king ordered a number of monkeys to be brought to the palace and asked his servants to feed them well and look after their needs. The leader of the monkeys was an old scholar well versed in statecraft, specially the works of Sukracharya, Brihaspati and Chanakya. The old monkey trained the younger ones also in statecraft.

The king had a stable of goats that his young sons used to ride. One of the goats was fond of food and would daily sneak into the kitchen at any time of the day and make a clean sweep of whatever was available in the kitchen. If the cook chanced to see him stealing food, he would throw at it whatever was handy, a stick or a brass pot.

The monkey leader saw this drama between the cook and the wily goat and thought: "I am sure this tussle between the cook and the goat will lead to the ruin of my tribe. This goat has become a slave to food. The cook will throw at it whatever is nearby. It may be a stick or if it is not readily available he may use an ember from the hearth to throw at the goat. This will set ablaze the goat's fur-covered body making him run into the stable that would soon catch fire and burn the horses. The great veterinarian Salihotra has said the fat of monkeys is the best medicine for burns. That will be the end of monkeys."

The monkey leader then summoned all the younger ones and told them that the feud between the cook and the goat would certainly do harm to them. In their own interest they should leave the palace as early as possible. He quoted the scholars saying:

"He who wants to live in peace

Must leave a house of daily strife.

Conflict breaks up kingdoms

Like bad words separate friends"

The younger ones, however, refused to listen to the advice of the old monkey. They told the leader, "Sir, you have become old and senile. We are not going to leave this palace where we have the best food available. What do we get there to eat in the jungles? We cannot eat the indifferent food in the forest."

Extremely unhappy at their response, the old monkey said, "You have no idea of the price you will pay for the comforts of the palace. They won't last long. I cannot see the end of our tribe. I am leaving. He who spares himself the spectacle of a friend in distress, of his house occupied by an enemy or of the division of his country, is the happiest."

The old monkey left all of them with a heavy heart.

Some days later, the wily goat entered the royal kitchen and the cook, failing to see anything handy to punish it, took out a burning piece of wood from the hearth and hurled it at the goat. His fur afire, he ran in panic into the stable where his burning body set ablaze the hay stacked there. Several horses perished in the fire. The king consulted expert veterinarians who advised him to use monkey fat as unguent for horses suffering from burns.

The king ordered all monkeys to be killed and their fat used to heal the burns of the horses. The old monkey was distressed by the death of her progeny and began planning as to how he could take revenge on the king for killing all monkeys. Wandering restlessly in the forest, the old monkey saw a lake full of lotuses. On deeper inspection of the lake, the senior monkey found footprints of animals and human beings entering the lake but not footprints leaving the lake.

The monkey at once realised that there must be some wicked crocodile in the lake and that it was better to drink water with the tube of a lotus. As he began drinking water, a monster emerged from the lake wearing a pearl necklace. The monster addressed the monkey and said, "You seem to be an intelligent chap. You drank water without entering the lake. I am impressed by the presence of your mind. Ask anything you want."

The monkey asked, "Sir, how many lives can you take in one go?"

The monster said, "I can swallow tens, hundreds and thousands at one time. All this I can do only when they enter the lake. Outside the water, even a jackal can challenge me."

The monkey said, "I have to settle scores with a king. If you can lend me the pearl necklace on your body, I will somehow persuade the king and all his men to enter the lake for hidden wealth. Then you can kill all of them."

Trusting the monkey, the monster gave him the pearl necklace. The monkey reached the kingdom of Chandra. People saw the dazzling necklace and asked him how he got it. The monkey told them about the lake. When the word reached the king, he sent for the monkey and asked him how he got the necklace.

On the monkey telling him everything about the lake, the king, led by the monkey, and accompanied by his family, ministers and followers, reached the lake. The monkey told the king that it was better that all his men entered the lake at the same time at dawn. But the monkey told the king, "My lord, you will not go with them. I will take you separately to a spot where you can get a large store of pearl necklaces."

According to the plan, all the king's men entered the lake at the same time and were killed by the monster. When nobody came out of the water for a long time, the king became suspicious and asked the monkey about the delay in his men coming out of the lake. The monkey immediately sprang to the top of a tree and told the king:

"O king, the monster inside the lake has killed all your people. You have killed my people. This is my reply to that treachery." Suvarnasiddhi concluded the story by repeating the earlier verse:

"He who is overwhelmed by greed

And doesn't weigh its consequences,

Will become a victim of deceit

Like King Chandra in this story."

Suvarnasiddhi then asked Chakradhara for permission to leave. Chakradhara said that it was not good to desert a friend in distress.

Suvarnasiddhi said, "What you say is true. Yet, it is always better to do according to what the wise men advise. Otherwise, I will have to repent later like you. As the learned have said, "Those who are not united will perish like the great bird which had two heads on a single torso but ate different fruits."

On Chakradhara's request Suvarnasiddhi began telling that story.

Tale of The Bird with Two Heads

Agreat bird named Bharunda lived on the banks of alake. He had two heads but a single body. One day, as the bird was wandering on the bank of the lake, he found a fruit, which was as delicious as ambrosia. One of his heads mumbled, "Oh what a fruit. I am sure the heavens have sent it for me. I am so lucky."

Hearing this, the second head said, "O brother, let me also taste the fruit you are praising so much."

The first head laughed and said, "Both of us have the same stomach. It makes no difference whether I eat it or you eat it. I shall give it to our beloved. She will be very happy." Bharunda thus gave the fruit to his wife. The second head was disappointed at this action of the first head.

One day, the second head found a poisonous fruit and told the first head, "You treacherous fellow. For what you have done to me, I will eat this poisonous fruit and avenge your insult."

The second head said, "You fool, if you eat that, both of us will die because we have the same body."

Ignoring his warning, the second head ate the poisonous fruit and both of them died.

After listening to the story, Chakradhara said, "Friend, what you say is true. You can go home but don't go alone. Haven't our elders said:

"Alone, do not eat delicious food,

Do not sleep when others are awake,

Neither should you travel alone

Nor ponder alone over matters."

"See how the Brahmin has survived because he had heeded his mother's advice and took a crab as his travelling companion."

"How was that?" asked Suvarnasiddhi.

Brahmadatta was a Brahmin boy living in a city with his old mother. One day, when he was planning to travel to another village, his mother told him not to travel alone but take someone with him. The boy said that the way to the village was safe and that he was leaving on an urgent business. He asked her not to be afraid.

Knowing that he was determined to go, the mother went to the well in the backyard and took out a crab and asked his son to keep the crab with him during his travel. The boy then put the crab in a camphor box and put that box in a vessel and set out on his journey. That being summer, the day was very hot and the Brahmin halted and took rest under a big tree.

From the hollow of the tree, a snake emerged and, attracted by the fragrance of camphor, swallowed the box containing the crab. The crab came out of the box and sliced the head of the snake and killed him. The Brahmin boy woke and found the dead snake and the camphor box. When he saw the crab coming out of the box alive, he at once realised what had happened.

He then remembered the words of his mother and thought he did well by heeding her advice that saved him from death. He also recalled the words of the elders:

"Those who feed on the rich

Do not help them in distress.

When their wealth is in tact

Everyone hovers around the rich."

Chakradhara concluded his story telling Suvarnasiddhi how important to always have a companion. He then agreed to Suvarnasiddhi taking leave of him.

Thus ends the fifth strategy Vishnu Sharman narrated to the sons of Amarashakti.

2

Hitopadesha

Hitopadesha is a collection of Sanskrit fables in prose and verse; it is similar to, though distinct from, the Panchatantra.

The Hitopadesha is known to be more than a millennium old. Originally written in Sanskrit, its stories have travelled to several parts of the world.

The work has been translated into most of the major languages of the world. An english translation, rendered by Sir Edwin Arnold, then Principal of Puna College, Pune, India, was published in London in 1861.

One of the most widely read Sanskrit book in India, Hitopadesha tales are short stories that have the priceless treasure of morality and knowledge. After Bhagwad Gita, Hitopadesha is considered to be the best seller in India. The tales from Hitopadesh written in a very logical and a clear way and one does not have to make much effort to figure out what moral is a particular story implying. The stories are inspired from the Panchatantra and are simple stories that involve birds and animals.

Hitopadesha has been derived from two words, Hita and Upadesha. It basically means to counsel or advice with wisdom. The author of Hitopadesha, Narayana Pandit says that the main purpose of creating the Hitopadesha is to instruct young minds in a way that they learn the philosophy of life and are able to grow into responsible and mature adults. The stories are very interesting and youngsters not only find it interesting, but also accept it easily.

It is said that this literary work was written almost a millennium ago by Narayana Pandit. Though it has been inspired from the Panchatantra, the variety of tales in the Hitopadesha is very vast. It has been translated into many languages and has been circulated all around the world. It is surprisingly popular in many countries and one of the most widely read children's book. Even in today's world, it continues to amaze people with its simple but meaningful stories and many people are still inspired by the tales of Hitopadesha. Its simplicity and logic is what makes it a favourite among children and their parents.

The Hitopadesha may thus be fairly styled "The Father of all Fables"; for from its numerous translations have come Esop and Pilpay, and in later days Reineke Fuchs. Originally compiled in Sanskrit, it was rendered, by order of Nushiravan, in the sixth century, A.D., into Persic. From the Persic it passed, A.D. 850, into the Arabic, and thence into Hebrew and Greek. In its own land it obtained as wide a circulation. The Emperor Acbar, impressed with the wisdom of its maxims and the ingenuity of its apologues, commended the work of translating it to his own Vizir, Abdul Fazel. That minister accordingly put the book into a familiar style, and published it with explanations, under the title of the Criterion of Wisdom.

The Emperor had also suggested the abridgment of the long series of shlokes which here and there interrupt the narrative, and the Vizir found this advice sound, and followed it, like the present Translator. To this day, in India, the Hitopadesha, under other names (as the Anvari Suhaili), retains the delighted attention of young and old, and has some representative in all the Indian vernaculars.

Story

The Right Choice

Once upon a time, there lived a girl named Smriti. She lived in Mumbai in a big family with her uncles and aunts. She was a cheerful girl and loved music and dance. But there was once problem. Her mom and grandfather always used to fight with each other. One day her mom got so angry with her that she decided to separate her home. Now, Smriti had to choose whether to go to Delhi and live with her mom and dad, or live with her grandparents in Mumbai.

Undesirable, she had to go with the parents. A week later, in Delhi, Smriti became ill. She was irritated with the situation and wished to go back to Mumbai. She told her mother that she wanted to go back. Her father met with a serious accident and they had no one to look after. Her mother also realized that their happiness was not complete. She realized that her daughter and husband missed the warmth and love of a family. He realized the mistake she made by leaving her Smriti's grandfather alone.

The next day, Smirti's mother went and apologized to the old man and all of them lived happily ever after.

The Diamond Ring

Willy, the merchant, had crossed the ocean and had arrived in a far away continent, where he had succeeded to make a small fortune by hard work and his own personal ability. When, a few years later, he returned home to his own country, he found on arriving at the port that all his relatives were at a nearby villa where there was a large party.

He was in such a happy mood and in the joy of the moment, he did not even bother changing his grey flannel suit which had become a little worn during the trip home.

When he entered the brilliantly lit room his relatives and friends gave him a rather cold welcome because they had noticed his modest suit and immediately imagined that he had come back a poor man.

A young Negro who happened to be accompanying him was very irritated at this and said to Willy: "What a wonderful reception you have received from these people. They have not even the decency to shake your hand after all these years that you have been away from home."

"Just wait and see!" whispered Willy, "they will soon change their looks!" Saying this he slipped a precious ring on his finger. All of a sudden the faces of all those present lit up and immediately Willy was surrounded by so many people that he didn't know what to do. A man shook his hand, a cousin threw his arms around him, and he had so many invitations from the people present that he thought that he would be unable to make any other appointments for several years.

"Has this beautiful, precious ring of yours the power of enchanting people?" asked the Negro.

"Oh, no!" replied Willy, "they se in this glittering ring something that makes them think I am rich, and, unfortunately, they place wealth above everything else."

"What blind people!" exclaimed the Negro. "It is not the ring that has drawn you to them but their desire for riches. Is it possible to appreciate more a piece of yellow metal surrounded by little stones than the goodness of my Lord?... And indeed how foolish are people who place their trust in riches rather than in virtues!"

Madam Rides the Bus

There was a girl named Valliammai who was called Valli for short. She was eight years old and very curious about things. Her favourite pastime was standing in the front doorway of her house,, watching what was happening in the street outside. There were no playmates of her own age on her street, and this was about all she had to do.

But for Valli, standing at the front door was every bit as enjoyable as any of the elaborate games other children play. Watching the street gave her many new, unusual experiences. Once a foreign soldier went past, and she watched him as he came near her house. What fair skin he had! Such nice clothes he wore! Women smiled as he passed them and tried to catch his glance. But some children, and even a few grown-ups, were scared by the sight of the soldier and hid inside their houses. Not Valli. She clicked her heels, saluted smartly, and said: "Salaam."

The soldier stopped and smiled at her. "And a good morning to you," he said, and then he went on his way.

Valli's joy knew no bounds. She yelled, and she danced, boasting to everybody that the fair-skinned soldier had actually spoken to her.

"Very brave she is, this one," said the neighbours. Her importance among the people on her street increased considerably.

Now, it is true that ordinarily there wasn't much traffic by her house, but this is no way meant that events didn't happen in the neighbourhood. Now and then, for example, she could see a neighbour coming or going on some errand or other. Occasionally a bullock cart would pass by, its wheels creaking and groaning for want of oil, and the bells tied around the animals' necks made a gentle tinkling sound. Sometimes a dog would dart across the street, pretending to be very busy; suddenly it would slow down, sniff around, and life a leg to wet some wayside plant, and then go rushing back down the street as though it had forgotten something somewhere and wanted to fetch it. And then, of course, there were the beggars, and the street vendors... Oh, there was certainly no lack of entertainment for Valli as she stood watching from her doorstep all day long.

The most fascinating thing of all was the bus that travelled between her village and the nearest town. It passed through her street each hour, once going to the town and once coming back. The sight of the bus, filled each time with a new set of passengers, was a source of unending joy for Valli.

Day after day she watched the bus, and gradually a tiny wish crept into her head and grew there: she wanted to ride on that bus, even just once. This wish became stronger and stronger, until was an overwhelming desire. Valli would stare wistfully at the people who got on or off the bus when it stopped at the street corner. Their faces would kindle in her longings, dreams and hopes. If one of her friends happened to ride the bus and tried to describe the sights of the town to her, Valli would be too jealous to listen and would shout, in English: "Proud! Proud!" Neither she nor her friends really understood the meaning of the word, but they used it often as a slang expression of disapproval.

Over many days and months Valli listened carefully to conversations between her neighbours and people who regularly used the bus, and she also asked a few discreet questions here and there. This way she picked up various small details about the bus journey. The town was six miles from her village. The fare was thirty paise one way-"which is almost nothing at all," she heard one well-dressed man say, but to Valli, who scarcely saw that much money from one month to the next, it seemed a fortune. The trip to the town took forty-five minutes. On reaching town, if she stayed in her seat and paid another thirty paise, she could return home on the same bus. This meant that she could take the one o'clock afternoon bus, reach the town at one forty-five, and be back home by about two forty-five....

On and on went her thoughts as she calculated and recalculated, planned and replanned...

Well, one fine spring day the afternoon bus was just on the point of leaving the village and turning into the main highway when a small voice was heard shouting: "Stop the bus! Stop the bus!" And a tiny hand was raised commandingly.

The bus slowly down to a crawl, and the conductor, sticking his head out the door, said: "Hurry then! Tell whoever it is to come quickly."

"It's me," shouted Valli. "I'm the one who has to get on."

By now the bus had come to a stop, and the conductor said: "Oh, really! You don't say so!"

"Yes, I simply have to go to town," said Valli, still standing outside the bus, "and here's my money." She showed him some coins.

"Okay, okay, but first you must get on the bus," said the conductor, and he stretched out a hand to help her up.

"Never mind," she said, "I can get on by myself. You don't have to help me."

The conductor was a jolly sort, fond of joking. "Oh, please don't be angry with me, my fine madam," he said. "Here, have a seat right up there in front. Everybody move aside please-make way for madam."

It was the slack time of day, and there were only six or seven passengers on the bus. They were all looking at Valli and laughing with the conductor. Valli was overcome with shyness. Avoiding everyone's eyes, she walked quickly to an empty seat and sat down.

"May we start now, madam?" the conductor asked, smiling. Then he blew his whistle twice, and the bus moved forward with a roar.

It was a new bus, it's outside painted a gleaming white with some green stripes along the sides. Inside, the overhead bars shone like silver. Directly in front of Valli, above the windshield, there was a beautiful clock. The seats were soft and luxurious.

Valli devoured everything with her eyes. But when she started to look outside, she found her view cut off by a canvas blind that covered the lower part of her window. So she stood up on the seat and peered over the blind.

The bus was now going the bank of canal. The road was very narrow. On one side there was the canal and, beyond it, palm trees. Grassland, distant mountains, and the blue, blue sky. On the other side was a deep ditch and then acres and acres of green fields-green, green, green, as far as the eye could see.

Oh, it was all so wonderful!

Suddenly she was startled by a voice. "Listen, child," said the voice, "you shouldn't stand like that. Sit down."

Sitting down, she looked to see who had spoken. It was an elderly man who had honestly been concerned for her, but she was annoyed by his attention.

"There's nobody here who's a child," she said haughtily. "I've paid my thirty paise like everyone else."

The conductor chimed in. "Oh, sir, but this is very grown-up madam. Do you think a mere girl could pay her own fare and travel to the city all alone?"

Valli shot an angry glance at the conductor and said: "I am not a madam. Please remember that. And you've not yet given me my ticket."

"I'll remember," the conductor said, mimicking her tone. Everyone laughed, and gradually Valli too joined in the laughter.

The conductor punched a ticket and handed it to her. "Just sit back and make yourself comfortable. Why should you stand when you've paid for a seat?"

"Because I want to," she answered, standing up again.

"But if you stand on the seat, you may fall and hurt yourself when the bus makes a sharp turn on hits a bump. That's why we want you to sit down, child."

"I'm not a child, I tell you," she said, irritably. "I'm eight years old."

"Of course. How stupid of me! Eight years-my!"

The bus stopped, some new passengers got on, and the conductor got busy for a time. Afraid of losing her seat, Valli finally sat down.

An elderly woman came and sat beside her. "Are you all alone, dear?" she asked Valli as the bus started again.

Valli found the woman absolutely repulsive-such big holes she had in her ear lobes, and such ugly earrings in them! And she could smell the betel nut the woman was chewing and see the betel juice that was threatening to spill over her lips at any moment. Ugh!-Who could be sociable with such a person?

"Yes, I'm travelling alone," she answered curtly. "And I've got a ticket too."

"Yes, she's on her way to town," said the conductor. "With a thirty-paise ticket."

"Oh, why don't you mind your own business," said Valli. But she laughed all the same, and the conductor laughed too.

But the old woman went on with her drivel. "It is proper for such a young person to travel alone? Do you know exactly where you're going in town? What's the street? What's the house number?"

"You needn't bother about me. I can take care of myself," Valli said, turning her face toward the window and staring out.

Her first journey-what careful, painstaking, elaborate plans she had had to make for it! She had thriftily saved whatever stray coins came her way, resisting every temptation to buy peppermints, toys, balloons, and the like, and finally she had saved a total of sixty paise. How difficult it had been, particularly that day at the village fair, but she had resolutely stifled a strong desire to ride the merry-go-round, even though she had the money.

After she had enough money saved, her next problem was how to slip out of the house without her mother's knowledge. But she managed this without too much difficulty. Everyday after lunch her mother would nap from about one to four or so. Valli always used these hours for her "excursions" as she stood looking from the doorway of her house or sometimes even ventured out into the village; today, these same hours could be used for her first excursion out side the village.

The bus rolled on, now cutting across a bare landscape, now rushing through a tiny hamlet or past an odd wayside shop. Sometimes the bus seemed on the point of gobbling up another vehicle that was coming toward them or a pedestrian crossing the road. But lo! Somehow it passed on smoothly, leaving all obstacles safely behind. Trees came running toward them but then stopped as the bus reached them and simply stood there helpless for a moment by the side of the road before rushing away in the other direction.

Suddenly Valli clapped her hands with glee. A young cow, tail high in the air, was running very fast, right in the middle of the road, right in front of the bus. The bus slowed to a crawl, and the driver sounded his horn loudly again and again. But the more he honked, the more frightened the animal became and the faster it galloped-always right in front of the bus.

Somehow this was very funny to Valli. She laughed and laughed until there were tears in her eyes.

"Hey, lady, haven't you laughed enough?" called the conductor. "Better save some for tomorrow."

At last the cow moved off the road. And soon the bus came to a railroad crossing. A speck of a train could be seen in the distance, growing bigger and bigger as it drew near. Then it rushed past the crossing gate with a tremendous roar and rattle, shaking the bus. Then the bus went on and passed the train station. From there it traversed a busy, well-laid-out shopping street and, turning, entered a wider thoroughfare. Such big, bright-looking shops! What glittering displays of clothes and other merchandise! Such big crowds!

Struck dumb with wonder, Valli gaped at everything.

Then the bus stopped and everyone got off except Valli.

"Hey, lady," said the conductor, "aren't you ready to get off? This is as far as your thirty paise takes you."

"No," Valli said, "I'm going back on this same bus." She took another thirty paise from her pocket and handed the coins to the conductor.

"Why, is something the matter?"

"No, nothing's the matter. I just felt like having a bus ride, that's all."

"Don't you want to have a look at the sights, now that you're here?"

"All by myself? Oh, I'd be much too afraid."

Greatly amused by the girl's way of speaking, the conductor said: "But you weren't afraid to come in the bus."

"Nothing to be afraid of about that," she answered.

"Well, then, why not go to that stall over there and have something to drink? Nothing to be afraid of about that either."

"Oh, no, I couldn't do that."

"Well, then, let me bring you a cold drink."

"No, I don't have enough money. Just give me my ticket, that's all."

"It'll be my treat and not cost you anything."

"No, no," she said firmly, "please, no."

The conductor shrugged, and they waited until it was time for the bus to begin the return journey. Again there weren't many passengers.

"Won't your mother be looking for you?" the conductor asked when he gave the girl her ticket.

"No, no one will be looking for me," she said.

The bus started, and again there were the same wonderful sights.

Valli wasn't bored in the slightest and greeted everything with the same excitement she'd felt the first time. But suddenly she saw a young cow lying dead by the roadside, just where it had been struck by some fast-moving vehicle.

"Isn't that the same cow that ran in front of the bus on our trip to town?" she asked the conductor.

The conductor nodded, and she was overcome with sadness. What had been a lovable, beautiful creature just a little while ago had now suddenly lost its charm and its life and liked so horrible, so frightening as it lay there, legs spread-eagled, a fixed stare in its lifeless eyes, blood all over....

The bus moved on. The memory of the dead cow haunted her, dampening her enthusiasm. She no longer wanted to look out the window.

She sat thus, glued to her seat, until the bus reached her village at three forty. She stood up and stretched herself. Then she turned to the conductor and said: "Well, sir, I hope to see you again."

"Okay, madam," he answered her, smiling. "Whenever you feel like a bus ride, come and join us. And don't forget to bring your fare."

She laughed and jumped down from the bus. Then away she went, running straight for home.

When she entered her house she found her mother awake and talking to one of Valli's aunts, the one from South Street. This aunt was a real chatterbox, never closing her mouth once she started talking.

"And where have you been?" said her aunt when Valli came in she spoke very casually, not expecting a reply. So Valli just smiled, and her mother and aunt went on with their conversation.

"Yes, you're right," her mother said. "So many things in our midst and in the world outside. How can we possibly know about everything? And even when we do know about something, we often can't understand it completely, can we?"

"Oh," said Valli, "I was just agreeing with what you said about things happening without our knowledge."

"Just a chit of a girl, she is," said her aunt, "and yet look how she pokes her nose into our conversation, just as though she were a grown lady."

Valli smiled to herself. She didn't want them to understand her smile. But, then, there wasn't much chance of that, was there?

Trojan Horse

It happened hundreds of years ago. Greece and Troy were at war. The Greeks had come in their ships to attack Troy. For ten long years, they besieged Troy but the Trojans would not surrender. There were strong and high walls around the city of Troy. No enemy could enter the city when the gates were closed. The Greeks made several attempts to break down the walls and the gates but failed each time.

But now, Greek soldiers had become homesick. They longed to go back to their homes across the sea to see their near and dear ones. But though they were tired and weary of war, they could not go back to Greece till Troy fell. Their main aim in waging the war with the Trojans was to recover Helen, the beautiful wife of Greek General Menelaus, who had run away with the Trojan Prince Paris. The Trojans had refused to send her back to Greece.

One day the Greek generals met in a council to decide their future course of action. Several Greek princes and warriors addressed the council. "We have been here for ten years," said Ulysses, a veteran Greek leader. "We have been here for ten years," said Ulysses, a veteran Greek leader. "We have already lost many of our gallant soldiers in our attempt to enter Troy. We have no hopes of taking the city by force. We must conquer it by deceit. Nothing is unfair in war."

Then Ulysses explained to them a clever plan that he had in mind to achieve their objective. All the members of the council were impressed by this plan and decided to put it into action.

Accordingly, the Greeks built a huge wooden horse. The horse was placed on a large platform with wheels underneath. A few of the bravest Greek warriors including Ulysses hid themselves in the hollow stomach of the horse. They securely closed the opening in the lower part of the wooden horse. The rest of the Greeks set fire to their tents and sailed away to a nearby island, not far from the city of Troy.

When the Trojans saw clouds of smoke rising from the Greek tents, with neither the Greek soldiers nor their ships in the sight, they could not believe their eyes. But soon surprise changed to Jubilation when word went round the Trojan camp that many people had seen the Greeks sailing away. The Trojans thought that Greeks were tired of the war and had no longer the energy and zest to fight. When they opened the gates and came out, they could only see the wooden horse left behind by the Greeks. They thought it was the idol of some Greek God.

They gazed at the gigantic horse in admiration and excitement and soon dragged it into the city of Troy. The capture of wooden horse was, to them, a symbol of their victory over the Greeks. They began to celebrate their success with feasting and merrymaking. "The danger is over, at last. We can sleep in peace now," they said to one another. Late at night, they went to sleep.

At the dead of night, when the Trojan were fast asleep, the Greek warriors who were inside the stomach of the horse came out quietly. They opened the gates of the city for other Greeks to enter. The Greek ships which had pretended to sail away, now turned back quickly in response to the signal from their leaders inside Troy. Soon, thousands of Greek soldiers rushed into the city. They killed thousands of Trojans men, women and children. They burnt their houses and looted the city. Even before the Trojans were fully awake, their magnificent city was in ruins. Before they could realize what was happening, Troy was in the hands of Greeks.

Thus, the Greeks succeeded in punishing the Trojans for dishonourable act of refusing to hand over Helen to them. The architect of their great victory was brainy and wily leader Ulysses who brought the long-drawn war to close by a masterstroke of cunning and foul play.

A Brother's Story

LET'S SHOW our love while we can, while people need us. That is something I learnt from an incident in Bhopal.

I saw a little boy daily near the Hanuman temple, always in a white tee and black pants, with a small Hanuman pendant around his neck.

He sat with a basket of fresh floral garlands. Be it at six in the morning or nine at night, he would try his very hardest to sell his wares.

I was a frequent temple goer and each time the boy would beg me earnestly to buy a garland. But somehow I never did. Even when I came out, he would follow me to my car, begging me to buy one at least.

Other boys sold flowers too, but none as persistently as he. I went back to the temple recently after a gap of some months.

The boy was there, seated exactly as before. I tried to avoid his gaze, assuming that he would follow me. But he did not budge.

I went inside the temple and came back. But the boy made no effort to sell his garlands.

I thought he was angry or just showing his own self-respect.

I suddenly missed the communication. I always had with this unknown boy and went to him. He looked at me but did not speak.

This was strange. I gathered courage and asked: "Bhaiya, why are you not asking me to buy your garlands?"

He said, "Didi, why should I ask? You are rich but you can't spend five rupees on my garland. Anyway now I am not so desperate. My sister was suffering from cancer and I had to work for her medicines. My father had left us. My mother makes the garlands and I sell them. We used the money for my sister's medicines. She passed away two months ago. You can now take one for free."

I bought them all. But I felt so small. I still repent that I did not respond then when he tried so hard.

Rishab's Rama

Rishab pushed open the door of his house and ran in. His bag flew from his back on to a nail on the wall.

"First time!" he shouted gleefully. He had been practising for months, and now the bag had flown to its right place almost on its own, as if it had a pair of wings.

"Is that you, Rishab?" called his grandmother, coming in from the kitchen. Rishab grinned to himself. His grandmother asked this question every single day. The running footsteps and the bag's slap against the wall told her who it was, but still their afternoons together always began with this question.

Later, after they had eaten and she washed the dishes, they lay down side by side.

Sometimes, when Rishab thought about which part of the day he liked best, he found it difficult to make up his mind. He loved the early morning when he woke up to the sound of his grandmother singing under her breath, as she picked flowers in the muddy little patch behind the house. Or the evening, when his mother got home from work, then his father.

But the afternoons were, he decided, the most peaceful. His grandmother and he would lie side by side, the sun streaming in through the window into the quite room. Or she would tell him stories, stories different from the kind he read, or heard in school.

Some days, she would sing him one of the hundreds and hundreds of songs she knew. She had a soft, trembling voice, but she knew what every word meant. Rishab could tell, from the way she sang, that she believed in the song. He could see how much she loved it.

Sometimes she would sing a story-song; a story from the Ramayana or the Mahabharata.

She told Rishab once, "Rama is called karuna-samudra. Do you know what that means?"

Rishab shook his head.

"Karuna is like pity," she said. "The gentle, sorry feeling you have when you see something that needs your kindness. Samudra of course is a deep deep ocean. So you see, there is no end to Rama's kindness, or his tenderness for all living things."

Then one day, Rishab came home later than usual. His grandmother stood at the door, waiting for him.

He went in with her, so full of news that he forgot to make his bag fly on to the nail on the wall.

"Pati!" he said, breathless, before she could ask him why he was late. "I saw a big procession today on the way home."

"Oh? What procession was that?" she asked him, taking the bag off his back.

"There was huge cardboard Rama with a bow and arrow. There were people with loudspeakers on a lorry. And everyone was shouting 'Jai Shriram! Help us to defeat our enemies!'"

Rishab was so full of the crowds he had seen-the colour, the noise and the marching that had reminded him of an army-that he didn't notice how silent his grandmother was.

"And then, when the procession had marched down the road, I ran after it till the market," said Rishab. "Look, one of the men with a trishul in his hand gave me this kumkum."

Grandmother didn't even look at it. "Put it away and come to eat," she said.

Rishab was so excited by what he had seen that he had forgotten how hungry he was.

Later, as they lay side by side, Grandmother suddenly said: "Rishab, when Rama, Sita and Lakshmana were in the forest, they once a yak. It had a very beautiful tail."

"Sita admired the tail very much. She thought she would like to take home a tail like that to remember her years in the forest.

"Rama decided to get the yak's tail for Sita.

"But the yak suddenly turned around. Now Rama could no longer see the tail. Instead, he saw the yak's large, trusting eyes, and its defenceless neck-stretched out as if it was offering it in place of its tail.

"Rama was filled with pity, with tenderness. Sita didn't get the yak's tail. But as they walked back to their hut, their faces-the faces of Rama, Sita and Lakshmana-were full of wonder at what they had seen: the beauty of love and trust between two living creatures."

Grandmother stroked Rishab's hair gently. "I know that look," she told him. "That face of Rama you don't need cardboard to see."

Rishab looked at her, a little puzzled by Grandmother's earnest face.

"Do you remember what I called the song I sang yesterday?" she asked him.

"Yes," said Rishab, "you called it prema bhakti."

"Do you remember what that means?" she then asked.

"A prayer that is love," he replied.

And Rishab remembered the song again. He saw a peaceful, loving, generous face, like Rama's when he spared the yak. This was the face of Rama that he saw in his head whenever he heard Pati sing.

"But Pati," he said, still puzzled, "this face looks different from the cardboard one. Are they two different Ramas?"

"Sleep now," said Grandmother, her voice barely above a whisper. "Rama lives in your heart, not on cardboard or in some building. And a prayer-or a song of love-does not need loudspeakers."

Then they fell asleep together, side by side, as if they had travelled a long distance that afternoon.

Katha

Noah Builds an Ark-Old Testament Part-V

But there was one man who loved God. He and his family obeyed God. This man was Noah. Noah always tried to do what God wanted him to do. God spoke to Noah one day and said, "Noah, I am going to destroy all the people on the earth. I will send rain for forty days and nights. All the earth will be covered with water. But Noah, because you love me and try to obey me, I will not destroy you and your family."

Then God said: "I want you to build an ark. You must build it like I tell you. Before it begins to rain, take your wife and your three sons and their wives into this houseboat. I also want you to take two of some kinds of birds and animals into the ark. Take seven pairs of the animals and birds which men use most. You must also take plenty of food for all the people and animals."

God gave Noah the exact measurements that he should use when building the ark. Noah went to work at once. He followed the plan God had given him. When the people who lived nearby saw Noah and his sons building the ark, they laughed. "Look at Noah. Isn't he silly to build such a big boat on dry land?" they said to one another as they watched.

It took a long time to finish, but Noah and his sons worked and worked. At last, the big houseboat was ready. It was very long and three stories high. There was room for Noah, his wife, his three sons, and their wives. There was room for all the animals and birds that God had told to take into the ark with him.

Then one day the sky grew dark. God told Noah that it was time to go into the ark. Noah did as he was told. He and his family went into the ark. They led all the birds and animals into the ark as God had asked. When they were all safely inside, God shut the door of the houseboat.

The Safeguard of One's Best Interests:

अनन्याश्चिन्तयन्तो मां ये जनाः पर्युपासते ।
तेषां नित्याभियुक्तानां योगक्षेमं वहाम्यहम् ॥

जो अनन्यप्रेमी भक्तजन मुझ परमेश्वरको निरन्तर चिन्तन करते हुए निष्कामभावसे भजते हैं, उन नित्य-निरन्तर मेरा चिन्तन करनेवाले पुरुषोंका योगक्षेम* मैं स्वयं प्राप्त कर देता हूँ ॥२२॥

* भगवत्स्वरूपकी प्राप्तिका नाम 'योग' है और भगवत्प्राप्तिके निमित्त किये हुए साधनकी रक्षाका नाम 'क्षेम' है।

'The devotees, however, who loving no one else constantly think of Me in a disinterested spirit, to those ever united in thought with Me, I bring full security and personally attend to their needs.'

Some people who interpret this verse entirely in a disinterested and detached fashion think it worth white only to devote themselves to the remembrance of God taking refuge in Him, to the uttar neglect of their mundane existense. In this connexion they quote they quote the following parable-

Once there was a Brahman who regularly recited the Gita, was a devotee of God and lived the life of detachment. He would spend all his time in reciting the Gita times and again with understanding, practising Jap of the Divine Name and meditating on His Manifest aspect. God was his only refuge. He did not care for his meals far less to speak of earning his livelihood. His parents had already departed to the other world. He had two brothers. All the three were married. He was eldest and the other two were younger to him. The two younger brothers afforded to meet the entire household expenses by functioning as family priests. One day the two younger brothers said to the eldest one-'It would be better if you could find some time for earning your livelihood'. The eldest brother said-'When God, the sustainer of the universe, who supports one and all is present at every place and at all times, it is merely childish to be fretful about earning one's livelihood. The Lord has taken upon Himself the responsibility of safeguarding one's best interests and needs by proclaiming in verse 22 of chapter IX of the Gita which runs as follows:

अनन्याश्चिन्तयन्तो मां ये जनाः पर्युपासते ।
तेषां नित्याभियुक्तानां योगक्षेमं वहाम्यहम् ॥

So, my brothers, it would be in the fitness of things if we leave ourselves to His will. Right from Brahma up to the lowest forms of creatures as well as the minutest atoms are all supported by Him. Moreover, He is avowed to safeguard the best interests and needs of those who taking refuge in Him constantly reflect on Him. It would better for us to devote ourselves exclusively to the study and teachings of the Gita and practice only the remembrance of and meditation on God with due reverence and devotion.'

The two brothers said-'Dear brother, you are right indeed but God won't provide for one sitting idle at home provided one has reverence for and trust in Him'-replied the eldest one confidently. Both the younger ones got a little irritated and said-'O brother, it is always easy to talk of lofty ideals. The fact is that the household expenses are met with the little earning we are able to make. You remain lying reciting the holy verses and indulge in lofty talks. You little know what a lot of trouble we have to undertake to make a little earning. You will be able to appreciate the difficulty only when you begin to live apart and run the household yourself. Then shall we see how you manage the affairs.' The eldest one patiently replied-'Dear brothers, if you deem it proper, I shall not feel any displeasure. Let me live apart. I do not want to be a burden on anyone. God knows best how He is going to provide me.' At this the two brothers spoke in a decisive tone-'All right, only tomorrow we shall make a partition as per our shares.' 'You may do as you think proper. I have nothing to demur about. My agreement lies with your'-said the eldest one.

The next day the two brothers partitioned whatever property and other belongings they had into three parts. For his share the Brahman devotee got a mud-built house, a little cash, a few ordinary clothes and ornaments and some cooking utensils etc. one third of the families they visited as priests were also apportioned to him as his share. But such was the mentality of their customers that in some family priest visited their house he was offered something as charity but none cared for the priest who stayed at home.

Thus as per partition the three brothers began to live separately, the Brahman devotee addressed his wife thus-'Whatever has been apportioned to us by my brothers is quite justifiable but we should henceforth take every care that we resort to God and non else. We should not pay visit to any house in order to ask for something nor should we accept anything even when it is offered to us. God himself safeguards the best interests and needs of people and it is he who will safeguard ours. For the present we shall manage with whatever has been apportioned to us by my brothers as our share.'

The Brahman's wife was a devotee of God and was devoutly faithful to her husband. She accepted her husband's proportioned with deference. She thought to herself-'We have already something to provide us with for the present. When the resources exhaust my husband himself will arrange for things in the way he deems proper.'

The Brahman devotee would get up at 4 o' clock and go to a tank a mile away from the city and there he would attend the call of nature and wash himself. Then after offering the morning prayers he would offer mental worship, tell the beads, meditate on God and thereafter would recite the whole of the Gita with due devotion concentrating on its meaning and after returning home at eleven would take food and perform other duties. Having taken his food he would again returning to the same tank at 1 o' clock in the noon time, practice Jap, meditation and self-study. Again at 4p.m. after easing and bathing himself he used to offer the evening prayers. After that having performed mental worship he would reverentially study the holy scriptures.

After the sunset he practised the Jap of the Divine Name and meditate on His aspect. Finally returning home after 8p.m. he would take his supper and go to bed at 10. At the time of both meals his virtuous wife would take her meals, only after feeding her husband. She considered it her supreme duty to make salutations to her husband daily to offer the best attendance to him, to abide by his bidding and to meditate on God and chant His divine names.

Thus the couple pulled on together. Daily expenses had, of course, to be born by them. After some time the little money they had was spent up. The wife informed her husband that all the money was spent up. The husband enquired of her if the clothings and ornaments too were used up to which the wife gave a negative reply. Now the Brahman's wife argued to herself that her husband meant to pull on for the present by selling off the clothings and ornaments. So she began to manage the household by disposing of them one by one. But how long could the clothings and the ornaments last? A time came when she had no more of them to dispose of. Then one day his wife informed him that there were no more of ornaments and clothings left in the house.

The husband said-'Worry not. Still we have the utensils and the house as well.' This made the Brahman's wife think that her husband consented to manage the household by selling the utensils and the house as well. Without any demur she sold out the house and the two shifted to another rented house. This enabled to them to pull on for some time more. Then they sold off the utensils but these could not fetch much money. At last they had nothing left except a 'saree' for the Brahman's wife to wrap herself in and a 'Dhoti' and a large napkin for the use of the revered Brahman.

One morning at 4 o' clock when the revered Brahman was proceeding to the forest, with folded hands the Brahman's wife very politely spoke to him thus-'My husband, we have nothing left with us now. You are left only with this holy book of yours- the Gita, your Dhoti and the napkin whereas only one saree is left for my use. There is no foodgrain in the house for cooking food this day. Whatever we had exhausted yesterday. 'The Brahman gave no answer to this and made his way to the forest as usual.

In the routined manner the Brahman went to the tank and after easing and bathing himself he performed the morning worship and practised the Jap of Gayatri (a divine formula). Subsequently when he was reverently reciting the Gita he came across the following verse which he prized much-

अनन्याश्चिन्तयन्तो मां ये जनाः पर्युपासते ।
तेषां नित्याभियुक्तानां योगक्षेमं वहाम्यहम् ॥

That day as the learned Brahman was reciting the verse he thought to himself and argued thus-'This verse does not seem to contain the utterance of the Lord probably it is an interpolation. Had it been the utterance of the Lord himself, would not the Lord ensure my wellbeing? I totally depend on Him but to this day he was shown me no favour at all.' Analyzing thus he obliterated the verse and barring this one began to recite the Gita as usual.

Noticing such a sentiment of the revered Brahman, the ruler of the hearts of entire creation, ever ready to fulfil the desires of His devotees, at once disguised as a pupil and riding a horse reached the Brahman's house and approaching his wife and placing before her a large plate filled with sweetmeats asked the whereabouts of the preceptor. The Brahman's wife said-'A mile away from home, there is a tank where he goes every day for performing the daily rituals and returns at about eleven.

It is ten now and he is expected to be back in an hour. Who are you and what for have you brought these sweets?' 'I am the disciple of the revered Brahman and have brought these sweets to make an offering to my revered preceptor and your good self, please accept these', replied the disciple. The Brahman's wife said-'The learned Brahman entertains no disciple nor he accept things offered by others. I have been instructed by him not to accept any offering made by others, please take it back.' The disciple said-'I quite agree with what you say. True it is that he does not entertain any disciple. He has not accepted nor will accept anyone as his disciple.

But I enjoy his special favour that is why he has accepted me as a disciple. I want to assure you that I am his only disciple.' 'I know full well that he never made any disciple. How then I take it for granted that you are his disciple. Whatever be the fact, in no circumstance I am going to accept these sweets. You may offer them to the learned Brahman when he returns'-said the Brahman's wife. 'Well, I leave this plate right here and the horse also tied nearby. I shall come back again to see the learned Brahman'-said the disciple. At this the Brahman's wife replied-'You may take this plate back with you and bring it again when he comes back. In no circumstance shall I keep it without his consent.' But the Lord was no ordinary human being. He walked away leaving the plate at its place when he was departing the Brahman's wife said-'But leave with me your name and address so that on his return the plate containing sweets may be sent back to your house.' The disciple asserted-'I am known to him and I enjoy his special favour; He has no disciple other than myself. Please tell him that the same disciple of His whom he had disfigured this morning had come. This will be sufficient to remind him of me.' Saying so the Lord walked away.

An hour later when the learned Brahman returned from the forest and entered the house he took notice of the plate full of sweets. A little agitated the Brahman sternly asked-whence have these sweets come? Who brought them and why have these been accepted?' With folded hands the Brahmans wife politely replied-'My master, I have not wilfully accepted them. A disciple presumptuously did so. He said he had brought them as offerings for the preceptor. Even though I did not accept them, he left them here in spite my resentment.' The Brahman said-'You are not unaware of the fact that neither have I ever made any disciple nor do I do so on principle.' 'That is true indeed. I too did not fail to tell him that neither you have ever made any disciple nor you do so on principle nor will ever make any in future. Taking my statement to be correct he stared that he knew it well that his preceptor did not make any disciple and that you had shown him special favour. That was why you had entertained him as your disciple and assured me that whatever he had stated was true.

In spite of all that I only said that I never heard of your accepting him as a disciple. I told him that in no way could I keep that present without your consent still he kept it here and walked away.' The Brahman remarked-'At least you should have asked for his whereabouts so that the things belonging to him should be returned to his house.' The Brahman's wife said-'I did ask him for it and to my querry he replied that his preceptor knew him, He added that only that morning you had disfigured him and you could not quite dismiss from your memory so soon. He requested me to tell you that the offering was made by your only disciple whose face was disfigured him and you that morning. Saying so he went away and while departing reminded me that the plate containing sweets was being left here, his horse was tied nearby and that he would turn up after words to see you.'

Hearing this the Brahman felt horripilation and extremely gladdened he spoke thus-'O wife, blessed you are for He was none else but God incarnate. You are fortunate to have a perception of Him. I lack in faith and am unfortunate that is why He did not grant me His vision. I did not observe fast even for a day and having lost all patience obliterated the very utterance of the Lord. The Gita has directly emanated from the lips of the Lord and an effort to obliterate it amounts to distorting the face of the Divine Being. Today while reciting the Gita when I came across the verse-

अनन्याश्चिन्तयन्तो मां ये जनाः पर्युपासते ।
तेषां नित्याभियुक्तानां योगक्षेमं वहाम्यहम् ॥

I felt dubious about the utterance of the Lord and thought that if those were the words of the Lord, He must have looked after my well-being-so this must be an interpolation. Arguing that why I effaced it. I am indeed the vilest sinner lacking in faith. Had I an atom of patience within me, I should never have done such a vile act. The supremely compassionate Lord is already safeguarding our wellbeing. And he did arrive as soon as we were left penniless. For the offence of disfigurement I was deprived of His perception. You are pure at heart, a devotee of undivided mind and a devoutly faithful wife. So he granted you His perception. No, I shall not enjoy the peace of mind till he does not turn up'. Later on when he looked out he was surprised to find the horse loaded. He at once unloaded the horse and having carried the bundle inside began to examine it. It was filled with precious stones worth lakhs of rupees. Seeing this the Brahman began to repent for his evil doing. He was again overwhelmed with joy and began to recite rhythmically the following verse from the Bhagawat-

अहो बकी यं स्तनकालकूटं जिघांसयापाययदप्यसाध्वी ।
लेभे गतिं धात्र्युचितां ततोऽन्यं कं वा दयालुं शरणं व्रजेम ॥

(How wonderful it is that the vilest Putana who weaned Krishna with her breast smeared with the deadliest poison in order to put an end to the life of Shri Krishna, merited and end worthy of a good mother (by the grace of the Lord). Why then should we forsaking refuge in such a compassionate Lord seek shelter with others)?

'Fie to me how have stained myself by falsely blaming the Lord who is so affectionate to the poor, the sanctifier of the sinner, the sustainer and the fosterer of all and the Lord of the universe. I am only the minion of pelf. If truly I were the minion of the Lord why should I have catered for fooding and clothing and why should the Lord have to come up with this treasure of precious gems? Had I the true knowledge of the true aspect and mysteries of the Lord, had I true love of Him, had I been rid of the lust for money, why should He delude me by offering these precious stones?' While saying so the Brahman was overwhelmed with excessive joy.

As it was getting very late the Brahman's wife requested him to take food-the God's gift. The learned Brahman said that as the Lord had promised he would partake of it only after His arrival. Evening drew on but the Lord did not turn up. Then the Brahman's wife requested him to take food-the divine gift. But the learned Brahman was too firm to be shaken from his resolve; he mechanically repeated the reply made earlier. When it was ten in the night-the time to go to bed and the Lord did not turn up, once again the Brahman's wife requested him to take food-the divine gift. But the revered Brahman would not and so bath fell asleep without taking anything at all.

It was 11 in the night. Knocking at the door someone called out in a very sweet voice-'O preceptor's wife, please open the door'. The Brahman couple were still far from getting any sleep at all. Hearing the sweet voice and the endearing address, the Brahman's wife started up and being overwhelmed with joy said-'O husband! See your Lord has come up at last'. The Brahman immediately rushed forward and flung open the door and fell in obeisance at the feet of the Lord. The Lord taking him up into His arms hugged him to His bosom. At that time the Brahman's condition was too strange to be described. He felt horripilation through the whole of his body, tears rolled down in torrents from his eyes and his voice was choked with excessive joy. Still anyhow he composed himself and spoke- 'O Lord, I have been only a minion of pelf. It is because of your supremely compassionate nature that you have taken pity on a wretched person like me. If my motive and conduct were to be taken in to account, I should not even as much get a place in the hell far less to speak of having your perception. I tried to bring infamy to a blameless and sublime person like you. A person vile like myself full of lust for money would be far to seek.

It was for the sake of money that I worshipped you. That is why you offered me these jewels for my satisfaction. I am too much motivated by desires that was why I thought you to be the caretaker of worldly welfare otherwise I should have craved for my spiritual wellbeing. Those who with a desireless heart surrender themselves to you alone, do not even aspire for this spiritual wellbeing but notwithstanding that you safeguard their best interests and needs. I was too unfortunate to be devoid of such reverence, love, faith, and self-surrender to make exclusive self-surrender to Supreme Being like you.'

The Lord said-'You are not to blame in this matter. You had surrendered yourself exclusively to Me. The delay in My arrival was caused an account of My faulty nature. But how is it that you have not taken your meal till now?' The learned Brahman replied-'When you had left the word that you would turn up to see me, how could I take food prior to your arrival? Be pleased to take food first, we too shall partake of the remainder afterwards.' 'Nay, we all shall dine together'-said the Lord. Then the Brahman's wife getting a hint from the Lord, offered food to both of them.

The revered Brahman overwhelmed with love took his share of food. Having dined the lord spoke-'Ask for whatever you desire, nothing is unattainable by you.' The Brahman said- 'When you have arrived here in person, does anything remain to be aspired for even now? My Lord, my only desire is that my heart should be rid of even the desire for my spiritual wellbeing and that I should have true and exclusive love of you. 'Saying-'Be it so' the Lord disappeared. Subsequently the Brahman's wife also took her share of food.

On the other side such was the state of affaires that since the time the two younger brothers had sought separation from the eldest one they became unhappy and grew miserably poorer and poorer. Such was their plight that they did not get anything even by borrowing or begging. When the news came to their ears that their brother had become so rich that his doors were always crowded with beggars, they also approaching their brother.

Seeing that his brothers had arrived, the learned Brahman who was a great devotee embraced them and enquired after their welfare. In reply they said-'How could we ever afford to be happy after being separated from a gentle man like you? We dare not show our faces to you. It is kind of you to take pity on us and entertain us with love.' The eldest one said-'No, brother, do not talk like that. The three of us are real brothers born of the same womb.

The fact is that we can never be separated. It was merely an unavoidable event. We should live cordially together as ever before. Who could be more affectionate well-wisher in this world other than one's real brother? Instead of being ashamed and repentant you should try to live with accord as before. My brothers; the credit of amassing this wealth you are beholding does not accrue to me. All this is the glory of the Lord. The Lord by all means safeguards the wellbeing of each and everyone who takes refuse in Him alone.

Just as a child confiding himself to the care of his parents moves about fearlessly and the parents naturally have to provide with all his needs in the same way, nay, even in a better way the Lord undertakes the work of upbringing and safeguarding those dependent on Him. He having full faith in whatever has been said in this verse (quoted below) you should meditate on God alone and devote yourselves to the study and teaching of the Gita regularly trying to understand its connotative and denotative meaning:

अनन्याश्चिन्तयन्तो मां ये जनाः पर्युपासते ।
तेषां नित्याभियुक्तानां योगक्षेमं वहाम्यहम् ॥

Since then the two brothers began to stay with their eldest brother and under hid advice began to practice Jap, meditation and the recitation of the Gita in a routined way and with in a short time through the adoration of God, attained God-realization by the grace of the Lord.

How far this story is true is not known, but from this story we must draw the moral that after taking refuge in God, He safeguards one's best interests and needs. So placing full reliance on this fact, we should try to surrender ourselves to God. The best thing is to meditate on God with a desireless mind regularly and at all times. One should try to develop disinterested and true love of God without aspiring for one's wellbeing one should aspire for true spiritual wellbeing. The realization of what remains unrealized is termed as 'Yoga' and the safeguard of what has already been achieved in the field of spiritual practice and contributes to what remains unachieved in one's effort towards God-realization. Such is the assurance given by the Lord. Knowing this and placing one's full trust in it one should surrender oneself to God and rid oneself of all fears and should not contemplate over anything except the contemplation of God.

Those who worship God for the purpose of material wellbeing and the safeguard of worldly interests are decidedly superior to those who do not adore God; for the seekers of worldly objects and the suffers have been described by him as noble and virtuous-Hindi. 'All these are noble devotees' but the man of wisdom and the devotee of undivided mind and disinterested spirit has verily been described by Him as His ownself because the man of wisdom having a desireless mind, has God alone as his ultimate goal. So it is desirable for us to become disinterested and enlightened devotees of undivided mind for such a devotee is extremely dear to the Lord. The Lord say:

तेषां ज्ञानी नित्ययुक्त एकभक्तिर्विशिष्यते ।
प्रियो हि ज्ञानिनोऽत्यर्थमहं स च मम प्रियः ॥

उनमें नित्य मुझमें एकीभावसे स्थित अनन्य प्रेमभक्तिवाला ज्ञानी भक्त अति उत्तम है, क्योंकि मुझको तत्त्वसे जाननेवाले ज्ञानीको मैं अत्यन्त प्रिय हूँ और वह ज्ञानी मुझे अत्यन्त प्रिय है ॥१७॥

Of these the best is the man of wisdom constantly established in identity with Me and possessed of exclusive devotion. For extremely dear I am to the wise man and he is extremely dear to Me.

Satya's Marriage

Satya was the most beautiful and most gifted girl in the world. She was a princess-the daughter of the rich and powerful King of Khosla. Her fame spread far and wide. Many royal princes asked the King of Khosla for her hand in marriage.

Satya reached the age of marriage and the King had to find a suitable match for her. Every one of the princes who wished to marry Satya was great in his own way. The King therefore found it difficult to choose one. He thought over the matter for many days and decided to hold a contest.

The King announced that any prince who could yoke the seven wild bulls he kept in his stables would win the hand of Satya in marriage.

A day was fixed for the marriage. Invitations were sent to all the suitable kings and princes to come and try their luck and their skill in the contest. The King also made all arrangements to celebrate the marriage in grand style.

New palaces were built for the royal guests. Large kitchens and huge dining halls were put up, and big feasts arranged. Famous musicians and dancers were invited to entertain the guests. The city was decorated and lit up.

The guests started arriving. Every king and every prince hoped that he would win the contest and marry Satya. Every one of them came in a large procession. In every procession there were elephants, chariots, horses, palanquins, and soldiers. The kings and princes also brought their ministers and court officials, and many servants carrying boxes of jewels and clothes.

All the guests were received with great honour. They were housed in beautiful palaces. They were feasted and entertained most splendidly.

On the marriage day, the royal guests set out in their best clothes and jewels. They assembled on one side of a large field, which was fenced on all sides. The King of Khosla arrived with his family, his ministers, court officials, and friends. He told the big gathering that his daughter, Satya, would marry the first prince who could yoke the seven wild bulls together. He then ordered the contest to begin.

The ceremony began with the beating of drums and the sounding of bugles. The pipers and trumpeters joined in. The music was exciting.

Seven large cages were then brought in. The attendants opened the doors of the cages. Seven huge, fierce-looking bulls rushed out. They moved about, challenging everyone.

Every prince desired to win Satya and wanted to get in first to try his luck. Many of them rushed in together, in the hope of yoking the wild bulls.

One king, who had won many battles and thought he was the strongest man to enter the contest, walked boldly towards one of the wild bulls. The bull charged at him with great force. He was tossed, and he fell to the ground. The bull followed him but the brave man got up and ran for his life.

A prince, one who had killed many wild animals, rushed at one of the bulls. The bull gored him and he fell down unconscious. Another prince approached a bull. But he then felt frightened and ran out of the field. The animal kicked one prince who tried to catch one of the bulls. He withdrew with a broken leg.

Everybody laughed when one of the kings caught the tail of a bull and the bull ran up and down, with the king dangling on its tail.

A prince tried to catch a bull by the horns; and soon he was seen flying through the air. The bulls trampled on one of the kings. Another king lost an eye; yet another lost an arm.

All the kings and princes tried their best. But none of them was able to catch the bulls and yoke them together.

Everybody was upset. Some of the princes said that the King of Khosla had set an impossible task for them. They said that the King must choose one of them to marry his daughter.

They argued that the marriage had been fixed and it must take place.

The King of Khosla was very sad that the contest had failed. He ordered the bulls to be put back in their cages and taken away.

Suddenly, a new prince arrived in a chariot. It was Krishna, with Arjuna as his charioteer. Krishna wanted to try his luck in the contest to win Satya.

The King welcomed Krishna and told him about the terms of the contest. Krishna accepted these terms and entered the field. The defeated kings and princes looked on.

The wild bulls were all standing in a row, with their heads raised high, as if celebrating their victory. Then they saw another man walking boldly towards them. They stared at him; he stared at them. For the first time the bulls seemed frightened. Krishna was strong and clever. He knew how to tackle these wild animals. Slowly, he walked around, caught the bulls one by one, and firmly yoked them together.

The kings and princes were surprised. There were loud cheers for Krishna. The drummers, pipers, and buglers went into action with exciting loud music. The King of Khosla greeted Krishna. He placed Satya's hand in Krishna's. There was joy on all sides.

Then the defeated kings and princes raised an uproar. They were shocked that Krishna had won the contest and thus won the hand of Satya. They rose up in anger and cried: " Who is this Krishna? Is he not a cowherd? Is he not the one who killed his own uncle? How can kings and princes of noble birth allow one of their girls to be married to a mere cowherd?"

The kings and princes talked and talked, and shouted at the top of their voices. They said it was below their dignity to allow a cowherd to marry Princess Satya. They wanted to fight it out with Krishna.

Krishna and Arjuna were about to leave with Satya, when the challenge came. Krishna walked to the chariot, jumped into it, and sat there with Satya by his side. He then asked Arjuna to deal with the kings and princes who had declared war on him.

Arjuna went to them and pleaded for peace. He said that Krishna had won the princess in an open contest, by fair means. He appealed to them not to create unnecessary trouble. But the princes, in their disappointment and anger, would not listen to Arjuna. They wanted to fight.

"Then get ready," said Arjuna. He took out his mighty bow 'Gaiidivam', and started shooting arrows that fell like a heavy shower on his foes. The princes shot back but they were no match for Arjuna.

Arjuna aimed his arrows in such a way that he did not kill anyone. His arrows hit the bows and arrows of his enemies, who were left without weapons to fight back. Still the princes wanted to continue the battle. Then Arjuna shot arrows, which destroyed the clothes worn by his enemies, leaving all the kings and princes quite naked on the battlefield.

In their shame, all the defeated kings and princes ran away.

Krishna then took leave of the King of Khosla and drove away with Satya by his side, and Arjuna as the charioteer.

The Amazing Adventures of Hanuman

Once upon a time, long ago, there lived in India a monkey-boy called Hanuman. His father was Vayu, the god of the winds, and his mother was a monkey princess. Although he was only little, Hanuman had magic powers. He was also naughty.

This is the story of some exciting adventures, which began in the beautiful valley of flowers, where one day Hanuman sat with his mother in the warm sunshine. Hanuman looked up into the sky and saw the sun.

"I like the sun", said the naughty monkey-boy.

"How beautiful it is, so warm, so warm, so golden and so bright. I'd love to hold it and play with it as if it were my very own!"

He reached up, caught hold of the sun and started throwing it up and down as though it were a ball. The sun was not pleased, and began to feel rather ill.

The sun called out to Indra, the god of thunder and lightning, who was riding by on his magic elephant.

"Help! Indra! Look at what this naughty monkey-boy is doing to me! Help!"

Indra was very cross with Hanuman.

The sky grew dark and storm clouds gathered.

"Put the sun back at once", he said in a mighty voice.

"NO", said Hanuman, who was not afraid.

In fury Indra shot a bolt of white lightning.

"Zaap!"

It hit the monkey-boy.

Hanuman fell to the ground, where he lay very still. His father Vayu, who was flying over the earth, had a feeling that Hanuman was in danger. He rushed back to the valley of flowers and found his little son lying with his eyes closed.

"Who has done this to my son"? he called out from the sky.

The god of the winds was furious and blew great winds and storms around the world. Then, all of a sudden, the air become still.

"I will stop the air from flowing everywhere until my son Hanuman breathes again!", said Vayu. Now this was very serious for the world. Plants, animals and people quickly began to feel weak, fall over and die. They did not have any air to breathe. When Indra, the god of thunder and lightning, flew by and saw what was happening, he felt very sad for the world.

"Anger is such a terrible thing", he said. "None of this would have happened if I hadn't got so cross. I must ask Vayu to forgive me". Meanwhile Vayu had taken his son Hanuman deep under the ground and was cradling him in his arms. Indra called some other gods to beg Vayu to bring air back to the world. "Not until Hanuman breathes again", replied Vayu.

So the gods promised to bring the monkey-boy back to life and said that when he grew up he would have more magic powers. He could grow as big or as small as he wished. His tail would be magic and he could fly high in the sky. He would lead an army of monkeys and even live as long as he liked!

"Lightning and thinder bolts will never harm him again", said Indra.

"Fire will never touch him", said the sun. Hanuman's father was happy now and kept his word. The air moved agin and all the plants, animals and people came back to life.

"What happened to us?" they asked. They couldn't remember anything!

Everything took place as the gods promised. Hanuman grew up to be the most fantastic monkey in the world. He lived in an enormous green forest. Sugriva, the king of monkeys, heard about Hanuman's special powers. He went to see him.

"Will you be my best friend and lead my army?" Sugriva asked. "Certainly", said Hanuman, and from that day on the two were always together.

At the other end of the forest lived a handsome prince called Rama and his beautiful, clever wife princess Sita. The news of her beauty spread far and wide. Now, down at the Southern tip of India, on an island called Lanka, there lived a wicked, jealous demon with ten heads and twenty arms. His name was Ravana.

'I will make Sita my wife,' he boasted,' even if I have to steal her!' He sent his wicked demons, disguised as golden deer, to lure prince Rama away from home for a day's hunting in the forest. As soon as Rama was gone Ravana leapt forward and with a terrifying R-o-à-r-r-r!' swept Sita up with his many arms. His evil plan was to fly back to Lanka and keep Sita a prisoner until she would agree to marry him. But Sita managed to take off her jewels and throw them down on the ground.

'I hope, I really hope, someone finds them,' Sita thought,' and takes them to my husband Rama.' Luckily, down below on the ground, the jewels landed just by Hanuman and Sugriva.

'The gods must be sending us gifts!' said Hanuman.

'I wonder who these belong to?' asked Sugriva.

The two set off into the forest to solve the mystery. Meanwhile, prince Rama had returned and was calling for his wife Sita. 'Where has she gone?' he thought, as he searched the forest for her. Hanuman and Sugriva found him wandering alone calling Sita's name.

'Who is Sita?' asked Hanuman.

'Sita is my wife, the princess,' said Rama. 'She has disappeared'. 'I see,' said Hanuman. 'Perhaps these jewels belong to her then.' 'Why, they are Sita's,' replied Rama. 'Where is she and who are you?'

'I am Hanuman and this is my king Sugriva. We will help you find her.'

'Thank you,' replied Rama. 'Please do your very best.'

Hanuman Searches for Sita

Hanuman flew south. He learned that Sita had been taken to the city of Lanka by the demon king Ravana. Hanuman grew tall and mighty and with one giant leap began to fly through the clouds to the walled city on the island. As he flew over the ocean a terrible sea monster saw his shadow.

'Grrrrr!' she said. 'I'm very hungry and I'd like to eat you.' She opened her mouth and swallowed him whole. 'Oh, Oh,' thought Hanuman, as he slid down her slippery throat. Hanuman landed with big THUMP! He was sitting on something soft. He looked down... he was sitting on a bed! Hanuman was floating inside the stomach of the sea monster! He peered through the darkness and saw bits of masts, bits of sail and ships and all sorts of things the sea monster had swallowed.

'I must get out of here,' thought Hanuman, looking around him. Then he had an idea. Hanuman made himself very small and flew around the monster's stomach tickling her sides. She began to squirm and thrash about.

'Hoo, Hoo, ha ha! Stop that at once,' she giggled. 'I am very ticklish and if I laugh too much I'll sneeze!'

But Hanuman wouldn't stop. The sea monster could take it no longer. 'I think I'm going to . ' She opened her enormous mouth wide. All at once Hanuman shot out of her mouth.

Ahh,Ahh...Choooo!' sneezed the sea monster.

She shut her great jaws suddenly as she remembered that Hanuman was supposed to be inside her. But he was already speeding away to the walled city of Lanka. When Hanuman arrived at Lanka he saw all sorts of demon guards everywhere. Some were fat, some were thin. Some were beet root red, some were banana yellow and some were even cucumber green. All were ugly and smelly. They grunted as they walked around.

'Oh dear,' thought Hanuman, as he sat on the city wall. He was still very small, so he managed to slip past the guards through the darkness without being noticed. Inside the white marble city he searched for Sita in all the rooms of Ravana's grand palace. Hanuman searched in the dinning hall. He searched in the kitchens. He looked down all the corridors. But he couldn't find Sita. Then he heard a great rumbling noise, like thunder, coming from a bedroom with a huge golden door. He quietly crawled under the gap in the door and found Ravana. He was fast asleep on a huge bed with all his ten heads snoring loudly.

'Grrrr-phew...Grrrr-phew!!'

'Well,' thought Hanuman, ' Sita certainly isn't here!'

Hanuman found Sita outside the palace sitting sorrowfully in a beautiful garden surrounded by sleeping demons. He bent down from the branch of a fruit tree.

'Pssst!' he said, beckoning to her. Sita looked up in surprise. 'Who are you?' She asked. "I am Hanuman,' he replied soft and low. 'I have been sent by Rama to find you. Now that I have I must return to tell him and we will come back and rescue you'.

'Oh, thank you!' Sita replied, cheering up a little. 'But be careful. Ravana is not only mighty but also cunning.'

Just then one of the demon guards was disturbed and woke up. 'An intruder in our midst!' he shouted to the other guards. 'We must capture him!'

They raced to attack Hanuman, who suddenly made himself grow tall and strong again until he stood high above the garden. Reaching down towards the earth he pulled two trees with their roots out of the ground and swung them around like clubs to keep the demons away. When Ravana heard what Hanuman was doing he was furious. There was a deafening sound as his ten heads all roared and shouts at once.

'A monkey doing all this damage in my garden!' he cried. 'Send my son to capture him and bring him to me.'

Ravana's son went and began shooting deadly snake arrows at Hanuman, but they didn't harm the mighty monkey-man.

Hanuman had a brilliant idea. 'Perhaps I should meet Ravana face to face,' he thought. Making himself small again he allowed himself to be caught. He was tied up and brought to Ravana.

'Please let Sita go!' begged Hanuman.

'Never!' snarled Ravana. 'How dare you! Set his tail on fire!' Several demons grabbed Hanuman's tail, but it suddenly began to grow longer and longer! It was knocking over the demons who could hardly hang on!

'Fools!' yelled Ravana. It's a trick! Grab his tail and set it alight!' Finally they managed to set the tip on fire and mighty roar went up from the crowd. But the fire didn't hurt Hanuman at all because his magic powers kept him perfectly cool. Hanuman's eyes twinkled as he had another idea.

'I know,' he thought. I can put my burning tail to good use!' He suddenly grew big again, breaking free of his bonds. With one bounded he leapt into the air, his tail burning brightly. He looked like a giant fireball He then flew over the city of Lanka setting fire to the roofs of the houses. Another roar went up from the demons, this time in astonishment.

'Oh, how I hate that monkey!' Ravana stamped his feet and cursed with rage. He waved his twenty arms wildly, while Hanuman dipped his tail in the sea.

' Ssssss...'

There was a loud sizzling noise, but Hanuman's tail was not burnt at all! Hanuman flew back to prince Rama to tell him what had happened. 'That's all very interesting. 'Rama said, 'but how can we rescue Sita?' 'Don't worry,' said Hanuman. 'I have a whole army of monkeys and I will help you rescue Sita.'

They marched down to the southern tip of India where they were faced with mighty ocean. ' How shall we cross?' asked Rama. 'My monkeys will build a bridge of rocks for you,' replied Hanuman. Using great stones and trees Hanuman and the monkeys built a strong bridge. Hanuman carried Rama on his shoulders and they crossed the sea to Lanka. The demon king Ravana sent his son to lead the demon soldiers. There they were lying in wait and ready for battle.

The Great Battle

When a fierce battle! Among the ugly, smelly demons and the poisoned spears and snake arrows, Rama fought bravely. Way up on the hillside Hanuman Picked up rocks and hurled them. Then the demon king himself entered the battled. Ravana's twenty arms were here, there and everywhere, cutting, thrusting, and circling like a whirlwind. Every time one of Rama's arrow hit one of Ravana's heads, another would just pop up in its place! The demon moved forwards to attack Rama's army.

'This is no good,' said Rama to Hanuman. How will we rescue Sita now?'

Hah! Sneered Ravana from afar. 'Foolish Hanuman. Foolish Rama you'll never get Sita back now because we're going to win the battle!' Hanuman flew close to Rama and whispered in his ear: 'Ravana's weak spot is his foot. There's only one sure way to kill him with a magic arrow kept hidden in his own palace!'

Rama looked up. Hanuman was already flying away to Ravana's palace. Soon he returned with the magic arrow. 'Here you are,' he said to Rama. 'Let's hope this works'.

It's our last chance,' said Rama, as he strung his bow. Ravana was getting closer. Fire was coming out of his ten noses and smoke from his twenty ears. Rama took aim.

'Z-I-N-G!'

The arrow flew straight and sweet through the air. It hit Ravana's foot and he let out an ear-piercing scream. Then he fell, dying, to the earth. Hanuman flew to Ravana's palace, freed Sita and returned her to Rama's waiting arms. They hugged each other.

'I missed you so much,' said Sita,' but Hanuman gave me hope.' 'It is thanks to Hanuman that you are safe and sound,' said Rama. 'It was nothing really,' said Hanuman shyly, as he looked at the ground. 'Come on Sugriva, we'd better be going now.'

'No wait,' replied Rama. 'You have done so much for us and we'd like to thank you.' Rama and Sita gave Hanuman and Sugriva some jewels as gifts. ' From now on you will be our brothers. Please accept our friendship and join us.' Hanuman agreed. There was great rejoicing in the land. Hanuman lived happily ever after in the green forest and had many more exiting adventures.

Satrajit was a pious man. He was a devotee of Surya, the sun god. He worshipped Surya for a long time. Surya was pleased. He appeared before Satrajit and asked him to name his wish.

Syamantakam

Satrajit was a poor man. He wanted to become rich. He asked Surya to help him to get rich.

Surya granted Satrajit's wish. He gave Satrajit a precious stone called 'Syamantakam'. Surya told Satrajit: "This will produce a good quantity of gold every day. Look after it well."

'Syamantakam' was a bright gem, shining like the sun itself. Satrajit took it home. People who saw it thought that 'Syamantakam' was Surya, the sun god, himself. They feared that something bad might happen because the sun god had appeared on earth. So they went to Lord Krishna for advice.

Krishna talked to them. He tried to calm their fears. 'Syamantakam', he said, was only a precious stone. There was no cause for anxiety about it. Krishna also told them that Satrajit was bringing the gem for him to see.

Satrajit went to see Krishna and showed him Surya's wonderful gift. "It is bright and wonderful," Krishna told Satrajit. "It shines like the sun. It can produce gold every day. People will come to know about this gold you get every day. Be aware of robbers."

Krishna added: "Perhaps it is risky for you to keep this precious stone. If you like, you can leave it here with me. I shall take care of it. You can come here every day and collect the gold it produces."

Satrajit was unwilling to part with 'Syamantakam'. He thought Krishna was trying to steal it.

"My lord," he said, "I received this gift after worshipping Surya for many years. I would like to keep it myself. I think even Surya would not like me to give it away. I beg you not to ask for it."

Krishna said: "I do not want the stone. I only wanted to help you to keep it safe. It is your property and you may take it home. You are free to do whatever you want with it."

Satrajit was happy. He went home. He took very good care 'Syamantakam'. Every day the bright gem produced a good quantity of gold and Satrajit became richer and richer.

Satrajit had a brother named Prasenan. This young man was very fond of rich clothes and costly jewels. One day, Prasenan was going to hunt in the jungle with a large number of people. He had put on his best clothes and costly jewels. But he thought he would look better if he wore 'Syamantakam' also.

Prasenan went to Satrajit and asked for the precious stone. Satrajit was fond of his brother. He loved him so much that he could not say 'no' to Prasenan's request. Satrajit therefore gave 'Syamantakam' to Prasenan and asked him to take good care of it.

Prasenan went hunting, wearing the bright 'Syamantakam'. The hunt was exciting. Prasenan chased a wild boar. The chase was long and Prasenan went far away his companions.

Suddenly a lion jumped at Prasenan.

Prasenan fought the lion single-handed. In fight Prasenan was killed.

The lion was attracted by the brightness of 'Syamantakam' and carried away the gem.

A huge monkey, passing that way, saw the lion. The monkey was attracted by the glow of 'Syamantakam'.

The monkey, who was very strong, chased the lion. The lion was killed in the fight with the monkey.

The monkey took 'Syamantakam', went to his home in a huge cave, and gave the gem to his children to play with.

Satrajit waited for his brother's return from the hunt. The people who had gone on the hunt with Prasenan had all come back. They were unable to tell Satrajit what had happened to Prasenan-how and where he had disappeared.

Satrajit hoped that Prasenan would soon return. He waited for many days. But there was no news of Prasenan.

Satrajit was sad. He began to suspect lord Krishna. He remembered that Krishna had wanted 'Syamantakam' and that he had not given it to him. Was it possible that Krishna had killed Prasenan and stolen the precious stone?

Satrajit thought hard. His suspicion of Krishna grew strong. But he was helpless. Krishna was the King. Satrajit could not accuse him of murder or robbery.

Satrajit, however, could not keep his thoughts to himself. He told some of his very close friends what he thought of the disappearance of Prasenan and 'Syamantakam'. He asked these friends to keep it a secret.

But each of these friends of Satrajit had his own very close friends. Each of them told a few people what Satrajit had said? They said Krishna had killed Prasenan and grabbed 'Syamantakam'.

These friends told their friends and the story spread far and wide.

In a few days, everybody in the country was talking about Prasenan and 'Syamantakam'-and Krishna's cruel hand in his or her disappearance.

Women could talk of nothing else. They wanted their children to be careful.

"Take good care of your ornaments," they told the children. "Krishna may steal them, if he gets a chance."

The children were frightened. They began to run away from Krishna-though they had always loved him.

One day, Krishna saw some children playing at the roadside. They ran away when they saw him. But Krishna heard what they were saying as they ran away.

One child cried: "Run, run! Run away from Krishna. He is a thief. He will even kill Children, to grab their ornaments. That is what my mother said."

The other children said that was what their mothers had told them, too.

Krishna was shocked. He wanted to know the cause of such ugly rumours against him.

Krishna went about in disguise. He moved among the people. The people did not know who he was. He heard the ugly rumours about him that had spread all over the country. Everybody seemed to believe that Krishna had killed Prasenan and grabbed 'Syamantakam'.

Krishna and his companions went to the jungle where Prasenan had gone for the hunt. After a long search, they found the dead body of Prasenan. But they could not find the precious 'Syamantakam'.

They continued the search. Soon, they discovered the body of a dead lion. They also noticed some footprints leading from the lion.

Krishna and his party trailed these footprints to the mouth of an enormous cave. The footprints led into the cave.

Krishna asked his companions to wait while he went inside.

It was a wonderful place. There was a long passage. On the walls on both sides, were beautiful painting-scenes from the 'Ramayana'. Krishna was surprised. He followed the story in pictures as he walked along the passage. The story ended when he entered a big hall.

Some children were playing in the big hall. They were playing with a brilliant gem. Krishna knew at once that it was 'Syamantakam'.

The children were frightened at the sight of a stranger. They cried out for help.

Suddenly, Krishna heard a thunderous roar. He saw a huge monkey rushing to attack him. There was no time to explain why he was there. The huge monkey jumped at Krishna. There was nothing Krishna could do except defend himself.

It was a terrible fight. The monkey lashed at Krishna, and Krishna fought back. The fight lasted a long time.

Now, this huge monkey was Jambavan, one of the heroes of 'Ramayana'. He had grown very old and had retired. With his many children and grandchildren, Jambavan was living happily in that beautiful cave.

Nobody had disturbed him there. Now, a stranger had come and frightened his children. Jambavan did not like it. He wanted to turn out the stranger.

Jambavan fought Krishna, and Krishna fought back. Neither of them would yield to the other. The terrific force of the battle shook the entire jungle.

Krishna had not gone there to fight. He did not wish to fight Jambavan, the veteran 'Ramayana' hero. Krishna wanted to stop the fighting somehow. So he rushed forward, caught hold of Jambavan, and threw him aside with great force.

Jambavan was surprised. Nobody had ever defeated him. He looked at the man who had thrown him down. Then he saw Krishna in form of Lord Vishnu. And within that form he saw the image of his old master. Rama.

Jambavan was sad that he had fought his own master. He fell at the feet of Krishna and asked for forgiveness. Krishna embraced Jambavan and said: "It was our bad luck that we had to fight each other. But I am happy to meet you, and to see you as strong as ever."

Jambavan shed tears of joy.

Then they sat down to talk. Krishna told Jambavan why he had come to the jungle and how he had come to the cave.

"My Lord," said Jambavan, "the precious stone you are looking for is here; I saw a lion with it and I took it from him. I gave it to the children to play with."

Jamabavan went in and brought 'Syamantakam'. He gave it to Krishna. Everybody was happy. Jambavan's children and grandchildren came out and asked Krishna for his blessings.

After sometime, Krishna took leave of Jambavan. Outside the cave, he joined his companions and went straight to Satrajit's home.

Satrajit was happy when he got back the precious 'Syamantakam'. He fell at Krishna's feet. He told Krishna how sorry he was for his evil thoughts and the ugly rumours. Satrajit begged for Krishna's forgiveness. He offered 'Syamantakam' to Krishna as a gift.

But Krishna did not want the precious stone. He was glad that he had proved his innocence. He was happy that he had won back the love and trust of the people, young and old.

Krishna was a very poor boy. He lived in the village with his mother. His father was dead. When Krishna was five-year-old, his mother sent him to school.

The road seemed very long. Krishna thought he had lost his way. He went on and on, till he saw the other village boys going to school. He joined them, and at last reached school.

He had a happy time at school. When lessons were over, he played games with the other boys. It was almost dark when he set out for home.

It was a long way back to home. It grew darker and darker. Krishna was very much afraid. He did not know what to do. So he began to run, and he did not rest till he was in his mother's arms.

Next morning Krishna told his mother that he did not want to go to school. "But," said his mother, "You had a happy time at school yesterday, my child, and learnt many beautiful things!

You said you loved your lessons. Why do you not wish to go to school today?"

"I love school and my lessons, mother," replied, "but I am afraid to go alone through the woods, they are thick and dark."

The poor mother stood for a minute, thinking what to say. She was very poor to send anyone with her son to school. At once the name of lord Krishna came to her mind. So she said to Krishna: "You don't know, my child, their lives in these woods another son of mine who is always there near the path. Whenever you are afraid, call out Him, 'O Cowboy Brother, come with me to school!' He will come at once and take care of you, and then you will not be afraid.""

And Krishna said, "Is it really true, mother, that my Brother, the Cowboy, will come to take care of me on my way to school?"

"Yes, it is true, my boy," said the mother, "He loves you as a brother does, and will never fail to come to your help when you call out to Him."

So Krishna set out like a brave boy. But he had not gone very far when he began to feel afraid. So he called out, "O Brother Cowboy, Brother Cowboy, come and play with me!"

A Boy appeared out of the tree, took the child's hand, and led him to school. When they came near the school, He parted from him, saying: "Call Me again on your way back to home."

Every day, Krishna, while going to and coming back from school, would call the Cowboy. They would play together all the way. The Cowboy was so kind and good that Krishna came to love Him as he had never loved anyone before.

And when, day after day, Krishna told his mother all about Him, she was not in the least surprised. She knew it was the Child Krishna who came to her son's help every day.

So time went on. Then one day the school master said:" tomorrow I want to give a feast. All of you, my boys, must bring presents."

So Krishna said to his mother that night, "Mother, our noble teacher is going to give a feast tomorrow. What should I take to him?"

The child's words made the mother very sad. She knew she was very poor and could not give anything to her little boy for his teacher. But at the same time she did not want her son to give no present to his Master.

So she said to him, "My boy, I am too poor to give you anything for your teacher. But, while going to school in the morning, ask your Brother to give you something." She knew that the child Krishna would help them.

So in the morning Krishna said to the Cowboy: "O Brother, my teacher is going to give a feast today. All the boys will be bringing presents. It will look so bad if I give him no present. I am too poor to give anything. Will you, give me something foe my Master?"

"What can I give you, O brother? What am I but a poor Cowboy? Here is a little bowl of milk. That's all I can give you, Krishna. It is only a poor Cowboy's present. But you must give it to your teacher, "said the Cowboy.

Krishna went to his master's house with the present. He waited behind a crowd of boys who were handing over what they had brought.

Krishna waited a long time, but no one saw him. The poor boy became very sad. At last the teacher happened to look at him. He took the small bowl of milk from his hands and went to empty it into a big pan. But great was his wonder when the little bowl filled up again. Again he tried to empty it, and again the little bowl was full. And so he went on emptying it again and again, but still the little bowl was full.

All those present there wondered what it meant. Krishna also wondered. He now understood for the first time that the Cowboy Brother was no other than the Child Krishna Himself.

The teacher asked him, "From where did you get this milk?" Krishna replied, "From my Brother, the Cowboy Brother, who lives in the woods."

"Who is He?" asked the teacher.

"One who comes and play with me on my way to school," replied Krishna.

"Can you show me your Brother in the woods?"

"Yes, if you come along with me, Sir."

So in the evening the teacher and Krishna went together to the place. When they got there, Krishna called: "Cowboy Brother! Brother Cowboy! Won't you come?" but no Cowboy appeared. Krishna did not know what to do. He called and called, but there was no answer.

At last the boy, full of grief, cried, "O Brother Cowboy, if You do not appear, they will think I do not tell the truth."

Then came a sound, as it were, from the deep woods, which seemed to say, "No, my little brother, I cannot show my face to your master. He still has long way to wait."

Zacharias and Elizabeth-New Testament Part-II

Elizabeth, Mary's cousin, was married to Zacharias. Zacharias was priest and served at the Temple in Jerusalem. Elizabeth and Zacharias had no children. Because they were old, they did not expect to have any.

One day when Zacharias was busy in Temple, an angel appeared to Zacharias. Zacharias was afraid, for he had never seen an angel before.

"Don't be afraid, Zacharias," the angel said. "Your prayers have been heard. You and Elizabeth will have a son. You will call him John."

Zacharias did not believe the message from God. The angel said: "Zacharias, because you do not believe, you will not be able to talk until the baby is born."

It was after this that Mary came to see Elizabeth. Mary was excited and anxious to tell Elizabeth her news. When Mary saw Elizabeth, the Holy Spirit told Elizabeth the wonderful news that Mary was to be the mother of the Son of God. Elizabeth said to Mary, "Cousin, you are indeed blessed among women."

Then Elizabeth told Mary that she, too, was going to have son whose name would be John. She told Mary that the angel said John would one day lead the people of Israel.

Mary was happy to hear Elizabeth's news. She and Elizabeth prayed together and thanked God for all that had happened. Mary stayed with Elizabeth for about three months. It was a happy time for them and often they would talk of the great happiness that would be theirs when their sons were born.

Later, when Elizabeth's son was born all her friends and family were happy and rejoiced with her. But Zacharias still could not speak. When the baby was eight days old, Elizabeth and Zacharias were ready to give him a name and present him to God.

"Call him Zacharias after his father," some said.

"No, he is to be called John," Elizabeth said.

"There is no one in your family named John," the friends said.

Then Zacharias wrote on a tablet, "His name is John." Then Zacharias was able to speak, and he praised God.

This John became one of God's prophets, John the Baptist.

Folktales

The Sadhu

Akbar came to the throne when he was only thirteen years old. In the years that followed, he built on of the greatest empires of his time. He lived in unimaginable splendour. He was surrounded by courtiers who agreed with every word he said, who flattered him and treated him as if he were a god. Perhaps it was not surprising that Emperor Akbar was sometimes arrogant and behaved as if the whole world belonged to him. One day, Birbal decided to make the great emperor stop and think about life.

That evening as the emperor was going towards his palace, he noticed a sadhu lying in the centre of his garden. He could not believe his eyes. A strange sadhu, in ragged clothes, right in the middle of the palace garden? The guards would have to be punished for this, thought the emperor furiously as he walked over to the sadhu and prodded him with the tip of his embroidered slipper. "Here, fellow!" he cried. "What are you doing here? Get up and go away at once!"

The sadhu opened his eyes. Then he sat up slowly. "Huzoor," he said in a sleepy voice. "Is this your garden, then?"

"Yes!" cried the Emperor. "This garden those rose bushes, the fountain beyond that, the courtyard, the palace, this fort, this empire, it all belongs to me!"

Slowly the sadhu stood up. "And the river, Huzoor? And the city of Agra? And Hindustan?"

"Yes, yes, it's all mine", said the emperor "now get out!"

"Ah", said the sadhu. "And before you, Huzoor. Who did the garden and fort and city belong to then?"

"My father, of course", said the emperor. In spite of his irritation he was beginning to get interested in the sadhu's questions, he loved philosophical discussions and he could tell, from his manner of speaking, that the sadhu was a learned man.

"And who was here before him?" the sadhu asked quietly.

"His father, my father's father, as you know."

"Ah", said the sadhu. So this garden, those rose bushes, the palace and the fort all this has only belonged to you for your lifetime. Before that they belonged to your father, am I right? And after yours time they will belong to your son, and then to his son?

"Yes", said the Emperor Akbar wanderingly.

"So each one stays here for a time and then goes on his ways?"

"Yes."

"Like a dharmashala?" the sadhu asked. "No one owns a dharmashala. Or the shade of a tree on the side of a road. We stop and rest for a while and then go on. And someone has always been there before us and someone will always come after we have gone. Is that not so?"

"It is", Emperor Akbar quietly.

"So your garden, your palace, your fort, your empire... these are only places you will stay in for a time, for the span of your lifetime. When you die, they will no longer belong to you. You will go, leaving them in the possession of someone else, just as your father did and his father before him."

Emperor Akbar nodded. "The whole world is a dharmashala", he said slowly, thinking very hard. "In which we mortals rest awhile. That's what you are telling me, isn't it? Nothing on this earth can ever belong to a single person, because each person is only passing through the earth and must die one day?"

The sadhu nodded solemnly. Then, bowing to the ground, he removed his white beard and saffron turban and his voice changed. "Jahanpanah, forgive me!" he said, in his normal voice. "It was my way of asking you to think about..."

"Birbal, oh, Birbal!" the emperor exclaimed. "You are wiser than any philosopher. Come, come at once to the royal chamber and let us discuss this further. Even emperors are but wayfarers on the path of life, it is clear!"

Scribe's Dream

There was once a poor scribe in the city of Agra. He copied other people's writings and books. He earned barely enough to support his family. But no matter how difficult it was, he and his wife always managed to feed themselves and their children. The scribe was proud of the fact that he had never borrowed a single copper coin. "We must never fall into the hands of the moneylender", he often told his wife. "For if we do, we will surely bee ruined."

The scribe worried so much about his lack of money and his fear to borrowing that his worries even found a place in his dreams. One night he dreamt that he had borrowed one hundred gold coins from the moneylender. He woke up in terror, thinking, "One hundred gold coins! Where, oh where will I ever find such wealth!" Still trembling from his nightmare, he woke his wife and told her all about it. They talked quitly for a while and soon the scribe began to feel better. He was able to lie down again and was soon asleep once more.

The next day, as the scribe's wife drew water from the well at the end of the street on which they lived, she told her friends of her husband's dream. "Imagine!" she exclaimed. "He dreamt that we had borrowed not one or two, but one hundred gold coins from the moneylender!" Her friends laughed with her. A few of them thought it was a very good story and repeated it to their husbands when they got home. The story spread and a few days later, it reached the moneylender's ears. He laughed when he heard it but his eyes begin to glitter greedily. That evening, he put on his turban and, picking up his walking stick, strolled over to the scribe's small house.

"I've come", he announced to the nervous and worried scribe "to remind you of the money you owe me."

"Money?" squeaked the scribe in a panic. "I owe you?"

"Yes bhai", answered the moneylender firmly. "One hundred gold coins. Surely you can not have forgotten?"

"One-one-one h-h-hundred gold coins..." gasped the scribe in a failing voice, tottering to the nearest chair.

The scribe's wife, who had been listening from an inner room, came hurrying out. "But it was only a dream!" she cried. "You cannot ask us to return money that has only been borrowed in a dream!"

"Money is money", the moneylender said, unmoved. "And money borrowed must be returned. You will have to start tomorrow. I am a kind man, a good-hearted man, and so I shall not demand it all back at once.

One gold coin a month will do. And then there will be the interest above that as well." And these words, he stood up and left.

The scribe began to moan softly. His wife sat down suddenly, her knees giving way beneath her. They sat is silent despair. Suddenly, from the depths of her misery, the wife had an idea. "Husband", she said, sitting up straight. "We must beg Raja Birble to help us. Only he can save us from utter ruin". At this, the scribe sat up. Strength and energy seemed to flow into his limbs. "I shall go to his house at once", he said "If anyone can save us it is he."

Birbal listened to the poor scribe's tale of woe. Then he brought out a bag of gold coins and emptied them on to a table. He counted out a hundred and put the rest away, they he placed a large mirror in front of the coins.

"Huzoor, huzoor!" the scribe said in a distressed voice. "I did not come here to beg or to ask you to pay the moneylender. Surely there is another way!"

"There is another", Birbal answered with a smile. "Compose yourself and go and call the moneylender to my haveli. Tell him his debt is about to be paid."

Full of doubts, the scribe hurried to the moneylender's house with Birbal's message. The moneylender smiled when he heard and got up at once to accompany him.

When they arrived at Birbal's house and were shown in, the moneylender spotted the pile of gold coins on the table. He smiled and smiled, unable to take his eyes of them. The mirror behind the coins made the pile look larger and more glittering.

"So the scribe borrowed a hundred gold coins from you in his dream, did he?"

"That is so", replied the moneylender, never taking his eyes off the coins on the table.

"Well", said Birbal. "You may take all the coins in the mirror," said Birbal. The real coins belong to me, but all those in the reflection are yours in return for the dream loan!"

The moneylender knew he had met his match. Without a word, he turned and left the house. Never again did he try to bully the scribe or anyone else in the city of Agra.

Sloth to the Rescue

Once upon a time there was a sloth. All sloths are lazy animals who live in trees.

The other animals of the forest knew that sloths were lazy, but they all thought that this sloth was the largest and laziest of them all, and quite good for nothing.

One day a bird flew into the tree and built her nest beside Sloth. As she sat on her eggs. She twittered to him and sang, making him very happy. He would nibble at nearby leaves and fruit, and listen to the little bird's song, but he was much too lazy to talk to her.

One day, when the baby birds had hatched from the eggs, the mother flew off to find some food. "Take care of my babies," she called to Sloth, but he didn't bother to answer.

While Sloth dozed on his branch, a snake came slithering up the tree looking for baby birds to eat for supper. All around monkeys chattered and birds cheeped warnings, but lazy Sloth slept on.

Nearer and nearer slithered the snake, not noticing Sloth, so still and green as he hung among the leaves.

When the snake saw the baby birds, he hissed a loud hiss right in Sloth's ear. Sloth woke up, for he hated hissing noises, unless he made them himself. He was so angry that he opened his eyes, and saw the slippery snake about to snatch the babies from the nest. Unhooking one hand, he clawed at the snake, who was so surprised that he fell out of the tree and slithered away home.

Then all the birds and monkeys were proud of Sloth, for he was useful, after all.

The Rabbit who Saw the World

Rufty Tufty was a rabbit who wanted to see the world.

"What is the world like?" he said to everyone he met. "It's a big flat place," said his mother. "No, it's square," said his father, and nobody could agree.

One evening Rufty Tufty saw Wise Old Owl sitting in an oak tree. "Mr. Owl," he squeaked. "Can you tell me what the world is like?" The old owl looked wise, then he said, "The world is round."

All night Rufty Tufty dreamed of a round world. As soon as he woke up he said "Goodbye" to his family, and set out to see for himself.

He hadn't gone far-hoppity hop, hoppity hop-when he came to the edge of the woods and saw a fence. Slipping through a gap, Rufty Tufty found himself inside a vegetable garden. As Rufty Tufty looked round the garden, and nibbled at a cabbage, he saw a large round pumpkin. "The world!" he squeaked to himself, and joyfully hopped over the cabbages to the place where the pumpkin stood. Rufty Tufty stretched out a paw and patted the pumpkin. "The world is hard," he thought. Then, giving a jump, he scrambled to the top of the pumpkin and looked all around, then slithered down the other side.

Just then Mr. Brown came home and saw Rufty Tufty near his pumpkin. He shouted and frightened Rufty Tufty so much that the little rabbit scampered back to the Window Woods.

"Mr. Owl is right," he told his mother. "The world is round and I have been all over it!"

The Elephant and the Mahout

Once upon a time a silly king ruled the kingdom of Magadh. He was extremely jealous of anyone who looked better than him, be it a man or a woman, a bird or even a beast!

The king had many elephants, but his favourite was the one and only white elephant. He had all the characteristics of a great human being! He looked almost divine with a six inches wide halo around his body. People's mouths fell open in awe whenever they saw him. The king was so proud of him that he named him Auspicious Elephant.

On festivals, the king was supposed to ride an elephant and take a round of the city. On one such occasion he chose to ride the white elephant. The mahout had decorated him with colourful patterns on his body. The king was pleased to ride such a magnificent elephant. He set out for his usual round of the city. Thousands of people stood on both sides of the streets to greet the king, but when they saw the brilliance of the elephant they began to praise him and ignored the king. He saw the same response of the people everywhere. Some awed by the elephant's halo had thrown flowers and garlands on him. Others struck by his beauty praised him aloud.

The king turned green with jealousy. He could not bear his people paying so much attention to his elephant. He was bursting with envy and anger. The poor elephant was no rival to the king, but an angry and jealous person can hardly think straight! In that state of mind he decided to kill the elephant. However he could not order his killing because the animal had already become so popular. The king thought of a wicked plan. He asked the mahout to cut short the city tour and returned to the palace immediately.

On his way back the king planned such a strategy that the elephant's death would look like an accident. He decided to take the elephant to the top of the mountain Vepulla and then manipulate an accident in the forceful waterfall.

When they reached the palace the king alighted from the elephant and asked he mahout, "So, you have been looking after this elephant. Haven't you?"

"Yes, Your Majesty," said the mahout awaiting further instructions.

"Have you taught him any tricks?" was the next question.

"Oh, I have taught him many tricks," the mahout proudly replied.

"Well, can this elephant climb the mountain Vepulla and reach the peak?"

"Yes, of course," replied the mahout.

'Then take him there. I went to see how, with this heavy body he manages to climb the steep mountain."

The mahout sat on the elephant and they headed towards the mountain. The king followed him with his retinue. In no time, Auspicious Elephant was on the top of the mountain. The king was on his fastest horse but he could not compete with him! The mahout very happily told the king, "Here were are!"

"Very well done!" said the king and quickly added, "Don't come down. Have you taught him to stand on three legs?"

The moment the mahout said, "Yes, I have," the elephant lifted one leg and calmly stood on the three.

"Bravo!" said the king. "Now make him stand on his two hind legs. Do you think he can do that?"

The elephant immediately lifted his front legs and was standing quite comfortably on the two hind legs. The mahout proudly patted him and asked the king, "Can we come down now?"

"Not as yet. I want to watch a few more tricks. Make him turn towards the waterfall and ask him to stand on the front legs," ordered the king.

The elephant now faced the waterfall and lifted his hind legs!

Everyone except the king clapped for him and showered praises on the mahout and the elephant. The king was enraged. His next move was rather dangerous.

"How about standing on one leg?" The king was sure that the elephant would lose his balance and would slip into the waterfall. But this was no ordinary elephant. Like a dainty dancing girl the elephant lifted his three legs and stood only on one with perfect balance of the body.

There were cheers all around but the king was exasperated. He had tried everything but he could not achieve his goal. As the last shot the king ordered an impossible feat. He asked the mahout, "Have you taught him how to stand in the sky?"

Now the mahout became suspicious about the king's intentions. Auspicious Elephant had the powers to fly and he could even stand in the sky. He was about to lift his body above the ground when the mahout whispered in his ears, "This king is asking you to perform all these tricks because he wants to kill you. He has malice and jealousy in his heart. Your life is precious. You are a very special auspicious elephant. Let us fly away to Varanasi. The king of Varanasi is a learned and noble man. Both of us will live happily over there, and serve the king."

"I think you are right. Let me put you on my back." The elephant picked up the mahout with his trunk and safely placed him on his back. Then he concentrated on his positive powers. He told the mahout, "Hold me tight. I am going to take off now."

The elephant with the mahout flew up and stood in the sky facing the king of Magadh. The king realized his mistake. He apologized to the elephant and asked him to come back but it was too late. The mahout's parting words reached the king's ears, "You are not worthy enough to possess such an auspicious elephant. He has extraordinary positive powers. He uses them to give happiness to others. And you have negative tendencies like jealously, arrogance, and conceit. You always want to harm those who are better than you. What a pity, you could not appreciate such a wonderful elephant who was so loyal to you. You even wanted to kill him! Please remember what I am going to tell you now. When a foolish person receives a huge inheritance he destroys it. The same has happened to you."

And they flew away. The king and ministers were speechless. Their mouths fell open.

On reaching Varanasi the elephant stood still in the sky above the palace garden.

"Hey look! There is an elephant in the sky!" screamed a child. The word spread like wildfire. Everyone was out in the streets to see the most unusual phenomenon. The whole city was struck with amazement! The moment this news reached the king he too rushed out. He was a wise and kind king. He addressed the elephant with respect, "I am indeed honoured that such an auspicious elephant and his affectionate mahout have come to Varanasi. If the purpose of your arrival is to help me with looking after my people then please descend here in my garden."

The elephant came down. He and the mahout were greeted with warmth and honour. The king instantly recognized their noble qualities.

Since the elephant was the Bodhisattva and the king had taken good care of him, his good fortune flowed in the king's life. His kingdom expanded, his riches multiplied and he devoted his life to the happiness of his people till the last breath.

3

Tenali Ramalinga

The Vijaya Nagar Empire has a prominent place in the pre-independence period of the Indian subcontinent. Sri Krishna Deva Rayalu, among the rulers of the Vijaya Nagar Kingdom, has transformed his regime into a Golden Era for the history books.

This was possible through Rayalu's courage, righteousness and revered patronage. A Poet named Ramalinga added feathers to the crown of reputation of Rayalu. Tenali Ramalinga or Tenali Rama, as he was famous by, belonged to a town called Tenali and that stuck as his Surname.

Tenali is an important town in Coastal Andhra Pradesh's Guntur District. Tenali is also famous as "Andhra Paris."

Rayalu's court known as 'Bhuvana Vijayam' (Global Victor) was strongly upheld by eight poets called "Ashta Diggajas" (Elephants taking care of all the eight sides). Those eight's combination was the strongest ever and was invincible for any scholar or Master of Arts and Sciences during those days. Tenali Ramalinga shined among the eight as a precious diamond in the diamond studded crown.

Bhuvana Vijayam was host for discussions, arguments, and competitions of the learned and masters, almost all through the rule of the King of Kings Sri Krishna Deva Rayalu.

The historians and chroniclers found a synonymity between Akbar-Birbal and Rayalu-Ramalinga. However, despite the commonness among the two combinations, a small line distincts Birbal and Ramalinga. While Birbal was famous for his delicate and involving humour, Ramalinga was stern and sarcastic in his wit to puncture the shields of proudness the others had.

The records also state that Ramalinga was instrumental in protecting the King Rayalu and his prestige many a time, coming to his rescue in critical situations. A popular story among the commoners narrates how Ramalinga protected the Vijaya Nagar Empire from getting into the clutches of Delhi Sultans through his timely wit interlaced with a perfect strategy.

The most popular stories about the lifestyle, combination, and coordination of Rayalu and Ramalinga spread the message of intellect, time tuning, and strategic stroking besides lively wit and humour.

Birth and Education of Tenali Ramalinga

Bhuvana Vijayam, the royal court of Sri Krishna Deva Rayalu comprised of eight wise and learned men collectively titled as Ashta Diggajas. Tenali Ramalinga was prominently one among them. He was also known as Tenali Ramakrishna.

Tenali Ramalinga was known for his attentiveness, alertness, time tuning, wit, and intelligence. Ramalinga said to be hailing from Tenali town, set it as his surname. In the modern times, Tenali is in Guntur district of Andhra Pradesh on the banks of Holy River Krishna.

Ramalinga was popular as Vikatakavi. Right from his childhood, Ramalinga was centre of attraction among the children of his age groups in the region. His versatile mentality, intellect and aggressiveness brought him laurels and fame.

A Saint passing by, one day watched Ramalinga closely and could identify the 'celestial spark' shining from within him. The Saint, as he was in the devotional path, also recognised the inherent qualities of command and intelligence interlaced in Ramalinga.

The Saint called Ramalinga by name and asked him to accompany to a place. With the natural quality of fearlessness, Ramalinga accepted the invitation without even asking, "where to?" The Saint and Ramalinga walked little away from the crowd and reached Goddess Mahakali Temple in the woods.

Arranging to perform a divine sacrifice to please the Goddess Mahakali, the Saint told Ramalinga, "My dear child! I am growing old and gradually losing the physical strength to perform puja to seek the blessings of the Goddess Mother."

He continued, "You are having all the qualities and blessings of the Mother to please Her and receive Her blessings." Preaching a mantra into Ramalinga's ear the Saint said, "Chant this mantra continuously and pray the Goddess every evening. Put in all your concentration and strength to please the Goddess. Goddess Mahakali will shower many boons on you."

After the sacrifice, the Saint left the place and never returned there. It had become a routine for Ramalinga to chant the mantra and pray the Goddess Mahakali every evening, at the designated Temple in the woods. Time passed by, and Ramalinga continued his prayers.

One day, Goddess Mahakali appeared in front of Ramalinga in the form of a Motherly figure. She was holding two small silver bowls in her palms. She started speaking to Ramalinga in a blissful tone, "My Child! I am pleased with the prayers you had been offering to me. I wish to bless you with a boon. You see the two utensils on my palms. One is filled with milk and the other with curd." Ramalinga was looking at her with shining eyes.

Goddess continued, "If you consume the milk, you will be a great scholar. In case, you wish to take the curd, you will be blessed with riches for all your life. However, take caution. You should take only one of them."

With a lightening speed, Ramalinga not bothered by the Goddess' words grabbed both the bowls from Her hands and gulped down the contents. Goddess Mahakali was puzzled with his act. "What did you do?" She questioned him. Unmoved Ramalinga answered in a requesting tone, " Hey Mother! Goddess Jaganmatha! What is the use of becoming a scholar without any wealth? Similarly, there will not be any purpose to the riches without intelligence. Hence, I thought I should have both of them and drank the contents of both the utensils. Kindly pardon me Mother, if I had done any mistake."

Mother Mahakali was pleased with his frankness and analytical evaluation at that tender age. Imposing some sanctions, She blessed Ramalinga with two boons before She disappeared. She said, "You will have both intellect and wealth. There will be problems with the riches you gather by associating with the rulers. The poetry you author will be filled with uniqueness."

Ramalinga was extremely happy over the happenings. He thought the boons were apt to his nature and versatile psychology.

There were many occasions wherein Ramalinga emerged as a centre of attraction with his versatile acts, wit, and humour filled conversations. Of course, sarcastic element was the prime composition of Ramalinga.

Ramalinga's Entry into Bhuvana Vijayam

Ramalinga was mischievous during his childhood. His childishness cheered some and troubled some. His activities were pleasure to some and humiliation to others. Once, while Ramalinga was pursuing his academics, the provincial ruler visited the school as part of checking the standards of the school.

He questioned the children in the classroom, "Who among you is the most intelligent?"

Silence spread in the class. No child dared to give reply to the King's question. Meanwhile, Ramalinga sprung up from his seat and answered with confidence, "I am the intelligent student in the class." The King appreciated Ramalinga's confidence and courage. Calling him closer, the King enquired him about several things and blessed him, "You will go places my child."

Similarly, Ramalinga grew big and made his presence felt in history.

Ramalinga practised poetry and composition along with command on language and grammar. Mingling with a group of minstrels, he learnt the art of spontaneous poetry composing techniques at Tenali.

He made himself a perfectionist in Sanskrit and Telugu (Andhra) languages. Gradually, in the natural process of growing up, he was married and was blessed with children. From then onwards, he was compelled to find ways to earn a living and feed his family.

He learnt that Vijaya Nagar ruler Sri Krishna Deva Rayalu was a revered patron for poetry and poets besides being a scholar in Kannada, Andhra and Sanskrit languages on par. Every poet and scholar with some skill in the vast Vijaya Nagar empire was longing for getting into the Bhuvana Vijayam, the royal court of Rayalu. Ramalinga headed for Vijaya Nagar with a similar thought and wish in him.

First, he approached the royal priest Thathacharya and laid his heart before him, after exhibiting his skills. Thathacharya promised Ramalinga to introduce him to the King Rayalu. Satisfied Ramalinga spent many a days in vain, waiting for the opportunity.

Ramalinga was vexed and started hunting for alternative ways that would gain entry into the court. He then located Nandi Thimmana, another scholar who had a permanent place in the royal court. Ramalinga approached Thimmana and appeased him with his expertise in spontaneous poetry.

Thimmana felicitated Ramalinga by presenting him with a Kashmir Shawl, which was presented to him by King Rayalu the previous day for his performance.

The next day, Ramalinga adorning the Kashmiri Shawl on his shoulders walked into the royal court. King Rayalu was discussing various issues with the courtiers at that time. Rayalu was surprised to see a stranger in the Shawl that was presented to Thimmana couple of days before. A straight question came from the King Rayalu, "Where did you get this shawl?"

With all humbleness Ramalinga replied, "My King! Thimmana could have satisfied you with his proficiency. I was fortunate enough to please that great personality with my poetry. Thimmana, pleased with my expertise..." he continued, "presented me this shawl felicitating me at his residence. I am wearing this to exhibit my competence."

Sri Krishna Deva Rayalu was impressed by the way Ramalinga presented himself in the court. The King also appreciated the intelligence and presence of mind Ramalinga had. Immediately Rayalu offered a position to Ramalinga in his court.

Thus was the entry of Ramalinga into Bhuvana Vijayam.

Mahabharata and Delhi Sultan's Wish

Mohammedans ruled parts of the subcontinent with Delhi as their capital for over two centuries. Few of the Mohammedan rulers maintained patience towards Hindu rituals and maintained communal harmony encouraging Hindu scholars and prophets.

Delhi was in Adil Shah's rule concurrently while Sri Krishna Deva Rayalu was ruling Vijaya Nagar. A war broke out between the two kingdoms for supremacy over one another. At one stage, both the rulers felt there was a need to establish peace in the region. Adil Shah invited Rayalu to Delhi for finalising the peace treaty.

Hoping to utilise the opportunity to establish a cordial relation between the two empires, Rayalu headed for Delhi with a big team comprising of poets, dancers, scholars and others. At Delhi, Adil Shah gave red carpet welcome to Rayalu. During the pleasant rounds of discussions, Adil Shah urged the scholars and poets from the Rayalu band to recite some sequences from the epic Mahabharata.

The visitors recited several sequences to please the Delhi Sultan. It was then that trouble shot up for the Vijaya Nagar ruler. Adil Shah expressed his wish and requested Rayalu to make his men rewrite the Mahabharata portraying him and his friends as Pandavas and his rivals as Kauravas. The total visiting team was shocked to hear the Sultan. They somehow managed to close the day's meeting immediately.

Rayalu was worried about the development. He called for an emergency meeting with the learned persons of his team. In the meeting, he sought suggestions from them to avert the problem. Everyone started scratching their heads to find an amicable solution. None could come out with any concrete proposal. After watching all this, suddenly Ramalinga raised and put his proposal before Rayalu.

He said, "My Lord! I think there is not much for you or us to get so much worried and burdened about the Delhi Sultan's wish about Mahabharata. You please leave the problem onto my shoulders and have a relaxed sleep. I will solve the problem without any problem." The King Rayalu had his own doubts about the safety of the kingdom and its people.

"Ramalinga..." Rayalu said, "...I am aware that you are a genius. However, it is not a common situation. Dealing with the Delhi Sultan is not an easy job. It is similar to fete on the edge of a sword. You should be very careful!" He was worried that if the problem was not dealt properly, there was a chance that Delhi Sultan might declare a war on Vijaya Nagar.

Ramalinga was stiff to his argument and assured everyone to leave the matter to him. The big heads of the meeting could not comprehend how Ramalinga was confident that he could solve this 'so easily!' Anyway, they told each other, as we could not come out with any proposal for the solution, let him handle this. The meeting finally nominated Ramalinga to take care of the situation.

Next morning, the court was packed with both the rulers and their henchmen. Adil Shah recalled his wish about re-composing of the Mahabharata. Ramalinga rose from his seat and saluted the Sultan. "Huzoor! All of our poets are into the job assigned by your majesty's wish. However, every one of us is stuck at one specific issue. It is not proper for us to discuss the subject in the court. If you can kindly permit me, I wish to present the poking issue before you in private."

Adil Shah thought that there should really be some problem and consented for the one-on-one meeting with Ramalinga in a separate room. Ramalinga folding hands and presenting all respects to the Sultan in his words started, "Your Highness! You are the king of kings! It was our pleasure to know about your inclination about our epics like Mahabharata. The poets and scholars started re-composing the whole epic, in accordance to your majesty's wish. You are being portrayed as Dharmaraja, eldest of Pandavas and your friends as Bhima, Arjuna, Nakula and Sahadeva."

Ramalinga paused a second and continued, "This is where we had to scratch our brains..." However he was not forth coming with the problem. Adil Shah waited and when it was clear that he has to get it out of Ramalinga he ordered, "What is the problem? Tell me clearly and quickly."

"You are aware Huzoor! That Pandavas are five. All the five were married to Draupadi and were sharing her equally..." Ramalinga stressed, "We are unable to portray your image as Dharmaraja in this regard, thinking about the prestige of the King of Kings...."

Long before Ramalinga could complete, Adil Shah hastened to say, "Stop this nonsense now. I cannot take this anymore. Stop rewriting Mahabharata immediately. I can never accept this."

Ramalinga tried to say... "Huzoor! We started to work as per your wish...now, how can we turn away from the word given to you by us...we..." "Look Poet!" Adil Shah raised his voice, "you should drop the Mahabharata topic as of now if you wish the friendship and cooperation between the two kingdoms to last long. Is that clear" and walked off the room.

Ramalinga bubbling with joy returned to his King Rayalu and his bandwagon of delegation and explained the whole sequence. Everyone including Rayalu appreciated the sharp intelligence and presence of mind Ramalinga had in solving the toughest problem just like that!

Thousand Gold Coins and a Handful Grain

Simhapuri was a prominent town in the Vijaya Nagar empire. There lived a stunning beauty named Vidyullatha. She was a rich lady and well versed with prose, poetry and composition besides dance and music. Vidyullatha was famous as a proud woman in the region.

A hoarding appeared on the compound wall of the woman's house quoting as, "A reward of one thousand gold coins would be presented to those who can win over the Lady in the house. The competitors are required to prove their upper hand in humour, wit and scholarship." This became a prestigious issue for the scholars in the region.

Many responded to the open invitation and barged into her house, individually, to test their fate through the fete. Surprisingly, everyone whoever walked into Vidyullatha's house lost in the battle and came out with chins down. The list of losers was steadily growing and after sometime there were no takers to the invitation.

Days were passing like this. One morning, a vendor with a load of firewood on his head started shouting in front of her house, "Firewood...strong firewood...excess heat generating firewood..." he continued the sequence for sometime. Vidyullatha thinking that his noise was growing unbearable walked on to the threshold and enquired, "How much do you sell the load for?"

An instant reply came from the vendor, "I will not sell this for money. If you can give me a handful grain I will give you all the load." Assuring him to give more grains, Vidyullatha ordered him to dump the load in the backyard and return to collect the grains.

The vendor unloaded the weight off his head then and there started to argue, "There is no bargain in this deal Madam! I will sell this to you only if you can give me a handful grain, did you get it" he stressed, "a handful grain." The rich woman got disgusted with the vendor's behaviour, "Hey you bloody vendor. Stop crying, I will give you what you wanted." She said, "throw them in the backyard and come here."

The Vendor was adamant and made his firewood load's price much more clearer, "There is no change in the deal Madam. I said a handful grain...that means nothing more or less...it should be a handful grain. If you cannot pay the price, you should pay me one thousand gold coins and wipe the invitation hoarding on the compound wall."

Vidyullatha yelled at him, "What nonsense are you trying to talk?" The vendor replied on par with her, "There is not any nonsense. I told you the price, you agreed for it and now if you cannot pay the price, stand by my wish. You should give the one thousand gold coins. That is it."

The fire broke out between Vidyullatha and the firewood vendor. Both started arguing and shouting at each other. The local people started gathering in front of the house to witness and know what is happening and why is the Lady was having a tiff with an ordinary vendor. Tired of shouting, both resorted to approach the provincial Court of Law for justice.

Vidyullatha presented her argument, "My Lord! This firewood vendor must have gone crazy. He is not ready to accede to my offer, though I wished to pay him more. He is sticking to his senseless argument to have a handful grain. He demands later for payment of a thousand gold coins and wiping away the invitation hoarding. I plead for justice."

The Judge looked at the vendor and asked him what was his problem. Folding hands the vendor started in a humble manner, "Yes Your Majesty. She was right to some extent. However, I am not crazy. I informed her beforehand that the load of firewood would cost her a handful grain."

He continued innocently, "When I was clear about a handful grain, she must have understood that I needed handful of grains. That was her mistake to mistake my quote for a handful grain. It means, one grain that fills the hand."

What more? Vidyullatha was speechless. Obviously, the verdict was in favour of the vendor. Vidyullatha was unable to comprehend that a handful grain meant so much. Shocked with the development and the judgement, she was compelled to pay him one thousand gold coins and wipe off the invitation from the compound wall.

The people of the region knew about this and told themselves that the years old proudness of Vidyullatha was shattered to pieces in a single stroke. By the way, the vendor was Tenali Ramalinga.

On hearing about the problem Vidyullatha created with her hoarding, Ramalinga took due permission from the King

Rayalu to take her to task. In the guise of firewood vendor, Ramalinga fulfilled his responsibility in all success.

The Last Wish-Mango Fruit

Once when King Sri Krishna Deva Rayalu was ruling the Vijaya Nagar Empire, the royal mother fell sick and was bedridden. The medical professionals of the court declared that there was no chance for her to survive this episode and that she grew too old to respond to any medication.

One morning, she summoned Rayalu to her presence. "My Dear Son! I realise that I am close to death's door. I also do not have any hopes that my health would become better. However, I have a last wish."

She paused and asked, "Can you accomplish it for me before my soul is taken away?"

Rayalu was the King of Kings. His mother was on the deathbed, expressing her last wish. How could he turn away from it? He gently said, "Mother! Please tell me I will definitely accomplish your last wish" he assured.

"I..." she added, "...wish to eat a mango fruit, can you get me one?" in a feeble tone the mother asked Rayalu.

It was early summer. Trees had just started bearing tender fruits. There was no guarantee that royal mother would live until the tender ones ripened on the tree, Rayalu thought. It was also an insult to his royalty, if he was unable to fulfil his mother's last wish.

Immediately the King ordered his soldiers to scan through the fields of the kingdom and bring some ripe mangoes at any cost, immediately. The soldiers plunged into action. They did their best and returned with a basket filled with ripe mangoes. Eventually, just before the soldiers could place the basket before their King, king's mother breathed her last.

Rayalu was taken aback, for being unable to fulfil the last wish more than for her demise. He was shook deeply with the thought that his mother was dead even before her quench for mangoes was fulfilled. He slowly started to sink day after the day with the thoughts that were ripping him.

Rayalu invited Royal Master Thathacharya, explained his struggle, and sought an advice that would take the suffering off from him.

Thathacharya thought for a while and told the King, "My king! Your mother was fond of giving alms to the poor and needy. Her soul would rest in peace, if you can fulfil her last wish through donations. Order for preparing mangoes with gold and distribute them to Brahmins of the country."

The news spread like wildfire in the kingdom that Rayalu was doling out golden mangoes to Brahmins in the memory of his mother. Brahmins from all over the empire started flooding into the capital to accept the golden mango from the King. Day in and out, long queues were always seen only to add people to its tail.

With this, the gold reserves in the exchequer were melting down rapidly. Rayalu not bothering about the consequences was incessantly involved in donating golden mangoes to the Brahmins. He never heeded to the pleas and warnings of the Chief Minister Thimmarusu in this regard.

Thimmarusu was in confusion and did not know how to stop the King. He approached Ramalinga and urged for a solution to this in the interest of the kingdom and its people. Ramalinga assured Thimmarusu that he would check it at the earliest. "Go home and have a sound night sleep, Chief Minister. Everything will be alright by tomorrow evening" Ramalinga sent off Thimmarusu.

Next morning, Ramalinga went near the long queues and watched what was happening. He then selected a yard close to the queues and sat there, ordering the queue maintenance persons to send each of the Brahmins to him before sending him to Rayalu for the golden mango.

Everyone knew that Ramalinga was one of the close associates of the King. They thought that Ramalinga was doing so on the orders of the King and started sending the Brahmins first to Ramalinga before sending them into the palace.

Ramalinga told every Brahmin that there was a slight amendment to the donation process. "The King Rayalu wished to donate the golden mangoes to those who bore a blister from him" Ramalinga explained. Brahmins desirous of the gold first had a burn on their backs and went for the King's gold.

This went on until afternoon. In the later afternoon, one Brahmin pleaded Ramalinga to give him two burns and two golden mangoes. Ramalinga immediately fulfilled the Brahmins wish.

Then the Brahmin approached Rayalu. As usual, Rayalu handed him one mango. The Brahmin immediately requested the King, "My Lord! I had two burns please give me two golden mangoes."

The King Rayalu did not understand what was happening. He enquired, "What burns?" Then the Brahmin narrated the entire story about Ramalinga and burns to Rayalu.

The King shivering with anger called for Ramalinga and questioned him, "Ramalinga, what is happening. Why are you doing this brutality on these poor and innocent Brahmins?"

Ramalinga very politely and innocently, as if nothing was amiss, explained. "My Dear King! I am an unlucky person. Recently my mother succumbed to a chronic disease. She wished all during her bed ridden period to cauterise her back so that she could become healthy and live longer."

Wiping the tears dropping on his cheeks, Ramalinga continued, "Probably she would have lived. Nevertheless, I did not heed to her requests. She died with it on her lips. I thought of presenting it to the Brahmins, as I failed to fulfil my mother's last wish.

However, me being a poor man cannot invite such huge number of Brahmins. Anyway, all of these had come on your invitation and I am trying to fulfil my mother's last wish in this manner. With all due respects to the King, I beg for pardon for my deeds, if I am wrong."

Rayalu analysed that Ramalinga was attempting to teach his a lesson. He then recalled Thimmarusu's pleas about the drastically dropping gold reserves in the exchequer.

Appreciating the presence of mind and loyalty, Rayalu immediately stopped the programme.

The Secret of Weaving Invisible Fabric

A gorgeous woman entered the royal court of Sri Krishna Deva Rayalu when he was busy with the courtiers. With all her pleasing manners, attire and conversation, she attracted the gathering that day. After a little dialogue with the King and his prime staff, she took out the most delicate and flimsiest sari from a small box that would hardly be sufficient to place a pair of ear-tops.

Exhibiting the saree to the royal court attendants, she addressed the king, "King of Kings! A group of divine weavers are working for me. They can weave similar delicate, thinnest and beautiful saris. They are capable of weaving celestial fabric, which cannot be seen with the naked eye.

"If we have your majesty's blessings and support in addition to appropriate allocation of funds, they can do wonders and exhibit before the honourable King."

Satisfied with the exhibit, Rayalu believed her words. Allotting required funds for weaving the celestial fabric, Rayalu asked her to get the job done with thorough research and of course within the year.

The gorgeous woman and her weavers enjoyed the comforts and treatment extended by the King to the royal court guests for one year. Even after the lapse of one year, there was no news from the woman about the research nor the weavers exhibited any products before the King.

Rayalu ordered some of his employees to inspect the weavers' guesthouse and enquire about the weaving of celestial fabric that was fit to be worn by the Gods. The royal employees at once left for the guesthouse.

The woman welcomed the inspectors and took them to the location where the weavers were working seriously not even noticing the presence of guests in the room. The inspectors were aghast when they entered the room. There were no looms, no thread spools, not even a string of thread in the room. All the weavers sitting there were pretending to draw threads and weave. Every act was as if they were weaving something, with empty hands. The inspectors could not realise what was happening there. They asked the woman about the invisible fabric. She threw a lovely smile at them and told in a low husky voice. "Gentlemen, the invisible or celestial fabric is visible to only those who are pure along with purity of their parents. Of course, I believe that you can see the clarity of design and beauty of the craftsmanship of our weavers."

The inspectors were worried of being branded as sinners, if they spoke truth about what they saw. They did not dare to probe against the guests. Moreover, they appreciated the delicacy, accuracy, and what not about the work being done at the guesthouse. They stood by the roles they played at the guesthouse, in front of the King Rayalu too.

The feedback of the employees augmented the enthusiasm of Rayalu. He was eagerly waiting for the finished products to be exhibited before him and the royal court members. Some days later, Rayalu ordered his men to bring the weavers to his court along with the finished products.

An unusually big gathering assembled in the royal court to witness the celestial fabric exhibition. As part of the introductory speech, the weavers addressed the gathering. They pointed out that the fabric was made from various divine materials. Hence, they would be visible only to those who are clean by soul along with purity of their parents. The whole gathering went silent for a moment, as no one could see any fabric in the hands of the weavers. Still, they maintained, out of fear of humiliation, that they were able to view the exhibit, started applauding the beauty, and praised the weavers.

Just then, King Rayalu accompanied by Ramalinga, entered the court to witness the exhibition. Weavers repeated their standard phrases. Rayalu stared at the hands of the weavers for a moment and whispered to Ramalinga, "I regret to say, I cannot see any material in their hands. Is that my own sin or my parents'?" "Nothing comes to be visible in thin air, My Lord!" replied Ramalinga.

Rayalu grew suspicious, "What do you mean?" he asked. Ramalinga in a low tone audible only to the King said, "King of Kings! These weavers are cheating our eyes and brains with their deceptive speech."

Rayalu urged Ramalinga to make public, the cheating of the weavers. Ramalinga turned towards the gorgeous woman and in an astoundingly inquisitive tone told her, "What a beauty! How rich are these textiles, Lady. The King of Kings Rayalu is anxious to view your stepped up decorum, if you wear those celestial material."

The lady understood that Ramalinga deciphered the secret of invisible weaving. She was confused for a moment. She could neither disregard the King's order nor stand nude in the crowded court in the guise of wearing something, which actually was nothing. She thought that the only way out would be to fall on the King's feet pleading mercy. Immediately she did so begging for pardon. This was how Ramalinga was once again instrumental in protecting his King.

Since then, nudity is being referred as wearing divine clothes.

Tenali Ramalingam and the Two Thieves

It was the practice of King Sri Krishna Deva Rayalu to visit the jails once a while and review the living standards of the convicted. During one of his visits, two of the jail inmates pleaded for cutting down their punishment period.

They explained that theft was one of the 64 arts in the epics and Vedas and started defining the art of stealing. However, they argued that they would shed the lifestyle and shift for one or the other profession to eke out their living. Rayalu thought for a moment brushing his moustache royally.

"It's alright thieves. First let me know about your expertise in the art and then decide. You both have to burgle at Ramalinga's house and return. If you emerge successful, then you will be set free immediately" Rayalu ordered them. "Hey you both listen. You should not deliver any physical blows to the households, take care" he added one condition.

The same night they were 'officially' let out for robbing Ramalinga's residence. Ramalinga was nurturing a beautiful backyard garden fondly. The thieves' duo crossed over the backyard compound wall and took shelter in the bean bushes to watch the surroundings first.

Ramalinga was not just another ordinary man in the crowd. He spotted the duo hiding in the bushes. He called his wife loudly, "My dear wife! Come here fast. The whole town is on fire with the news about some convicts jumping jail and are said to be at large well within the town. We should immediately protect all our jewellery and other valuables..." watching carefully around the bushes, increasing the pitch "...bring that bundle with all our gold and jewellery."

A minute later, Ramalinga and his wife with great effort brought a heavy bundle into the backyard and dropped it into the well. Dhhhhhhhhhhhabbbb....spppppplsh sounds of a heavy weight dropping into the water in the well echoed for few seconds. The thieves looked at each other with sparkles in their eyes.

They never thought it would be so easy to rob Ramalinga. Meanwhile, the couple went inside the house and closed the door. After sometime, snores were heard from the bedroom of the house. Slowly the thieves drew themselves out of the bushes, taking care they do not make any noise and went close to the well. While one of them stood guard, the other one slipped into the well. In a minute, the thief came out of the well and discussed with the other that there is much water in the well. The jewellery bundle cannot be taken out as it is. It would be better if some water was drawn out to snatch away the bundle, they decided.

Immediately they started drawing water from the well one after the other bucket. Water started flowing continuously in the backyard spreading all the ways. In the shade of trees and darkness, Ramalinga covering his head with a shawl took one farm tool and started guiding the water to the plants and trees in the yard. As it was too dark and the thieves were concentrating on drawing the water alone, they did not notice Ramalinga doing this.

After drawing water from the well for three to four hours continuously, the thieves were tired. One of them again went into the well and came back, "You, come I need help to bring the bundle out, it is too heavy." Both of them slipped into the well together again. With great effort both of them brought the bundle out and fell on the ground like logs of woods after opening it.

To their dismay, it was not a bundle of jewellery but a bundle of small boulders and rocks. They never understood until then that Ramalinga hid his precious items somewhere in the house and dropped this into the well.

Ramalinga called them, "Hey dear thieves! Please draw few more buckets of water from the well. Only two of the plants are to be watered. Please hurry up it is close to dawn. Kindly help me quick and little more" like sprinkling chillies on the wounds of burglars.

Both of them were stunned on hearing Ramalinga's voice. They told each other, "Run! It is Ramalinga!" and sped away crossing the wall with all the tired bodies.

The so-called argument of the thieves about the art of stealing and their expertise did not work on Ramalinga at least.

Ramalinga Dares to Criticise Rayalu's Composition

Sri Krishna Deva Rayalu and his court Bhuvana Vijayam comprising Ashta Diggajas was taken as a model by many kings and kingdoms in and out of the Indian subcontinent. Rayalu was known for his fondness towards literature and his patronage towards poets and composers.

The Ashta Diggajas in Bhuvana Vijayam are Allasani Peddana, Nandi Thimmana, Dhurjati, Madayya Gari Mallana, Pingali Surana, Tenali Rama Krishnudu, Ayyala Raju Rama Bhadrudu and Rama Raja Bhushanudu.

Rayalu was compared to one of the greatest ever kings of the country King Bhoja, for his inclination towards developing literature and composition. Rayalu himself was a scholar in Sanskrit, Telugu (Andhra) and Kannada. Most famous among the Telugu compositions of Rayalu were Amuktha Malyada, and Vishnu Chitheeyamu. Both the compositions were based on God Vishnu's devotees.

Life sketch of devotee Vishnu Chitha, Goda Devi's devotion and God's testing were the key elements. Goda Devi was a devotee of Lord Krishna right from her childhood. She adored Him ad finally she marries Lord Krishna. The heartfelt expressions of Goda Devi about the Lord Krishna and her lifestyle were decoratively in Amuktha Malyada. Though Amuktha Malyada was written in Telugu, it was majorly filled with usages of Sanskrit language and was not generally understandable by the common people. However, the scholars and persons with proficiency in Sanskrit applauded the book. They appreciated the expression of feelings, narration style and presentations of grammar and usages.

A criticism was in circulation about Amuktha Malyada during those days. It was said that Allasani Peddana authored it and named to be written by Rayalu. Critics also cited a line from sonnets written in both Amuktha Malyada and Manu Charithram starting with "Neela Meghamu Daalu Deelu Cheyu Gajalu...".

Allasani Peddana wrote Manu Charitram, sometime later to Rayalu writing Amuktha Malyada. There was also a discussion that Allasani Peddana with high regards to King Rayalu took the sonnet and presented it as it was written in Amuktha Malyada. Anyway, the criticism and discussion for and against Amuktha Malyada went on for quite sometime.

One day, Rayalu during the literature discussion in Bhuvana Vijayam asked the present poets and experts to comment over Amuktha Malyada. No one knew what the King actually wished to hear from the gathering. Almost all the renowned poets and scholars did not dare comment either for or against the book of Rayalu, thinking not to lose the place and position in the Bhuvana Vijayam.

Waiting for some time, Ramalinga raised. In a single sentence he said that he carried no two feelings about the book.

He furthered, "My Lord! A right critic will never bother who the author was. The critic will always be concentrating about the subject, presentation, narration and standards of language. Any criticism should be based on the occasion. It is also to be recalled that for any matter there definitely will be both constructive and destructive criticism in the world."

Rayalu asked Ramalinga to first explain the lacunae in the book. Ramalinga commented there were one or two usages that were irrelevant to the context of the situation. Rayalu was irritated on listening this. "Ramakrishna! Don't you note the circumstances to wit on? I'm not convinced with your sarcastic comment. Refer to the text and pass the comment carefully quoting it," roared the King.

The whole court was silent and the King's tone echoed in. Ramalinga took out a copy of Amuktha Malyada and recited a stanza from the text,

"*Aanishtha nidhi geha seema nadu reyalinchinan mroyunem,*

the nagendra sayananu punya kathalum divya prabandhanu sam,

dhana dhyanamu naasthi sakaluhuthansthushna thanasthapu va,

po nasthyo danaleshtavam chaknapaya bhokthavya mastalkulu"

"Referring to the last two lines of the above stanza I recited, I feel that it was like asking a guest to have lunch from a plate that is not served with any eatables. The situation is different here and this explains something different, which is irrelevant" said Ramalinga. All the members of the Bhuvana Vijayam looked at Ramalinga appreciating. Still, they were worried what would be the reaction of King Rayalu on this straight criticism on his book.

Rayalu reacted strange to the expectations of the courtiers. With his natural affection and inclination to constructive criticism and especially scholars, "Ramalinga! That was good to note your evaluation style. You are right. There definitely will be constructive and destructive criticisms on any material. I request all the members of the Bhuvana Vijayam to take

Ramalinga as model and express their comments freely on any book or composition. There is no need to consider who is the author and what is his or her status."

The courtiers continued to shower their appreciations long even after the court was adjourned for the day.

This was the courage, cleverness and presence of mind Ramalinga had.

Ramalinga Humiliates Rama Raja Bhushana

It was one of those finest days at Bhuvana Vijayam. King Rayalu along with his Ashta Diggajas was enjoying the literary discussion session that day.

Rama Raja Bhushana was known to be a romantic poet, authoring prose and poetry reciting women and their beauty. Rayalu asked Rama Raja Bhushana to frame a stanza on the beauty of women, extempore.

Rama Raja Bhushana rose from his seat and thought for a second or two and immediately composed,

"Naanaa soona vithavai vaasanala naa ghraaenchu saarangame

Laa nannolla datanchu gandha phalithabal, kakan bondiyo

Shaa naasaa kruthii booni sarva sumassourabha samvasamai

Poonen brekshana maalika madhukaree punjambui lirvankalakun"

Rayalu was impressed about the way Rama Raja Bhushana described the beauty of woman instantly. Pleased over, Rayalu appreciated him and felicitated him with one thousand gold coins.

Ramalinga, as everyone knows is not for sitting quite on any happening. He sprung off his seat to say, "My Lord, Rama Raja Bhushana bought this poem from Nandi Thimmanna for one thousand gold coins. It is surprising how come you know the exact price of the deal. It would not be profitable to him if you pay him exactly the same price at which he purchased..."

Hearing this the total gathering immersed in laughter. Rama Raja Bhushana had no way to counter Ramalinga, though he wished to, as the damage was already done. He could only manage sitting calm grinding his teeth on Ramalinga.

Some days later, one fine evening Rama Raja Bhushana along with his disciple was passing through the street in which Nandi Thimmana's residence was located. A subject discussion was going on in Thimmana's house during that time. Rama Raja Bhushana could locate Ramalinga from distance, participating in the discussions.

Loudly Rama Raja Bhushana told his disciple describing the session as,

"Vaakila Kaavali Thimmana

Vaakita Kavi Koti Maadhavakitakaade"

The sarcastic poetry described that the session was like an assembly of pigs that gathered near the threshold of Nandi Thimmana.

Hearing this, Ramalinga picked up the tone in which Rama Raja Bhushana was speaking. Immediately he stopped the discussion and said,

"Prakrutha, Sanskrutha, Ghaarjhura

mookee krutha kukavi thunga mustha thathikin

Vaakila Kaavali Thimmana

Vaakita Kavi Koti Maadhavakitakaade"

This meant that the discussion session would resemble similar to the gathering of pigs, for those who composes prose and poetry with a mixture of nonsense, brutal language, and irrelevant issues.

Rama Raja Bhushana taking the meaning immediately rushed off the place along with his disciple.

That was how Ramalinga humiliated Rama Raja Bhushana.

The Weird Wells' Wedding Invitation

During the period when Sri Krishna Deva Rayalu was ruling the Vijaya Nagar Empire with Hampi as his capital,

Mohammedan Sultans were ruling Delhi. The Sultans were powerful and were ruling many parts of Northern India. They were always attempting to invade on Hindu ruled kingdoms and grab them into their fold. For declaring war the Sultans used to find one or the other ploy.

The Delhi Sultan once got an idea to insult and instantly he sent a wedding invitation to Sri Krishna Deva Rayalu. Going through the contents of the invitation, the royal court Bhuvana Vijayam and the King Rayalu went speechless. The invitation read as:

Wedding Invitation

We proposed to perform marriage to the newly dug Well in our kingdom

We have the pleasure of inviting all the wells in your kingdom to attend the ritual and their (the wells) presence is solicited.

Delhi

Date:XX/XX/XXXX

Sd/-

The Sultan of Delhi.

The tremor did not stop there. A warning letter was attached along with the invitation. The warning letter said that in case the King failed to send all the wells in the concerned kingdom, such action would be treated as an insult and will be liable to face the fury of the Delhi sultan.

Rayalu, on receiving the invitation along with the letter through a personal messenger from the Sultan of Delhi could not understand what to do about this invitation. This is because; everyone knew that sending wells from one place to another is practically above impossible. Rayalu was in total confusion what to do and what to reply. Thinking for sometime to find a solution to this problem, in vain, Rayalu forwarded the puzzling wedding invitation and warning letter to the Chief Minister Thimmarusu and sent a message to come out with a viable solution.

Thimmarusu found the invitation to be too strange and the problem like a complex puzzle. What an invitation? Thimmarusu thought, inviting wells of Vijaya Nagar Empire to the wedding of a well at Delhi! Even Thimmarusu could not draw out any thought close to solution that can be effective in avoiding any rift between the two kingdoms.

Thimmarusu approached King Rayalu and expressed his inability to draw out any solution. Rayalu was much more tensed on hearing his Chief Minister. Then, Thimmarusu convinced Rayalu that there was no need to get so much worried, as there is a man in the service of the King, who can draw a best amicable equation.

Rayalu asked about the person Thimmarusu was referring to. Immediately, Thimmarusu told the King that it was none other than poet Ramalinga.

Taking the King's permission, Thimmarusu headed to Ramalinga's residence and explained the whole sequence along with the worries of the King Rayalu. Ramalinga in a cool fashion studied the invitation and the warning letter. He told Thimmarusu, "Dear Chief Minister Thimmarusu!

The Delhi Sultan must be attempting to humiliate the Hindu rituals and customs. You know Hindus have a ritual of performing enlivening (Prathistha) to the newly dug wells. A wonderful thought must have struck the Sultan's mind to perform marriage to the well instead of prathistha to the well."

He continued thinking for a moment, "There is no problem either with the invitation or the warning letter. There is nothing to worry. You go home peacefully and relax." Ramalinga assured Thimmarusu, "I will give out the best solution to this problem in the Bhuvana Vijayam tomorrow."

As usual, the Bhuvana Vijayam started its session the next morning, but there was no charm or shine in anyone's face including the King Rayalu. All of them were worried about the solution to the Delhi Sultan's created problem. Amid the gloomy atmosphere, Ramalinga rose from his seat and started reading a reply prepared by him on behalf of King Rayalu to Delhi Sultan,

"To His Excellency, the Sultan of Delhi...

We acknowledge your invitation inviting our wells for the wedding of a well in your kingdom. We are glad and grateful that you remembered us for the memorable occasion. On receiving your invitation, we immediately read the message to all the wells in our Kingdom.

Those wells are resenting your wells, as they did not attend their (wells in Vijaya Nagar Empire) wedding.

Hence, we keep you informed that if your wells personally come to Vijaya Nagar and invite, our wells will definitely oblige the invitation. Therefore, you are requested to send your wells here to invite our wells personally to the wedding ritual. Once your wells come here, our wells and we together will come to Delhi for the wedding.

Hoping to welcome your wells at the earliest,

Vijaya Nagaram (Hampi)

Date:XX/XX/XXXX

Yours' sincerely,

Sri Krishna Deva Rayalu,

"Vijaya Nagar Ruler"

The total gathering of the Bhuvana Vijayam cheered at once on hearing the reply intellectually composed by Ramalinga and appreciated him.

This reply was sent to Delhi Sultan with a personal messenger. Sultan of Delhi was shocked with the reply received and questioned the messenger, "how can we send the wells with you?"

Receiving no reply from the messenger, without any second thought Sultan dropped the proposals of humiliating Hindu rituals along with the thought of waging war unnecessarily on Hindu ruled kingdoms.

Moreover, the Sultan appreciating the intelligence and wit King Rayalu had in replying his invitation and warning, sent many gifts and Farmans with the messenger to Rayalu.

How an Elephants' Fleet Junks in a Mosquito's Throat?

Among the Ashta Diggajas in the Bhuvana Vijayam of Sri Krishna Deva Rayalu, the King for his ingenuity, quick wittedness, and fast filling of stanzas when at test particularly favoured Ramalinga. Rayalu was renowned as Andhra Bhoja and Poets' Paradise. With his inherent qualities of wit and sarcasm, Ramalinga was growing big and closer to Rayalu day after day. With no change in the rule, the more you grow the more envious you become, the other courtiers like Rama Raja Bhushana were against the growth of Ramalinga's association with the King Rayalu. Whenever there is a possibility, those courtiers, and Rama Raja Bhushana had been working out for damaging Ramalinga's image and sling mud on him before the King. Ramalinga efficiently countered these efforts and trials of courtiers all the time.

At one stage, as these personalities were unable to compete with Ramalinga in wit and ingenuity decided to humiliate Ramalinga. They handed over the responsibility of insulting Ramalinga to the main entrance guards. Those poor soldiers were lured by the bribe amount courtiers had offered them. A line was given to those guards for stopping Ramalinga at the entrance itself. The line was "Kunjara Yudhambu Doma Kuthuka Jochen" meaning an elephants' fleet is stuck in a mosquito's throat.

Ramalinga as usual was walking into the Bhuvana Vijayam premises and the guards stopped him. He questioned why were they blocking the way. The soldiers told Ramalinga about the line and asked him to enter the premises only after reciting the first three lines for the last line they recited to him. Ramalinga boiled and trembled with anger on those soldiers. Immediately he understood what and who was behind the soldiers. With harsh words he completed reciting,

"Ganjayi Thravi Thurakala

Sanjathamu Goodi Kallu Chavi Gonnava?

Lanjala Kodaka! Yekkadara!

Kunjara Yudhambu Doma Kuthuka Jochen."

Long before those guards could understand the meaning of the poem, Ramalinga walked stiff into the main court hall.

After sometime, while the King Rayalu was into one of the pleasure rounds of literary discussions, the guards entered the hall and complained that Ramalinga disgraced them with the poem at the main entrance. After listening to all the details narrated by the guards, Rayalu ordered Ramalinga to extempore compose a poem taking the same end line with a situation in Mahabharatha.

Ramalinga raised from his seat and after salutations to the King Rayalu recited,

"Ranja Chedi Pandavulari

Bhanjanulai Viratu Golva Palapadirakata!

Sanjaya! Vidhinemandunu

Kunjara Yudhambu Doma Kuthuka Jochen!"

Pandavas in Mahabharatha are like a fleet of powerful elephants. Losing in the gamble with Kauravas, they had to live incognito for some time. During this period they served a weak ruler Virata. By all Gods! It is the fate of those Pandavas to serve such a weak person in spite of being renowned warriors. This is similar to a fleet of strong elephants being stuck in the throat of a small mosquito.

Rayalu clapped in all praise of Ramalinga for his ingenuity and wit filled narration. In the full house, Rayalu hugged Ramalinga and appreciated him agreeing that Ramalinga's words are like double-edged swords. This state of affairs brought Ramalinga more close to Rayalu.

All the attempts to trap Ramalinga and cut down his image before the King Rayalu by the envied courtiers and poet Rama Raja Bhushana blew off like a piece of raw cotton in Ramalinga's intelligence whirlwind.

Ramalinaga and Ramayana Recital

Vikrama Simhapuri (presently Nellore town) was part of Vijaya Nagar Empire under the rule of Sri Krishna Deva Rayalu. This place was famous for wicked and cunning women. These women with their uncommon intelligence added to their beauty and appeal used to defeat scholars and experts to transform as their domestic slaves and servants.

A prostitute Kanchana Mala among them was too notorious in this regard. In the name of satisfying Ramayana recital, she framed twisty and wicked rules, which made all the competitors lose in their 'battle' against the woman.

The lady's "reputation" along with her condition filled Ramayana recital issue spread all over the region and no one was dared to step into her house to compete with her. In case any one ventured, lured by the stunning beauty of Kanchana Mala they too were definite to lose and become either a slave or a servant to her.

One day, Ramalinga visited Vikrama Simhapuri on his personal accomplishments. Completing his job, he sat with some scholars, reputed persons of the locality, and enquired about the happenings and specialities of the town. The gathering in a synchronised tone explained Ramalinga about Kanchana Mala and her urge for satisfactory recital of Ramayana epic. One of the associates there said that, "it was her celestial beauty and the quantity of reward that was driving scholars to her, who are finally seen serving her losing the competition."

One of the senior and aged poet of the region told Tenali Ramalinga cursing her, "she is not at all a woman, and she is wicked of the wicked. It is you, the right person, to defeat and smash her proudness."

He continued, "You should teach her a right lesson and release all the scholars suffering in her service."

Ramalinga thought, 'Oh! Kanchana Mala is that highly impious.' He said to the persons around him, "That being the case, I should definitely compete with her...by the way...what is the test she is winning on?" he questioned. One of them explained that she demands the competitor to recite Ramayana and satisfy her. Every time she says the recital was not satisfactory and orders the competitor to become her slave." "Poor fellows, what they can do? The condition of the test was to take out a word 'satisfied' from her after the performance."

"Enough! It is alright!" Ramalinga told all of them, "She just needs to be satisfied with a Ramayana concert, I will do it. One of you keep her informed about my willingness to satisfy her" Ramalinga said and headed towards his accommodation. Not one, but all of them got up to inform Kanchana Mala about Ramalinga's compliance to recite Ramayana at her residence thinking, 'Yes! Now the time has come for breaking her.'

Ramalinga, in the evening attired in a disguise went to Kanchana Mala's residence. "Welcome! Hearty Welcome! O learned man, Welcome" Kanchana Mala invited him.

He told Mala, "I have come to recite Ramayana as if it is happening in front of your eyes."

"That was good. Then, are you aware of the reward and punishments?" Mala questioned.

"I am aware of those Kanchana Mala! I have a request..." paused Ramalinga. "Please tell me Sir" Mala immediately responded, "Before I complete the total recital you should not say anything. You should do what ever I say as part of the presentation. After I complete the narration you can reward me if you are 'satisfied' or punish otherwise" Ramalinga sarcastically stated. She agreed to it and the story began.

Ramalinga started with the birth of Rama, Lakshmana, Bharatha, and Sathrughna. It continued with Rama Lakshmana accompanying with Sage Vishwamithra to protect the celestial sacrifice, killing Thataka, releasing Ahalya from curse, Rama's marriage with Seetha breaking Lord Shiva's bow, and Rama's migration to forests along with Seetha and Lakshmana on stepmother Kaika's wish.

Ramalinga was narrating the episodes with an excellent expression and mannerism in a right modulation. Nowhere, Kanchana Mala locked to be satisfied as she was commenting 'You are not satisfying me.' He advanced with the story narration about Ravanasura kidnapping Seetha, Rama killing Vali, deploying Hanuman to Lanka with the assistance of Sugriva. Again Mala screamed, "I am not satisfied with your performance."

Controlling himself from exploding with anger, Ramalinga convinced her "Kanchana Mala! You are telling me that you are not satisfied with my performance. However, this would be the best of performance on earth. OK. Let us leave that. Now get ready, you will witness Ramayana happening in front of you."

"Hehehehe...yeah please continue, I am in fact waiting for that," she said.

Ramalinga jumped on to her selectively decorated cot and said, "This is how Hanuman jumped on to the Peak of Mahendra Mountain." Standing erect on the bed he took another flight and landed on another cot, "Like this Hanuma jumped on to another mountain's peak." From there he jumped close to Kanchana Mala and started throwing powerful fists on her back, "this was how Hanuman hit Lankini, who blocked his way from entering Lanka."

Mala started shouting to the top of her voice, "Oh God! Mother! This man is killing me." Ramalinga in a commanding tone, "I told you not to hinder me in the middle. Now shut your mouth, Listen completely..." jumping like an ape, Ramalinga took out a lighted wisp hanging from the wall. "Hanuman returning from the Ashoka garden after visiting Seetha started torching Lanka and its men like this..." he gave fire to Mala's clothes and ignited almost all the clothes and inflammables in the house.

While Mala was attempting to extinguish fire on her clothes, Ramalinga repeated beating her all over stating that was how Hanuman thumped the demons in Lanka. Mala other than shouting loudly and protecting her from the fire could not do anything.

Few seconds later, after lighting all the household material, Ramalinga coolly went to the backyard stood near the well, "this is how Hanuman put out the fire set to his tail by the demons" and started taking bath drawing water from the well.

Looking at the house in fire, Kanchana Mala went astray and ran out of the house like a mad woman. Ramalinga's sarcastic comments irked her further more, "Who else can narrate Ramayana so lively Kanchana Mala, did you enjoy that?"

Cursing, yelling, screaming Kanchana Mala said, "fraud, cheat, he said he will recite Ramayana for me and set the house on fire." With disturbed clothes and hair, she ran to he local Court of Law and approached the judge. She sought justice from the judge explaining the whole episode. Meanwhile, Ramalinga reached there without any tension appearing on his face.

The Judge questioned Ramalinga, "What is your answer to her allegations?" Ramalinga folded hands at the Judge and appealed, "Your Majesty! I do not bear any fault with me. It was she, who wished to witness a lively Ramayana recital to her 'satisfaction'." Describing all the past and present deeds of Kanchana Mala, Ramalinga said, "Mr. Justice! I believe I am not at fault. In case the honourable court finds any, I am ready to take the punishment."

The Judge understood that it was the wicked and proud nature of Kanchana Mala, which brought her to this turn of life. He scolded her for cheating and humiliating scholars and learned persons in the name of Ramayana recital and rewards. The judgement made it clear that Ramalinga did not have any fault to punish and freed him. In addition to this, the verdict released all the learned men who were serving her as servants and slaves. Ramalinga received all the appreciations from the people of the town.

Ramalinga Wins the War before Drawing Swords!

Rama Sastry was a renowned scholar in reasoning, logic, and grammar. A wish lied in his heart to compete with Ashta Diggajas in Bhuvana Vijayam of Sri Krishna Deva Rayalu. The wish strengthened with the passage of time. With the desire in him, he appeared before the King Rayalu, one day when he was in his usual literary sessions with the eight jewels of his court.

"Hey King of Kings," Rama Sastry presented salutations to Rayalu, "You are the beacon of the Vijaya Nagar Empire!

With your pleasant looks poetry, literature and composition are flourishing in this region. I bow to you with all respects." Sastry continued, "The hear and say about the Ashta Diggajas in your Bhuvana Vijayam, their command over various divisions of literature. They all are reputed and their names are uttered with respect in the scholars and learned circles. I seek your kind permission to question them and know about their efficiency in their concerned arenas."

King Rayalu on listening to the humble request of the visiting intellectual, "Dear learned person! I too carry a thought to know the standards and excellence of our Ashta Diggajas. I would be happy if that wish is accomplished through you Rama Sastry. You attend the court tomorrow and let there be a professional competition." Rayalu ordered his courtiers to arrange a guest accommodation to the visitor.

Satisfied Rama Sastry presenting salutations to the king again and left Bhuvana Vijayam.

The next day, Rama Sastry presented himself in the court with all preparation. Allasani Peddana, Nandi Thimmana, Rama Raja Bhushanudu, Madaya Gari Mallana, Dhoorjati, Ayyala Raju Rama Bhadrudu, Bhattu Murthy, and Tenali Ramakrishna besides full house attendance to watch the competition fill the Bhuvana Vijayam. All the seven among the Ashta Diggajas were tensed with the reputation they heard about Rama Sastry about his command and expertise in logic, reasoning, and grammar. Sastry's name is taken with scare and respect, as he defeated those personalities who were graded to be aces in that division of literature. All the seven were nervous thinking whether there is a possibility of winning the visiting scholar or not.

While Sastry was sitting in all comfort, confidence and the seven of the Ashta Diggajas were worried; Tenali Ramalinga was seated in all ease and pleasant. Ramalinga after salutations to the King Rayalu and taking his permission started speaking, "Mr. Rama Sastry! Are you good in poetry." Rama Sastry thinking that as an insult to him was about to enrage on Ramalinga. However, recollecting that he is present in the royal court of King Rayalu stopped himself from doing so.

Gazing Ramalinga top to bottom sarcastically said, "Do you think that I am no good at that stupid...verses? Do you consider even that a scholarship?"

Instantly replied Ramalinga, "That was good to know Mr. Rama Sastry that you are good in stupid poetry. We understood that very well with your words. So nice of you." Sastry questioned, "Ramalinga, are there two categories as stupid poetry and bright poetry?"

"That was your statement, Rama Sastry!" Ramalinga bounced back, "you asked me whether I think you are no good in stupid verses. That's all right. Let us keep that aside for now, I request you to keep us informed what are you scholar in?"

"I am reputed for my scholarship in logic and grammar. On both the subjects I have excellent command," replied Rama Sastry.

Ramalinga innocently said, "Mr. Sastry! For quite some time, I have a doubt in a grammar sequence. Can you clarify, if I ask you that?"

"Sure!" Sastry answered with all pride and proud filled tone, "you don't have to hesitate any more."

"What is the grammatical rule and theory to be followed for a word, 'Thriyambaka'" Ramalinga furnished his suspicion.

Rama Sastry moved his body as if he was in laughter within. Later, he said that "is that a doubt? Don't you know even that? Thri + Ambaka= Thriyambaka. This is known as Dwigu Samasam (A theoretical regulation in Telugu (Andhra) Grammar for combining two meaningful words into one.) God! How is that you are placed so high without knowing such a common basic, strange!" commented Sastry.

"Hey! Is that all?" Ramalinga was ready for another bout of sarcasm, "If this is what you know, and can define then your scholarship is like a dead wood."

When the two were about to get into the actual and real round of debate and discussion, King Rayalu stopped them and adjourned the competitive session for the next day, as he was to take care of administrative and other affairs.

News spread in the city like wildfire that Ramalinga and Rama Sastry are about to have a literary war in the Bhuvana Vijayam, the next day enthusiasts, scholars, poets, composers and others flooded into the galleries of the court.

When almost all the distinguished personalities of Bhuvana Vijayam including the visitor Rama Sastry, King Rayalu entered the court and occupied the royal throne. All those present in the court saluted the King and took their respective seats. Ramalinga was not seen, and noticing this Rama Sastry grinned within. Sastry thought Ramalinga was scared and was not present. Just then, Ramalinga carrying something fastened in a nice cloth entered in a hurry and sat after saluting the King and the court.

Those present in the galleries whispered among them looking at Ramalinga surprisingly. After the King waved for continuation of the debate and discussion, Rama Sastry questioned, "Ramalinga can I know what is the title of the book you carried in?" Ramalinga not hesitating a moment replied, "This is king of standard books titled, 'Thilakashta Mahisha Bandhanam'." Rama Sastry puzzled on hearing such title, curiously he leaned forward and repeated, "What? Thilakashta Mahisha Bandhanam?"

"Yes! Mr. Rama Sastry!" Ramalinga said, "Thilakashta Mahisha Bandhanam! Haven't you read this book earlier? Presuming that this standard book would be helpful for our debate and discussion, I brought this along."

Rama Sastry could not figure out what to do. First, he never knew that such books of standards existed, secondly, Ramalinga brought that along with him. 'What to do if he countered my argument and presented one or the other citations from the book in support of his counter-argument? I will be closed and my skills and expertise, command would never be respected again.' Rama Sastry thought for a while and decided to do something. Turning towards the King Rayalu he said, "My Lord! Ramalinga brought Thilakashta Mahisha Bandhanam with him to standardise his argument and counter-argument in the session. That being the case, I should also bring some standard books to support my logic and reasoning. If the King kindly grant me permission to bring those from my guest accommodation, I would return immediately..."

King Rayalu acceded his plea and consented, "It's alright, proceed." Rama Sastry threw himself out of the court like a whirlwind.

Time was passing by and Rama Sastry did not return. Rayalu was compelled to postpone the session for the next day, as the session cannot continue without the competitor's presence.

The next morning, again the court was waiting for Rama Sastry. He never appeared. King Rayalu ordered his soldiers to verify and inform the court about the disappearance of Rama Sastry. Soldiers returned like a ball hit to the wall and explained that Rama Sastry in the dark of the night went away with his luggage. Probably this could be the result of the realisation that, he is definite to lose in the debate and discussion. From protecting himself from the humiliation, Rama Sastry should have left not informing anyone.

The total presence in the Bhuvana Vijayam including King Rayalu could not stop getting into laughter. Looking appraisingly at Ramalinga, Rayalu said it was an excellent performance.

"Ramalinga!" Rayalu asked, "Recite to the court some good contents of the book you brought along, Thilakashta Mahisha Bandhanam, to the court."

"Hahahahah...Hahhahaha..." Ramalinga said, "with all due respects to the King, is that you also mistook this bundle to be a book? Look at this..." and opened the bundle. Again there was hilarity in the court, as it was a book, it was a tender Sesamum plant tied with reign rope for buffalos. Both were fastened in a nice cloth. Looking at the contents of the bundle, there was amusement for the courtiers and onlookers.

Ramalinga explained, "Thilakashta means a Sesamum plant and Mahisha Bandhanam, a rope used for tying a buffalo, both put together, Thilakashta Mahisha Bandhanam. That is it all. No standards and no books. Rama Sastry fell into dilemma on hearing this name, he did not try to take the title and think. In all confusion, he fled the city."

King Sri Krishna Deva Rayalu appreciated the intellect of Ramalinga and felicitated him for protecting the reputation of Bhuvana Vijayam. That was how, Ramalinga won the battle long before drawing any sword!

Ramalinga Attempts to turn a Dog into a Cow!!!

The first rays of Sun were spreading on the world driving away all the evil and darkness from. Just then King Rayalu woke from deep sleep. Yawning he came out of his palace room and clapped calling, "who is there?" Running came a soldier, "Yes My Lord!" bowing his head to the King.

"Go right away and bring the barber along" ordered Rayalu. Taking the instruction, soldier left saluting the King. Rayalu re-entered his room and just rested in the easy chair in there. Immediately he went into sound sleep again. The barber rushed in on hearing the call of King Rayalu. Eventually, he slowly entered the room of the king to find Rayalu sleeping in the armchair. Sensing the King to be too tired the barber never wanted to wake him up. Putting all his experience and expertise, barber completed his job shaving the beard and cutting hair. Finishing his work barber left the place in all silence.

After sometime, Rayalu opened his eyes. He did not find the barber waiting by the door. Angrily he clapped for the attendant and shouted at him to bring the barber in a moment. Slowly he got off the armchair and casually put his hand on the chin, Surprise! It was like a freshly done. Rayalu grew suspicious and walked in front of the mirror and looked at his image in there. The hair was cleanly cut and beard was neatly shaved.

Meanwhile the attendant brought the barber before him. Rayalu was impressed about the barber's job and appreciated him, "You Barber! I am satisfied for your job. I wish to bestow a boon, go on ask one I will accomplish."

"Master!..." hesitantly barber presented his good old desire, "Since long, My Lord...I carry a wish to become a Brahmin. Kindly bless me with this, I do not need any thing, as my family and me do not have anything short with the your Lord's mercy."

Rayalu was stunned to know barber's desire. However, he assured, "This is not any big boon, tomorrow itself your wish will be fulfilled." He waved the barber to leave, and summoned for some Brahmins.

"Dear Brahmins! I promised the barber to transform him as a Brahmin. You should do it with all your knowledge and keep my word. All of you will be rewarded suitably," Rayalu ordered. On hearing the sound of 'rewarded' Brahmins were lured and told the king, "As you wish My Lord! We will transform the barber into a Brahmin."

The news of barber turning a Brahmin spread in the city and all the Brahmin community whimpered silently, because if they speak louder the King might know of it and they would face punishment. They thought, 'it is not fair for the King Rayalu to order so for transforming the barber into a Brahmin. This might give way for many others to long for the wish...this is against Dharma.'

Thinking long in vain what to do, they approached Tenali Ramalinga seeking a solution. Understanding the whole episode, Ramalinga tried to inject some confidence into the members of the Brahmin community. He told them, "All of you have some peace and rest. I will try my best to avert this extreme incident from happening."

The next morning, the Brahmins who were ordered on to the job took the barber to the Coast of Suvarna Mukhi River and started chanting some hymns standing around him. King Sri Krishna Deva Rayalu was watching the performance sitting at a distance and was supervising what was happening.

At the same time, a little far from this place,

Ramalinga was chanting something or the other standing by the side of a black dog. He was pretending to ignore what was taking place near the place.

While the Brahmins continued chanting the hymns, Rayalu slowly walked close to Ramalinga and asked, "Ramalinga! What are you doing to the dog?" With all natural submission Ramalinga told, "I am transforming this black dog into a white cow."

Rayalu laughing sarcastically, "Ramakrishna... hahahah... hahahaha... how can this black dog, perhaps, any dog turn into a white cow if you chant some hymns after giving it a dip in the holy river?"

Innocently Ramalinga said, "King of Kings! Kindly forgive me for my foolishness. But, why can't this black dog be turned into a white cow, when a barber is being transformed into a Brahmin?" King Rayalu stopped laughing and started to think. He understood that Ramalinga was doing this to open his eyes. Immediately he called the barber and told him, "Hey You barber, it is not possible to turn you as a Brahmin. Leaving this desire ask for another one."

The barber submissively saluted, "Master! I am happy with your kindness, I do not need anything" and left for home. Rayalu as usual, felicitated Ramalinga for opening his eyes and protecting from doing things against the Dharma.

Ramalinga's Prostrate Adoration to "Donkeys"

Thathacharya was the royal teacher to the King Sri Krishna Deva Rayalu. He was a Vaishnavite (Vaishnavites believe Sri Maha Vishnu as the Supreme God) by practice and was having a defiant opinion and behaviour towards the Smarthas (Smarthas follow the tradition instituted by Sri Adi Sankaracharya). While moving out, he used to cover his head and face with his upper garment (cloak) to avoid seeing Smarthas in the town. People watching Thathacharya doing this time and again titled him unofficially as 'stupid ritualist'. The learned category of Smarthas and other practices were finding ways to teach a lesson to Thathacharya.

They could not decide upon how and when to make tit for tat. The scare spread among them was that Thathacharya is the royal teacher to the King Rayalu and his family. If something goes wrong and kindles fury in the King, who should face it? With all these thoughts, they started searching who is efficient to do this job for them. Their search ended after touring and scanning through all the faces in the kingdom. That face belonged to Ramalinga. In a group all the learned people went to Ramalinga's residence to see him.

Ramalinga was little surprised to see all of them together at his threshold. Clipping some smiles on his lips, Ramalinga invited them folding hands to the scholars' battalion,

"Welcome to you all the learned personalities of the capital city. Welcome. It is my pleasure to see you all together."

Dhurjhati took the initiative to explain the problem that was boggling their minds,

"Ramalinga! We are all here to discuss a problem with you seeking a solution. The royal teacher Thathacharya is behaving beyond limits and is humiliating the Smarthas regularly. This might end up elsewhere, if he is not taught a right lesson. We all strongly believe that you are the right man who can do it in a sensible way. Please do not dishearten us. You should take this matter up."

Rama Raja Bhushana seconded supporting Dhurjhati,

"Dhurjhati was right Ramalinga. You should plunge into action for a right solution to this problem."

Ramalinga thought for a while, when all the other members of the group were coming out with one or the other statement against Thathacharya.

"Dear friends..." Ramalinga assured them, "All of you had put a heavy and burdensome job on my shoulders...Let me see what can I do about this. This is all the blessings of the Goddess Kali. You don't worry; I will take care of Thathacharya and his Vaishnavite proudness."

Though Ramalinga personally watched Thathacharya's misbehaviour towards Smarthas, he could not do anything. 'Now, the time has come. Nevertheless, how to go about this? What would happen if King Rayalu is irked on taking Thathacharya to task?' Ramalinga was waiting for the time tuning. While all this was going on, King Rayalu learnt about the indecent mannerism of Thathacharya. He was hurt with the behaviour of Thathacharya and thought that if this continued, it might give way to communal differences in the kingdom. Thinking so, Rayalu summoned Ramalinga to his private chamber in the palace. Ramalinga was present before the King as quickly as possible after hearing the call.

"Ramalinga!" King Rayalu said in a low tone, "I wish to discuss an important issue with you."

"Yes My Lord, as you Please!" Ramalinga replied.

"This is a matter that should be handled completely undercover. I thought you are efficient to handle this matter. I am assigning this job to you. Are you ready?" Rayalu questioned.

"Yes my king, every word of yours is an order for me."

"It came to my knowledge that the royal teacher Thathacharya is humiliating Smarthas. I also noted that people are disgusted with him for this, in fact some of the courtiers also pleaded me to handle him and stop him from doing so. He is my family master and an elderly person. What and how should I tell him to correct his deeds? Now, it is up to you. Think wise and do something to check him from continuing with this" Rayalu ordered Ramalinga. Ramalinga promised the King, "My Lord! I will do my best to solve the problem and bring some change in the ideology of Thathacharya about Smarthas."

Leaving the palace, Ramalinga was overwhelmed with joy. He was waiting for a right opportunity and it has come through his way in the form of King's order. The next morning Ramalinga went to see Thathacharya. No sooner Ramalinga approached the main gate, he could see Thathacharya coming out of the house. While approaching the gate, Thathacharya watching Ramalinga standing there took his upper garment and started covering his face. Ramalinga immediately said in a loud tone,

"Hey Master! I am the beloved disciple for you. Why is that you are covering your face on seeing me?"

"Ramalinga!" Thathacharya replied, "I will tell you a secret, just because you are my beloved disciple. Smartha culture is a sin filled one. Anyone who sees a Smarthite will be born as a Donkey in his or her next birth. That is why I protect myself by covering my face from attracting the sin of seeing a Smarthite. Keep this to yourself and don't reveal anywhere."

Ramalinga was more humble then, "My dear master! You know me. If I hear something, that totally remains within me.

That will not come out even after my death. You don't have to worry about this. Now, if you permit me I will take leave" "Go ahead", Thathacharya sent him off.

On way home, Ramalinga was almost jumping with joy. All these days he was breaking his head to find ways to teach a lesson. That was a fine day, because Thathacharya himself guided for an excellent way. Ten days passed off. Coolly, with Ramalinga waiting for an opportunity. On the eleventh day, King Rayalu along with Thathacharya, Ashta Diggajas and other scholars visited a garden on the outskirts of the city as part of his relaxing routines. The day was spent off in a pleasurable manner. While all of them were returning a herd of donkeys were seen coming in the opposite direction. Immediately, Ramalinga ran from behind the King and started paying prostrate homage to the donkeys falling on the ground before the herd. King Rayalu was completely surprised with his behaviour. He shouted, "Ramalinga have you gone mad? Why are you saluting those donkeys?"

"My Lord! Kindly pardon me. I did not go mad or crazy. This donkey is Thathacharya's brother-in-law. That one his grandfather, that stout one is his maternal uncle and the one with those spots is Thathacharya's father."

Ramalinga continued, "I am blessed to see all these persons reborn as donkeys. There are here in this form for the sin of looking at Smarthas in their previous birth. I am pleased to see all of them together. Please My King do not mistake me. I am not lying. You can confirm this with the respected royal teacher Thathacharya. He does practice to cover his face to protect himself from the sin of seeing Smarthas."

King Rayalu looked at Thathacharya, who already had hung his chin down in shame. Since then, Thathacharya stopped both humiliating the Smarthas and covering his face on looking at people, belonging to other traditions and cultures. The King felicitated with a great gift to Ramalinga in his private chamber for treating the royal master with a right lesson.

Thathacharya-Demon Chanting Hymns

Tenali Ramalinga clearly understood that Thathacharya

was furious on him. He is just a court poet, while Thathacharya is the royal family teacher and priest. If Ramalinga tried to confront directly with Thathacharya, that might ruin him similar to the situation, a lamb smashing her head when it collided with a mountain to knock it down.

Analysing all the situations in detail and taking comparison of the strengths, Ramalinga decided to encounter Thathacharya with intelligence and not directly waging a war in the open. Since then, Ramalinga started enquiring about the weaknesses of Thathacharya. In this process, one day Ramalinga managed to speak in isolation with Thathacharya's night watchman Bhadrudu. Carrying a small package in hand, Ramalinga addressed him, "Hey you, Bhadrudu! If you can give me a small information, all the 100 Varahas in this package will be yours."

Bhadrudu's eyes sparkled on hearing '100 Varahas'. It was equal to his two months salary and instantly he started calculating about what he could do with that sum. Ramalinga intercepted his thinking, "What are you thinking?"

"Nothing Sir! What should I reveal to you?" he asked in a humble tone. Bhadrudu carefully caught the package thrown at him while Ramalinga asked him, "Nothing very important. Tell me what is the schedule of our master Thathacharya after dusk, that's all."

Bhadrudu did not smell anything wrong about Ramalinga enquiring about Thathacharya and immediately replied, "There is no daily night routine for the Master Sir. However, twice a week, he goes towards the East Street after its dark and returns in the early hours. Ah! By the way, this night he will go on his way to the East Street."

"That's alright Bhadrudu! Keep this matter within you, as a secret," stating this Ramalinga left the place briskly.

That night Ramalinga reached the East Street before Thathacharya passed through and stood under the shade of a big tree by the side of the street. After waiting for sometime, he could spot Thathacharya walking into the street from a distance. Ramalinga started shadowing him in the darkness until he walked into the house of a sex worker. Reaching close,

Ramalinga could hear the door being locked from inside in the silence of the night. This was what I am waiting for, Ramalinga said to himself and sat in front of the house.

While Ramalinga was waiting, Thathacharya came out of the prostitute's house just before the dawn when it was still little dark. Immediately, Ramalinga rushed and stood before him. "Good Morning! Master Thathacharya! I now understood the saying 'Demons chanting hymns'. I will make your secret to everyone and expose your real nature," he threatened Thathacharya. Thathacharya started shivering on hearing Ramalinga. It would be the end of respect if he exposed this matter before the elite class, he should be persuaded not to do so. Thathacharya thinking so said, "My Dear Ramalinga! You are my dearest of the disciples. Please do not remember this after we leave this place. I will do good to you. I will give you whatever you wish for." Jumping with joy within himself, Ramalinga thought that was the time to take revenge out of him. "Dear master! I have a wish to sit on your shoulders for a distance, since long. Please carry me on your shoulders for a distance and I will forget about all this," Ramalinga announced.

'If I don't do what he says, I should lose hopes on retaining the reputation. Then, it will be like swimming all the seven seas and dying in the pothole in the backyard. I am little blessed, it is still dark, I cannot be so easily spotted by people if I carry him now itself." So went on Thathacharya's thinking and making Ramalinga sit on his shoulders started walking down the street and was passing through a street close to King Rayalu's bedroom in the palace.

Exactly during that time King Rayalu woke up early and was strolling in the balcony. In the loosening darkness, the King identified Thathacharya carrying someone on his shoulder. Immediately he called his gatemen and ordered them, "you fellows! Look at the man carrying another man down there on the street. Bring the person sitting on the shoulders of the carrying man kicking and hitting him from there, to me." Immediately, the soldiers sprung into action.

The always alert and wise Ramalinga understood the situation and got off the shoulders. "Master Thathacharya!

Kindly pardon me. I am a sinner by riding your shoulders, a learned man. Now, let me be relieved of at least part of the sin by carrying you on my shoulders." Somehow, though Thathacharya was hesitant, Ramalinga managed to convince, shouldered Thathacharya, and started walking.

Hardly walking a few yards, the soldiers appeared before them and threw Thathacharya on the ground from Ramalinga's shoulders. From there, they started dragging him to the King's presence kicking and hitting him mercilessly. Ramalinga with a great effort managed to stop his joy flowing from inside, said to the soldiers, "What are you doing soldiers? Whom do you think you are beating up? He is Royal Family teacher Thathacharya. It is not fair for you to do so with him. You leave him, hear my words..."

The soldiers replied Ramalinga with a rough tone, "Go on! Go your way! Get away from here. We are doing this on the King's orders" and pulled Thathacharya to the presence of the King. Rayalu was furious on noticing Thathacharya being booted by the soldiers. "You Stupids! What did I tell you and what are you doing? You all should be beheaded for humiliating revered Thathacharya."

Shivering soldiers bowed to the King and pleaded, "Oh My Lord! It was not our mistake, when we entered the street taking your order; Thathacharya was on the shoulders of poet Ramalinga and we following your orders dragged him here. That is it all. You can confirm this with Master Thathacharya before beheading us." Thathacharya was in a big soup. If the whole story was narrated, it again links with the night haul. If that comes out, it is the beginning of the end. With great pain Thathacharya told, "My Dear King! They were right Ramalinga was carrying me on his shoulders."

Rayalu regretted for the happening and asked the soldiers leave the place without punishing them. Later, he got Thathacharya treated for the wounds he suffered on taking the beating of the soldiers. Ramalinga crookedly was in all laughter the whole day for giving Thathacharya a right lesson.

Bibliography

Abol, Tabol : *The Nonsense World of Sukumar Ray,* Puffin Books, New Delhi, 2004.

Aston, N.M. : *Dalit Literature and African-American Literature,* Prestige, New Delhi, 2001.

Badhwar, Inderjit : *The Chamber of Perfumes,* Tara-India Research Press, New Delhi, 2004.

Bakshi, G.D. : *Dances with the Cranes : Poems on Reincarnation,* Sharada, Delhi, 2004.

Bhattacharya, Malini : *Giving Away the Girl and Other Plays,* Seagull Books, Calcutta, 2003.

Bradby, Anne : *Shakespeare Criticism,* Atlantic, New Delhi, 2004.

Bradford, Barbara Taylor : *Children's Stories of the Bible, From the Old and New Testaments*, World Distributors Limited, Manchester, 1968.

Carpenter, Humphrey; and Pritchard, Mari : *The Oxford Companion to Children's Literature*, Oxford University Press, Oxford, 1999.

Carroll, Lewis : *Alice's Adventures in Wonderland, and Through the Looking Glass*, Octopus Books Limited, London, 1984.

Desai, Rakesh : *W.H. Auden's Poetry : The Quest for Love,* Atlantic, New Delhi, 2004.

Dowson, John : *A Classical Dictionary of Hindu Mythology and Religion*, Rupa & Co., New Delhi, 1993.

Firdous and Niaz Zaman : *Galpa : Short Stories by Women from Bangladesh,* Writers.ink, Dhaka, 2006.

Garg, Rita : *Evelyn Waugh as a Satirist,* Vishvabharti Pub., New Delhi, 2006.

Ghosh's, Amitav : *The Shadow Lines : Critical Essays,* Atlantic, New Delhi, 2002.

Goel, Sandeep : *The Dum Dum Bullet : Adventures of a Corporate Soldier,* Penguin, New Delhi, 2004.

Gupta, Rashmi : *Adolescent Hero in the Works of Katherine,* Atlantic, New Delhi, 2003.

Habib, Mohammed : *Hazrat Amir Khusrau of Delhi,* Cosmo, New Delhi, 2004.

Iyer, Pico : *Abandon : A Romance*, Penguin, New Delhi, 2003.

Jaaware, Aniket : *Simplifications : An Introduction to Structuralism and Post-Structuralism,* Orient Longman, New Delhi, 2001.

Jacobs, Joseph : *English Fairy Tales*, Puffin Books, London, 1994.

Jan, K.M. and Shabnam Firdaus : *A Guide to English Literature,* Atlantic, New Delhi, 2003.

Joshi, Roswitha : *On the Rocks and Other Stories,* UBS Pub., New Delhi, 2004.

Joshi's, Arun : *Novels : His Vision of Life,* Sarup and Sons, New Delhi, 2004.

Kakar, Sudhir : *Indian Love Stories,* Roli Books, New Delhi, 2003.

Kapoor, Kusum Mercy : *The Heart Does not Give Reasons,* Writers Workshop Books, Calcutta, 1999.

Karnani, Chetan : *Eminent Indian English Writers : An Assessment,* Rawat, Delhi, 2001.

Knappert, Jan : *An Encyclopaedia of Myth and Legend: Indian Mythology*, Harper Collins Publishers India Pvt. Ltd., New Delhi, 1993.

Lawrence's, D.H. : *Novels : A Stylistic Approach,* Classical Pub., New Delhi, 2002.

Macdonald, George : *The Princess and the Goblin*, Watermill Press, New Jersey, 1985.

Mehta, Krishna : *Kashmir 1947 : A Survivor's Story,* Penguin, New Delhi, 2005.

Miller, Olive Beaupre : *My Book House*, The Book House for Children, Chicago, 1951.

Mishra, B.M. : *The Poetry of T.S. Eliot,* Atlantic Pub., New Delhi, 2003.

Mohit K. Ray and Rama Kundu : *Salman Rushdie : Critical Essays,* Atlantic, New Delhi, 2006.

Moon, Vasant : *Growing up Untouchable in India : A Dalit,* Vistaar Publications, Delhi, 2002.

Naikar, Basavaraj : *Indian Response to Shakespeare,* Atlantic, New Delhi, 2002.

Naipaul, V.S. : *A House for Mr. Biswas : With an Introduction by Ian Buruma,* Penguin, New Delhi, 1992.

Naravane, V.S. : *Adventures Among Masterpieces : Fifteen Literary Memoirs,* V.S. Naravane, Allahabad, 2002.

Nirad C. Chaudhuri : *The Autobiography of an Unknown Indian,* Jaico Publishing, Delhi, 2002.

Pradhan, Ram Prakash : *The Woman in the Novels of Saul Bellow,* Atlantic Pub., New Delhi, 2006.

Prafulla K. Mishra : *Ethics, Erotics and Aesthetics,* Pratibha Prakashan, Delhi, 2004.

Prem, P.C.K. : *A Handsome Man : A Novel,* Abhinav Publications, New Delhi, 2001.

Premchand, Munsi : *Gaban : The Stolen Jewels,* Oxford University Press, Delhi, 2000.

Pulinbihari, Sen and Kshitis Roy: *Rabindranath Tagore : A Tribute,* Hope India Publications, New Delhi, 2006.

Purkiss, Diane : *Troublesome Things: A History of Fairies and Fairy Stories*, The Penguin Group, London, 2000.

Rao, R. Raj : *The Boyfriend : A Novel,* Penguin, New Delhi, 2003.

Riaz, Ghulam Fariduddin : *Baramasa : Seasons of Rural Life,* Oxford University Press, New Delhi, 1988.

Roy, Pabitrakumar : *Rabindranath Tagore,* Munshiram Manoharlal, New Delhi, 2002.

Rubin, David : *Of Love and War : A Chayavad Anthology,* Oxford University Press, Delhi, 2005.

Shakespeare, William : *Complete Works,* ELBS and Collins, London and Glasgow, 1964.

Sharma, Ramachandra : *Home and Away : A Collection of Kannada Short Stories,* Katha, New Delhi, 2001.

Sharma, Vishnu : *Panchatantra,* Rupa & Co, Calcutta, 1993.

Silva, Neluka : *The Gendered Nation : Contemporary Writings from South Asia,* Sage, New Delhi, 2004.

Singh, Nandita : *Philip Roth : A Novelist in Crisis,* Classical Publishing, New Delhi, 2001.

Sinha, Nandita : *Nadine Gordimer's My Son's Story : A Critical Study,* Asia Book Club, New Delhi, 2005.

Swaminathan, A. : *A Critical Study of Charlotte Bronte,* ABD Pub., Jaipur, 2005.

Tarun J. Tejpal : *The Alchemy of Desire,* Harper Collins, New Delhi, 2005.

Tillotson, Giles : *Jaipur Nama : Tales from the Pink City,* Penguin Books, New Delhi, 2006.

Tolkien, J.R.R. : *The Lord of the Rings*, Unwin Paperbacks, London, 1981.

Yadav, Ajay Singh : *Darkness Before Dawn,* Light House Books, Bhopal, 2000.

Zheleznova, Irina : *A Mountain of Gems—Fairy Tales of the Peoples of the Soviet Lands*, Foreign Languages Publishing House. Moscow, 1983.

Zipes, Jack : *The Penguin Book of Western Fairy Tales,* Penguin Books, London, 1993.

Index

G

H

I

J

K

L

M

N

O

P

R